# Try This

danyelle freeman

An *Imprint* of HarperCollins*Publishers*

# Try This

## TRAVELING THE GLOBE
## WITHOUT LEAVING THE TABLE

HarperCollins books may be purchased for educational,
business, or sales promotional use. For information please write: Special Markets
Department, HarperCollins Publishers, 10 East 53rd Street, New York, NY 10022.

FIRST EDITION

*Designed by Claire Naylon Vaccaro*

Library of Congress Cataloging-in-Publication
Data has been applied for.

ISBN 978-0-06-188178-7

11 12 13 14 15   OV/RRD   10 9 8 7 6 5 4 3 2 1

*For my mom and dad,*
*who taught me that the two most*
*important things in life*
*are family and food.*
*I'm eternally grateful for your limitless love*
*and your encouragement to dream.*
*You will live in my heart always.*

*And for Amanda and Heath,*
*who fill my every day with love and laughter.*
*Everyone should be lucky enough*
*to have a sister and a brother like you.*
*Thank you for your support and, most importantly,*
*for always sharing your food with me.*
*(As if you had a choice.)*

*I am not a glutton.*
*I am an explorer of food.*

—ERMA BOMBECK

# Contents

## ACKNOWLEDGMENTS

Infinite thanks to Libby Edelson for bringing out the best in this book. I simply couldn't have done it without you. And to Daniel Halpern for believing that I had a book in me in the first place, then making it happen. You are a dream maker. Profound thanks to Verlyn Klinkenborg for making me a better writer and showing me how to love language as much as I love food. Oceans of gratitude to Dr. Allan Lans for making me a better person and keeping my head on straight—well, as straight as possible anyway. Thanks to Jennifer Joel for your support and assistance in making this book a reality. Thanks to Michele Lamorte for your diligent research and library expertise, and also to Maris Ackerman.

Thanks to Monica, Jonathan, Erin, and Jimmy for making me strong enough to believe I can do anything. Thanks to Roger, Justin, Jimmy, and Eleanora, who encourage me every morning. And, of course, thanks to my truly amazing friends—Dana, Dylan, Liz, Tori, Robin, and Jess—for seeing me through the best of times and the worst of times and sticking by me through it all.

# Introduction

Some people read romance novels in their free time. Others prefer thrillers or fashion magazines. Some spend their commutes flipping through gossip columns, while others scrutinize the business section. Me, I read menus. And in New York, menus are everywhere you look. They're prominently posted in restaurant windows or handed out by sidewalk hawkers at busy corners. Instead of avoiding eye contact or moving to the other side of the sidewalk, I'm the girl who asks for one, even when I'm not solicited. I'll spot a menu guy as I'm darting down the street, late for an important meeting, and beeline over for one of my own. Reading menus soothes me.

It doesn't have to be anything fancy. Hell, if I pass a burger joint, I'll check out the flimsy paper menu. Some chefs make their own ketchup or pickle their own pickles; some serve homemade potato chips or sweet potato fries instead of skinny potato fries; some bake their buns in-house or melt cheddar or blue cheese over their patties instead of the same old American cheese.

And burgers are just one juicy possibility: there's a universe of food and chefs with different opinions on what delicious tastes like. Some think delicious tastes like pillows of freshly made ricotta ravioli bathed in a sweet, tangy tomato sauce or barely seared scallops in lemongrass-laced coconut milk sauce; some a corn tamale studded with moist shreds of pork; others delicate, nearly translucent soup dumplings filled with minced crab, pork, and a rich broth. The possibilities are endless.

Long before I imagined a career in food, I made it my job to visit every respectable restaurant in my Zagat guide. Instead of a bubble bath or late-night TV before bed, I'd pull out my highlighter and mark up my little maroon book. When I graduated from college, I moved to Manhattan to conduct my food-obsessed fieldwork while experimenting with careers in psychology, acting, sitcom writing, jewelry design, and film development. Before then, I had never slurped noodles at a ramen counter or tasted a French bouillabaisse. I'd never gone out for Indian curry or do-it-yourself Korean barbecue. I had a lot of eating to do. Culinary matters quickly became all-consuming. I skipped auditions to linger over dim sum in Chinatown and took extra-long lunch breaks from my film job to try the new Vietnamese spot on the other side of town. Sometimes I'd eat two full meals in one night or one meal at two different restaurants on the same night. Every spare dollar went to investigating a new restaurant and sampling as many dishes as I possibly could. After dinner, I'd crawl under the covers, pick up my maroon book, and cross another conquest off my to-do list, scribbling my own review in the margin.

I read every review in every magazine and newspaper I could get my hands on. I'd make Sunday night foodie calls to set up the coming week's dinner dates. I began inventing excuses to avoid dining out with friends who proved themselves unadventurous at the dinner table. I judged my dates by what restaurants they chose, what they ordered, and how they ate it. I eliminated potential mates on the basis of dietary restrictions. I was on a mission to try anything and everything. Restaurants were my drug of choice. I couldn't get enough. Most twenty-two-year-old girls longed for Jimmy Choos and piles of Prada. I dreamed of dinner at New York's Le Cirque and Monaco's Le Louis XV. It was exhausting. It was exhilarating. I started blogging about my meals, just so I could maintain my serious restaurant habit. I was addicted to restaurants, so I thought it only fitting to call myself "Restaurant Girl."

This kind of obsession runs in families. When I was a child, my parents braved gang wars for good food. Literally. On Sunday evenings, we would drive from Short Hills, the quiet, suburban town in New Jersey where I grew up, to the then gang-riddled Elizabeth, New Jersey. My parents locked the car doors and made me, my brother, and my sister hunch beneath the windows to avoid potential gunfire—all in the name of veal cutlet, ravioli, and mushroom pizza at Spirito's. I've now eaten in many four-star restaurants, and that dingy joint still serves the best garlic salad, veal, ricotta ravioli, and fountain soda I've ever had. My parents have passed away, but my brother, sister, and I dutifully return to Spirito's a few times a year, just to make sure we aren't romanticizing those garlic-filled Sundays with our parents.

Spirito's opened over sixty years ago, and it's still going strong— and still cash only. They don't take reservations, they use an old manual register to make change, and the checks are all handwritten by waitresses with beehive hairdos and pencils tucked behind their ears. They refuse to write down your order and yet, somehow, never get it wrong. If you ever end up on a flight that connects at Newark Airport, you'd be wise to take a later plane. Most local taxi drivers should know Spirito's by name, so ask one to take you and see for yourself. (And bring me back a ravioli, please.)

Both my parents were foodies before the word even existed. On weekends our family motto might as well have been: "Will travel for food." Our family field trips to New York weren't so

much about seeing the Statue of Liberty or the Christmas tree
at Rockefeller Center as they were about paper-bagged chestnuts
and street cart pretzels spackled with salt. That was before dinner.
Then we'd head down to Little Italy for unspeakable amounts of
pasta, shrimp scampi, baked clams, and veal scaloppini. Our final
stop was always Ferrara's, just down the street, for biscotti, torrone,
and chocolate gelati. Summers at the shore meant saltwater taffy,
vinegar-doused French fries, and caramel apples. We'd settle into a
slippery plastic booth at some fish shack and, wearing plastic bibs
and wielding claw crackers and wet naps, feast on steamers, fried
clam strips, and lobster rolls. If we came on the right night, we'd
find sautéed soft-shell crabs on the menu. My mom made soft-
shell crabs any chance she could. She wasn't the best cook—more
concerned with eating than cooking—but her sautéed soft-shell
crabs were better than any I've had in a restaurant or picked up
fresh from the store. (I'm still on the hunt for a better rendition.)

Both my parents grew up in poor families, but that didn't stop
either of them from eating well. If all they could afford was bread
and cheese, they ate the freshest bread and freshly sliced (never
packaged) cheese. We didn't eat at the kind of restaurants that
required reservations, but we ate splendidly.

When my mom didn't feel like cooking, we went to local diners and reviewed their workmanship in the kitchen. We grimaced
at diners that served canned strawberries with their waffles or
skimped on the chocolate chips in our pancakes and gave bonus
points to diners that used semisweet chocolate chips instead of
milk chocolate. On school nights we mostly stuck to local spots,
where we got our fix of saffron-stained seafood paella and garlic
shrimp from our favorite Spanish restaurant, or Italian classics—
eggplant rollatini, mozzarella in carrozza, shrimp francese, escarole
and beans, and gnocchi in tomato sauce—from our favorite Italian
restaurant.

Now I eat out six nights a week at some of the best restaurants in the country. But I'll still chase a Mister Softee truck down the street for vanilla soft serve dipped in that liquid fudge that forms a magic shell in fewer than sixty seconds. (I've clocked it.) Good food is good food. I love boardwalk fries with malt vinegar just as much as I love seared foie gras with fresh figs. I love a Gray's Papaya hot dog and signature papaya drink, which tastes like a virgin piña colada, as much as I love caviar and Chablis. I love peanut butter, period; if you care about your stash, hide it from me. It's my kryptonite. I scour the city in search of the best peanut butter cookies, cakes, and ice cream. I can't pass a street vendor without slipping him a dollar or two for a bag of honey-roasted nuts. African food never interested me until I tasted a West African groundnut stew with a thick peanutty broth flush with shreds of chicken, tomatoes, garlic, chile peppers, and yam—and so thrilling that I began experimenting with other peanut-loving cuisines. I fell for the tempestuous kung pao chicken, a classic of Chinese cooking, where roasted peanuts mingle with diced chicken and chile peppers, and green papaya salad showered with peanuts at SriPraPhai, a Thai restaurant in Woodside, Queens.

I wasn't always an experienced eater, or an adventurous one, for that matter. Before I moved to New York, I had never tried truffles or gnawed on Memphis-style barbecued ribs. I stopped eating meat after a bad experience with a ham sandwich in sixth grade and didn't resume eating it until after high school. I had never tasted sweet shrimp sushi or scallops sashimi. I had no idea roasted suckling pig could bring a girl like me to her knees. I was hooked on new smells, tastes, and textures. I made it my mission to try something new every day, and life has been a delectable adventure ever since.

Not everyone lives in New York or in a major city, of course. But no matter where you live, there are dishes to discover, exciting and unfamiliar foods to long for. One of the best gastropubs in the country is called Feast, and it just so happens to be located in

Houston, Texas. One of the best sushi restaurants in the country, Sushi Sasabune, is on the island of Oahu. You'd expect to find flaky, buttery biscuits and fried chicken in Durham, North Carolina, but I was ecstatic and surprised to find great Greek there, too, at Niko's. There's great Vietnamese (The Jasmine Deli) in Minneapolis, Minnesota; Thai (Lotus of Siam) in Las Vegas; and Indian (Shalimar India) in Portsmouth, New Hampshire. There are dishes to discover wherever you live, even at your old local favorite. If you always order beef with broccoli when you go for Chinese, try something new this time. Try kung pao chicken or prawns in lobster sauce.

As clichéd as it sounds, the world really is your oyster. Don't let yourself get stuck in a rut, because there's a new restaurant around every corner, each one uncharted territory. They may not all be in your backyard, but they're right down the road. There are hundreds of cultures around the world with hundreds of cuisines and dishes, sauces, noodles, desserts, curries, spices, and wines for the sampling. Every plate is your playground. There's no time to waste on a mediocre meal or one you've ordered countless times before. With so much wonderful food from so many different regions of the world, there's also plenty to learn, and I say this from personal experience and mild embarrassment.

A few years ago I had my birthday dinner at The Spotted Pig in New York City's West Village. There were twelve of us, all fairly fashionable New Yorkers (myself included, of course) who ate out at least five nights a week. We thought we knew our way around a menu, certainly much more than we knew our way around our own kitchens. But when the server handed out the menus, everyone became unusually quiet. The menu was written in English, but it might as well have been in a foreign language. Rollmops? Devils on Horseback? Champs? Not one of us could identify half of the offerings. Was there a glossary in the house? Even now—after working professionally in the food business for five years—I still have questions. And I'm not alone. Just a few months ago, I overheard a fellow food critic ask his server what Jansen's Temptation is. (It's a Swedish potato and anchovy gratin.) I had to look it up the first time I saw it on a menu, too. We speak a whole new language of food today. We don't just eat Chinese food anymore: We eat Szechuan, Cantonese, or Hunan, and that means things like ma po tofu, flowering chives, and sea cucumber. You may not have been to Korea, but you can get Korean barbecue right here, and it's as different from Turkish barbecue as Turkish barbecue is from Texas barbecue.

I'm writing this book for anyone who's ever looked at a menu and had a question. Anyone who's had a plate put in front of him and wondered what the hell they were about to eat. Just because a cuisine is foreign to you doesn't mean you have to feel like a tourist at the table. Every region's cuisine has its own food language— and you can learn to speak it by tasting different foods on your own. Master that, and you'll be able to navigate a restaurant like a food critic, and before you know it, you'll become as insatiable as me. The key is eating with confidence. There's no reason to be intimidated—not by a place setting that includes a dozen different kinds of silverware and certainly not by the menu. It's not rocket science. It's food. Like anything else worth knowing, you just have to learn the basics—the tricks of the trade, the dos and don'ts, the way to get the most of every single morsel that crosses your tongue.

Eating out is a little like sex. Once you get the hang of it, you can't get enough. You want to try everything on every menu. That's the reason I can't be monogamous to a restaurant or even a chef. I'm always hungry for something new. Life is a feast. Devour it.

# · 1 ·

# British Cuisine

*It takes some skill to spoil a breakfast—*
*even the English can't do it.*

JOHN KENNETH GALBRAITH

Not long ago, if you had told someone you were traveling to London, his or her response might have sounded something like, "The food's terrible, but London's a terrific city." Instead of must-try restaurants, they would rattle off must-see sights, like Big Ben or Westminster Abbey. Most Americans had ruled out British cuisine entirely as an unappetizing mush of overcooked vegetables, strangely named puddings, and processed condiments.

And then, in 2005, gastropubs arrived on our shores, courtesy of The Spotted Pig. Before that, the "gastropub" was a foreign concept in America—it is a thoroughly modern, and thoroughly British, invention. Back in the late 1970s and early 1980s, during the height of England's Thatcher-era recession, savvy restaurateurs began taking over old pubs that had lost their leases. Gradually they started serving more than just the same old tired pub grub: pickled eggs, mushy peas, ploughman's plates, and the like. By the early nineties, the gastropub—a mash-up of the words *gastronomy* and *pub*—was in full flower in the United Kingdom. Arguably America's first gastropub (and definitely New York's), The Spotted Pig is the brainchild of American restaurateur Ken Friedman and visionary British chef April Bloomfield. April had cooked at the illustrious River Café in London and worked for a stint at Alice Waters's Chez Panisse in Berkeley, California. The Pig looked like your average local watering hole—tight tables, backless bar stools, beer on tap, and kitschy paraphernalia (in this case, all porcine-themed) in abundance. But the laidback facade belied the unexpectedly adventurous cooking coming out of the kitchen: a seasonal mix of Italian and ingeniously reinvented pub classics. Suddenly Manhattan trendsetters were delightedly grazing on shepherd's pie, rollmops, and Devils on Horseback.

At first people flocked to The Pig for the wickedly juicy Roquefort-topped burger, delicate nibbles of ricotta gnudi with fried sage, and British-style, cask-conditioned ales. If April ever took these now classics off the menu, the "piggies" would riot. (That's my nickname for the pub's groupies.) But when you earn the foodies' trust, they'll try anything. Slowly but surely, the piggies got hooked on more and more adventurous dishes, like sautéed veal kidneys, grilled beef tongue, and crispy pig ear salad.

I was particularly seduced by the complexity of the smoked haddock chowder laced with pancetta and the smoky-sweet Devils on Horseback—bacon-wrapped prunes dusted with chile powder and stuffed with pickled pear. Count me in for anything "on horseback," because that means it's wrapped in bacon. (Oysters wrapped in bacon are called "Angels on Horseback," because their edges curl up like angel wings when cooked.)

Where do the English come up with all these strange names for food? One of my favorites is Bubble and Squeak, a fanciful name for a fried leftover hash. It's typically made with cabbage, potatoes, and any other vegetables left over from Sunday lunch, often the largest meal of the week. For the life of me, I couldn't figure out if the potato was the bubble or the squeak. It's neither. The dish is actually named after the sound the leftovers make when they're sizzling in the pan. If you come across pork belly faggots, those are England's answer to meatballs, a blend of offal and pork meat. I keep hoping I'll see spotted dick on a menu somewhere, so I can order it just for shock value. "How's your spotted dick? Any good?" Or, "I've been craving spotted dick all week." Spotted dick sounds like a delightfully mischievous carnivore's dish. Nope. It's a humble sweet pudding "spotted" with raisins or currants. And while I find "rollmops" an amusing name for a bar snack, I've yet to acquire a taste for these salty, sour nibbles of pickled herring "rolled" around pickled onions. (But I'm still trying.)

The British do a lot of pickling and preserving. In the medieval era, when most of these dishes came into being, fresh fruits and vegetables were available for only a few months of the year. Pickling and preserving fruits and vegetables in the summer guaranteed there would be food to eat come fall and winter. This was a matter not just of survival, but also of culinary boredom. I mean, how dull would meals get if your only options were bread, meat, cheese, and potatoes? The Brits jazzed up monotonous, heavy braises and sandwiches with something pickled on the side. At The Spotted Pig, pickled beets accompany the grilled beef tongue, and serving a crock of seasonal pickles with the meal is practically obligatory at every gastropub. Unlike in the States, where "preserves" suggests something sweet, English preserves run the gamut from sweet to savory and even spicy. Clerkenwell, a newfangled watering hole on the Lower East Side in New York City, serves orange marmalade alongside toast at brunch, and onion marmalade alongside chicken liver mousse at dinner.

And in the end nothing happens without English mustard, which is much hotter than standard American-style mustard. Sandwiches, sausages, you name it. Dijon or good old yellow mustard just doesn't cut it. The British chef and TV celebrity Nigella Lawson even travels with English mustard in her purse (Colman's, the quintessential English mustard, comes powdered in pocket-size tins). The Brits are also attached to good old American Tabasco sauce, dousing everything from fried fish to soup with it. In fact, England loves Tabasco sauce so much that Queen Elizabeth II awarded its maker a royal warrant. (That's a good thing apparently.) It was first exported there in 1874. During World War II, the queen mother had her staff hunting down Tabasco sauce when it was in short supply! But HP sauce belongs to England. This malt-vinegar-based, fruit-and-spice sauce is named after the restaurant inside the House of Parliament, which devised the recipe and first served the sauce, all the way back in 1896. Horseradish, curry powder, and paprika are also all commonplace, and notably piquant, English seasonings.

As ketchup is to fries, all of these condiments seem like they were designed for salty, breaded, deep-fried bar snacks. Just like traditional pubs, most gastropubs serve snacks, too, like spiced almonds, chicken liver pâté, and pork rinds. At Wilfie & Nell, a popular gastropub in the West Village, I had my first Scotch egg. This is one husky bar snack—a hard-boiled egg wrapped in sausage meat, then breaded, seasoned, and fried. (The best ones have runny egg yolks at the center.) I also devoured UK-style pigs in a blanket—only the blanket in question was made out of bacon, not dough!—and chips doused in tart, malt vinegar.

If you order chips at a gastropub, you'll get fat French fries—sort of like American steak fries. (Want potato chips? Ask for crisps. Want a baked potato with your steak? Ask for a jacket potato.) Chips are the thick-cut English version of fries, but that's not the only difference. Most gastropubs fry their chips not once, but twice (sometimes even three times) in duck or beef fat. My problem with most thick-cut fries has always been their failure to live up to my crispy standards. Turns out, all they needed was another dip or two in the fryer. Thrice-cooked fries (excuse me, chips) are nirvana.

At The Breslin, Ken Friedman and April Bloomfield's newest gastropub, the thrice-cooked chips emerge from the kitchen golden and crisp, pillow soft at the center. But The Breslin is more than just The Spotted Pig 2.0. It's definitely not safe stomping ground for vegetarians, timid eaters, or offal-fearing diners. "The menu sounds like my worst nightmare," my sister said when this gastropub opened. I, on the other hand,

> **• TASTY MORSEL •**
>
> Offal *refers to butcher shop floor scraps, such as organ meats and entrails, like feet, head, and tongue. Historically those who couldn't afford "prime" cuts of meat bought inexpensive, protein-rich scraps instead.*

gushed to anyone who would listen about their braised beef shin and ungodly rich, smoked pork belly draped over a mound of buttery mashed potatoes. Sure, my meal could've sent me into cardiac arrest, but what a way to go.

This is a serious house of animal worship. "I love pig. Long live the middle white pig!" Bloomfield says. When in doubt, assume anything that comes out of The Breslin's kitchen has been fried in animal fat. The boiled peanuts and the spiced beans are both fried in pork fat. The onion soup is half onion, half bone marrow; the smoked salmon is spackled in bacon. This is head-to-tail dining—stuffed pig's foot for two (how romantic), fried headcheese, and, if you're brave enough to sit at the chef's table, whole roasted suckling pig and lamb's head. I remember glancing up from my Flintstones-size pork belly and giggling as I ob-

lled with hipsters dining on animal parts. The
wnright uncivilized, not to mention hazardous to
waistline. But it tastes good going down, and it's
t only because the meat is humanely raised on
local farms, but also because every last scrap is put to use—and
sustainability is in style. But this is the way the British ate for centuries. The majority of their diet came from meat, and nothing
ever went to waste. Kidney pies, faggots, and lamb tongue sandwiches were synonymous with home cooking. Just as Americans
snack on potato chips, the Brits snack on pork rinds (scratchings)
and roasted or fried pork skin. English comfort food consisted of
stews, meat puddings, vegetable mash, and pork pies.

English pies can be savory or sweet, so read the fine print. Case
in point: mincemeat pies are ironically meat-less. They're dessert
pies filled with minced dried fruits and spices. But savory pies
came first. Have you ever had a Cornish pasty? It's one of England's first meat pies, created way back in the 1200s by miners'
wives. A Cornish pasty was a miner's bagged lunch—an individual handheld pie with a crusty lid and a crimped edge to hold it
with—filled with meat, potatoes, and vegetables on one end, and
dessert on the other. Miners' wives carved their husbands' ini-
tials in the pasty's crust, so that a miner could identify his pasty
in the darkness. The piecrust also protected the worker's food
from arsenic in the mines. Nowadays the Brits still eat pasties and
pies, but most cooks use butter and oil instead of suet (rendered
animal fat akin to lard), and the crusts are buttery and rich. The
Breslin's mini beef and Stilton pie is a flaky-crusted flavor bomb
with sharp Stilton blue cheese, succulent beef, and vegetables.

Wilfie & Nell serves two very tasty pies: a handheld meat pie
and a shepherd's pie—dense with peas, carrots, potatoes, and Guin-
ness-braised lamb—topped with a clever mashed potato crust.
Shepherd's pies are always made with lamb—sheepherders' meat,

in other words—and cottage pies are always made with ground beef. If a menu lists plain old meat pie, you can assume it's made with beef as well. There are various English pies filled with everything from steak and kidney to mutton (lamb that's at least twelve months old). A tart is a small meatless pie with no top crust, filled with vegetables and cheese. One of my favorites is Clerkenwell's pea and leek tart with a poached egg on top. Beef Wellington is neither a type of pie nor a tart. It's more like an extra-large "pig in a blanket" of beef tenderloin coated in mushroom paste and pâté, then rolled up in a puff pastry.

Since nothing goes to waste, leftover meat scraps and offal are also ground up with seasonings and whipped into mousses and pâtés, or molded into terrines. Most gastropubs have one or two on their menu. April Bloomfield doesn't do anything in moderation. Instead, The Breslin has four homemade terrines, including a sweet rabbit and prune and a criminally unctuous headcheese terrine that comes with pickles, piccalilli (turmeric-flavored relish), and mustard, of course.

Stuff the ground meat into casings and you have sausage, better known in England as bangers. The first time I had bangers was years before the gastropub revolution. I was actually in pursuit of a cup of tea, so I stopped into a little haunt called Tea & Sympathy in Greenwich Village. For a second, I thought I'd accidentally walked into someone's apartment. There were bookshelves lining the walls, an antique sideboard, vintage teakettles, and other bric-a-brac scattered around the room. I had just eaten lunch, but I looked at the menu anyway. How could I resist a dish called bangers and mash? Mind you, I had no clue what it was, but I was game. It turned out to be a glorious mess of sausages perched on mashed potatoes and smothered in onion gravy (champs). We all have our British food "turning point," and this was mine. I'd heard British food was god-awful, but this was homey bliss. I was back the next

day for more. Sometimes I'd stop into Tea & Sympathy for a snack
of mashed potatoes and onion gravy. You could get even a side of
gravy in which to dip your chips.

This tiny tea shop did so well that the owner decided to open
a fish and chips shop—affectionately referred to as "chippies" by
the Brits—called A Salt & Battery right next door. I don't think
I was ready for Bloomfield's stuffed pig's foot straight out of college, but I was definitely ready for fish and chips. This clever combination first became popular with working-class families when
the English started fishing in the North Sea. I'd had a few soggy
American renditions before but nothing as wickedly crunchy and
fluffy as the fish at A Salt & Battery. The secret to English fish and
chips is the batter. Who else would think to spike the batter with
beer? Seltzer works, too. It's the bubbles that make the fish batter
extra light and crispy.

The options for battered fish at this chippie went way beyond
the standard cod—there was haddock, sole, pollack, even whiting
(and shrimp cakes!). After much deliberation, I went with the
haddock—the guy behind the counter said it was the one that all
the British expats ordered. The haddock was flaky and moist, a
splendid canvas for the light, salty batter. Skinny, skinless French
fries would've been overwhelmed by such firm fish, but not these
fat chips. The whole mess came bundled in an old issue of the
*Guardian*—a British daily newspaper. It doesn't get much more
authentic, especially since the chef's father ran a chippie himself.
In true chippie form, Mat Amfeld—the chef in question—serves
sides of mushy peas, mashed potatoes, and baked beans, and bottles of curry sauce and malt vinegar line the counters.

In the United Kingdom, fish tends to be prepared three ways—
fried, smoked, or deviled. Subtle is not an option. You don't see
much deviled mackerel—spiced with paprika, pepper, and English mustard—on gastropub menus in America, which is too

bad because it's fantastic. Instead you'll find salads aggressively dressed in anchovies and warm smoked salmon or cold smoked whitefish. Kedgeree, one of England's finest breakfast foods, is a mix of flaked smoked haddock, hard-boiled egg, cream, rice, and curry powder.

I know breakfast is the most important meal of the day, but the English take it a tad too far. A "full English breakfast"—emphasis on the full—comes with fried eggs, bacon, sausage, grilled tomatoes, mushrooms, baked beans, and toast. It's delicious going down, but I always want to get right back into bed after. Are the English storing up for winter? Do they wake up with a collective hangover every morning? (This is great, greasy hangover food.) I tell myself, "Don't do it this time, Danyelle. You'll regret it." I try to coax myself into fried eggs with just bacon, but sausages and black pudding (a type of sausage made primarily from congealed beef or pork blood) both sound tempting, too. Again, I've polished off five greasy food groups before noon. Oops. For those who prefer not to consume 90 percent of their allotted daily caloric intake before 10:00 A.M., there are always scones or English muffins. In America we frequently settle for Thomas' midget muffins, but those don't even come close to the real thing. A legitimate English muffin rises to one inch and comes dusted with cornmeal. The dust at the bottom of a Thomas' bag is farina, not cornmeal. No dice.

Some people mistake an English muffin for a crumpet and vice versa. A crumpet resembles a puffed-up minipancake with big pores. A crumpet is spongy, while a muffin is dense. But they're both cooked on the griddle and accompanied by a battery of condiments such as lemon curd, a sweet-tart custard made from lemon juice, sugar, and eggs; clotted cream, a thick, almost buttery spread made from scalded milk; and marmalade, as well as jam, preserves, and jelly. Though those last three are made with the same basic in-

gredients (fruit, sugar, and pectin), they use different parts of the
fruit. Jelly is made from juice only, jam from thick fruit pulp, and
preserves from whole pieces of fruit. Marmalade is just jam with
fruit zest added to it. I prefer chunky preserves. And, of course,
English muffins, scones, and their condiments pair perfectly with
tea, particularly in the afternoon.

When tea was first introduced to England in the mid-1600s,
only the wealthy could afford to drink it, as the tax on tea was
sky high. (Unless you skipped the taxes and smuggled it into the
country, which happened with some regularity.) King Charles II
and his Portuguese wife, Catherine of Braganza—habitual tea
drinkers—first introduced tea to England in 1662, and shortly
thereafter the wealthy followed their royal lead. In 1676, King
Charles II imposed a heavy tea tax (Scrooge!), which only got
heavier and heavier, reaching 119 percent by the middle of the
eighteenth century. We all want what we can't afford. I long for
a spoonful of caviar daily, but I need a roof over my head, and
something's gotta give. In 1784 William Pitt the Younger low-
ered the tax from 119 percent to 12 percent, and finally there was
tea for the masses. But the ritual of afternoon tea didn't origi-
nate until the 1840s, when a hungry duchess, Anna Maria Stan-
hope, couldn't wait for dinner, so she requested that bread, butter,
small cakes, and tea be brought up to her boudoir at the stroke
of 4:00 P.M. every day. Before you knew it, she started inviting
friends over for afternoon tea and snacks. The notion of afternoon
tea served with dainty tea sandwiches and tiny cakes became a
countrywide ritual.

Think of afternoon tea as a mini-meal with savory and sweet
courses. I endured a five-course afternoon tea at Lady Mendl's Tea
Salon on Irving Place in Manhattan, which started at three and
ended at five-thirty in the afternoon—and all I wanted were the
scones! These savory-sweet biscuits usually come plain or simply
seasoned with raisins, nuts, or spices. The focus is the rich bis-

cuit and its sweet accompaniments. Tea parties traditionally begin with dainty sandwiches on buttered bread with the crusts cut off. They can be as simple (and dull) as peeled cucumber with salt and lemon on white bread or as flavorful as curried chicken salad or smoked salmon on pumpernickel.

Don't expect to find dainty tea cakes on British dessert menus. Instead imagine desserts as rich as the mains—as rich as a beef pie or a braised beef shin. Sticky toffee pudding is a naughty, gooey deal closer. But it's not pudding the way we Americans think of it. (American-style puddings do exist in England. They're traditionally made with suet, but most chefs now use butter.) Sticky toffee pudding is sponge cake infused with chopped dates or prunes, then lacquered with a thick toffee sauce. A trifle cake also starts off harmlessly enough—the base is also simple sponge cake—but it's then layered with egg custard, cream, and sherry-soaked fruit. If you'd rather skip the cake part, try an Eton Mess, made with fruit, cream, and meringue. The Breslin produces an Italian-inspired Eton Mess with lemon ricotta cream. But the best dessert card they're holding at The Breslin is their Stout Syllabub, which would make the menu for my hypothetical last meal. Traditional English syllabub is a thick, frothy dessert composed of wine, sugar, and cream (some chefs substitute cider for wine and milk for cream). The Breslin's rendition is made with a rich, dark stout beer and cream—more like a velvety, stiff mousse than a frothy, silky liquid. What cinches it for me is the cloud of crème fraîche that caps it, sprinkled with crunchy, caramel-coated rice puffs. I hope someone reads this and brings a Stout Syllabub to my bedside.

Anything with treacle in its name should satisfy your sweet tooth. Treacle—also referred to as golden syrup because of its honey color—is evaporated cane sugar syrup. This thick, nutty syrup was England's first sweetener before processed sugar became widely available. Treacle sweetens pudding, tarts, and cakes and lends them a wonderful stickiness.

Need a little something to wash down all that pudding and pie? For all intents and purposes, beer is a basic British food group. A pub that doesn't serve beer is like an American diner that doesn't serve cheap coffee. Beer is the oldest alcoholic beverage in existence and the third most popular drink in the world. You can get your daily beer intake from ale or lager. Ales are bold and complex, while lagers are more simple and subdued. Porters and stouts are ales, while pilsners are a type of lager. If your bartender tells you something's hoppy, he means that it's distinctly bitter and fragrant. (The less hoppy a beer is, the less bitterness and aroma it has.)

America and England have different takes on what constitutes a pint—whose would you guess is bigger? That's right, the British Imperial pint at twenty tall ounces beats out the sixteen-ounce American pint. At a stateside pub it never hurts to ask whether or not they serve an Imperial pint—you never know, you might just impress your date and your bartender by knowing your stuff.

## Table Setting and Modern Manners

Unlike traditional pubs, the atmosphere at a gastropub seems less focused on manners. They're laid-back watering holes with spirited snacks, sandwiches, and burgers you eat with your hands. And as long as your pinky finger is sticking up properly on your teacup hand, you're ready for afternoon tea. Whether you're at a tea party or a pub, remember to tear off a piece of bread before buttering it. The English eat most things with a knife and fork. When you're finished, put the prongs of the fork face up on your plate. (It's the opposite in the United States.) The proper way to pick up your peas is by crushing them onto the back of your fork. Spoons are for soups (unless you're having tea). Oh, and never touch another man's ale or his fish and chips, especially while he's watching football. That's a perfect storm I wouldn't want to get caught in!

# · 2 ·

# Chinese Cuisine

*You don't sew with a fork, so I see no*
*reason to eat with knitting needles.*

MISS PIGGY

According to my mom, I've been eating hot
and sour soup since I was one. When I was
growing up, my family ate Chinese food at
least once a week. Unlike the stereotypi-
cal Jewish family, we didn't restrict ourselves to Sunday night scallion pancakes.
(But that stereotype is pretty accurate. I'd
wager more American Jews eat Chinese on Sundays than Shab-
bat dinner on Fridays. And don't get me started on Christmas.)
Our family haunt was a restaurant called Hunan Spring, located
in Springfield, New Jersey. With its chintzy green booths, match-
ing carpeting, and a cashier's station at the front entrance, Hunan Spring looks more like a diner that serves grilled cheese and
greasy breakfasts than a Chinese restaurant. No matter how many
times I visited, I was always surprised when the blue and white
porcelain plates of food appeared, piled with snow peas and squiggly, soy-sauce-stained noodles.

Hunan Spring sits right next to the tracks for the commuter

train that carries passengers between New Jersey and New York City. Whenever I happened to be on that train, I pressed my face up against the window to watch the stone building whiz by, recounting everyone's order in my memory. As a kid, I always started with hot and sour soup, a nourishing option during snowy winters in the suburbs. I'd wrap my hands around the porcelain bowl and steal a little heat from the muddy broth. I'll admit it's not the most attractive soup to stare down into, but its pleasures are many—a deeply tangy broth full of slippery black mushrooms, silken tofu, shreds of pork, wood ear mushrooms, lily bulbs, and crunchy strands of bamboo shoots. There's a subtle but invigorating heat that comes from all the black and white pepper in the broth. My mom and dad each got hot and sour soup, too, and my brother and sister always ordered egg drop soup. (A beaten egg dropped in chicken broth was all my brother ever wanted when he got the flu.)

We'd nibble on complimentary bowls of fried noodles that we dunked in fluorescent orange duck sauce while my dad proceeded to overorder. We'd start with appetizers (practically a full dinner in and of themselves): juicy pot stickers, scallion pancakes, and spring rolls packed with shreds of chicken, shrimp, and Chinese vegetables. Some foods are just meant to be greasy, and the scallion pancakes at Hunan Spring were deliciously so. The edges were crispy, the interiors laden with silky layers laced with scallions— little sponges ideal for soaking up the salty-sweet dipping sauce that traditionally accompanies them. If you had asked me what was in the plum sauce I was dipping everything else in, I would've stared at you blankly. I certainly didn't know the difference between plum sauce, hoisin sauce, and duck sauce. I ate by instinct. I liked crisp spring rolls better than doughy egg rolls. I liked the crunchy edges of pork pot stickers with ginger dipping sauce, the feeling of cold, slippery noodles in sesame sauce as they crossed my tongue, and the clean, pronounced flavors of prawns mingled with firm string beans.

We always had the same debate over whether to get moo shu shrimp or moo shu chicken. I loved the moo shu pancakes—small, springy rounds reminiscent of crepes. So long as some form of moo shu appeared on the table, I didn't really care, and no one else ever seemed to mind too much who won out on that particular night. Besides, the only difference was the protein; the rest was stir-fry goodness: a tangle of scrambled egg, julienned cabbage, wood ear mushrooms, bean sprouts, carrots, and—fingers crossed—shrimp. We dabbed our pancakes with thick hoisin sauce, added the eggy stir-fry, and made ourselves "Chinese tacos."

We were a family of five living in the 'burbs and we ordered like one: we got beef and broccoli; moo goo gai pan, a "fun to say" stir-fry of chicken, button mushrooms, water chestnuts, and broccoli; and chicken fried rice. To this day, my brother, sister, and I still sneak in an order of chicken fried rice whenever we have Chinese food. There's something utterly comforting about fluffy rice studded with scrambled egg, crunchy scallions, peas, and torn chicken. Family dinners always ended the same way: with a pot of black tea, sliced oranges, and fortune cookies. Probably because we never failed to order enough to feed a small army, we never left Hunan Spring without leftovers, and my dad would promptly scavenge them the minute we arrived home (right before he tore open a sleeve of Mallomars). We were suburbanites raised on Chinese-American food, an abridged version of mild Cantonese fare: General Tso's chicken, chop suey, and lo mein.

Nonetheless I thought Chinese-American cooking was Chinese cooking. Every few years my family ventured into Chinatown in downtown New York for the Chinese New Year parade, some celebratory peanut cookies, and a new fake designer bag for my mom. I'd skimmed the menu at Hunan Spring tons of times, but I never once tried the "Hunan beef" or even asked a server what was in it. I didn't know the difference between Szechuan or Cantonese or Beijing cuisine. I didn't know I owed Beijing a debt of gratitude for hot and sour soup or Szechuan for kung pao chicken. If I had grown up near or even in Chinatown in downtown New York, San Francisco, or Los Angeles, I might've known my chop suey from my chow mein, but suburbia doesn't offer much in the way of a local "hot pot" spot or an eatery that specializes in soup dumplings or Beijing food. It was only when I moved into New York postcollege that I realized I'd been eating "fake designer bags" all along (so to speak), geared toward suburbanites like myself.

As I ate my way through New York's Chinatown, I learned that there are four major regional cuisines—Cantonese, Beijing, Szechuan, and Shanghai—each with its own styles and specialties. The thing about China is that it's huge (it is home to one-sixth of the planet's population, after all). Some regions of China have access to water and seafood; others don't, so they eat lots of meat instead. Some regions have access to rice, while others rely on noodles and dumplings. And just like every person I know, different regions have different preferences. Some prefer spicy, others sweet; some opt for dark sauces, others light. Most of the dishes I'd eaten growing up were ostensibly Cantonese, with a dash of all the other regional cuisines tossed in for good measure. But I knew nothing of Szechuan cooking and its tongue-tingling peppercorns or the hundreds of hot pots those peppercorns set ablaze. I had never had the pleasure of experiencing Shanghai cuisine, with its signature dark and sweet sauces or its miraculous soup dumplings. Though I'd nibbled on Cantonese, I had no idea that it was a vast cuisine comprised of many diverse regional food traditions, like Hong Kong's roasted meats and dim sum, or that Beijing deserved the credit for barbecued Peking duck. But I was about to find out.

## Beijing Cuisine

The thing about food addicts is they're always looking for partners in crime, so they figure out your weaknesses, and mine was hot and sour soup. A friend took me to The Peking Duck House, a Beijing-style spot on Mott Street in the heart of Chinatown. "I don't eat duck," I protested on the subway ride downtown. "You will," he responded without an ounce of doubt in his voice. "But I thought we were getting soup," I begged. "We are. Beijing is known for two things: Peking duck and hot and sour soup." The first thing I did when I sat down was scan the menu for my soup. The soup was excellent, but I was dead set against trying the duck. That is until it arrived at the table. Really, it was more like a ceremonial presentation: a whole duck, with skin lacquered deepest bronze, and irresistibly aromatic.

After we had admired the high gloss of the bird for a few captivating moments, our server picked up a knife and carved it, just like my father used to do with the Thanksgiving turkey. Except in this case, it was the skin—not the meat—our server was after. He carefully carved out delicate crackling squares, placed them on their own plate, along with a feast of accoutrements that included steamed flour pancakes, finely sliced scallions, cucumbers, and a bowl of hoisin sauce. I followed my friend's lead and spread a thin layer of hoisin in the middle of my still-steaming pancake, added a few scallions and bits of cucumber, and finally, a shiny piece of skin. I folded it all up, closed my eyes, and took a bite. It was gloriously crisp and sweet. The first square of skin is the acid test, the cracklier the better. (In order to get that crackly skin, the duck is basted in soy sauce and sugar and hung to air-dry before being roasted.) Then came the succulent, lean meat, which we added to the second round of pancakes. (Peking duck is traditionally served with steamed buns, but most restaurants stateside serve it with steamed pancakes instead.) When there was nothing but hoisin sauce and a sliver of cucumber left, my friend looked my way and said, "I thought you don't eat duck?"

Beijing is most famous for its iconic Peking duck, with good reason, but is also known for its dumplings, noodles, braised shark's fin, and steamed breads. Their signature dishes include hot and sour soup and moo shoo pork. (Beijing cuisine is also known as Mandarin or Peking cuisine.) We tried the perfectly crisped pan-fried pork dumplings bursting with juicy ground meat and steamy pork buns stuffed with sweet, roast pork. But nothing etched itself in my memory quite like that glorious Peking duck.

## Cantonese Cooking

I was hooked. So the next week my friend whisked me to a Cantonese spot called Great NY Noodletown that specializes in Hong Kong–style roasted meats. There is no decor to speak of, just harsh, fluorescent lighting, cheap convention-hall-style tables and chairs, and a chef hacking up highly perfumed, five-spice-scented ducks and hogs near the entrance. (Five-spice powder is a hand-mixed spice blend that corresponds to the five tastes: sweet, sour, bitter, pungent, and salty. The spices can vary according to the chef, but it's usually a mixture of Szechuan peppercorns, cloves, cinnamon, star anise, and fennel.) Great NY Noodletown is a crispy-skinned wonderland of not just duck served every which way, but pork and chicken, too—many of them dangling from hooks right in the storefront window.

Noodletown's roast duck is excellent, especially the shredded duck with pea shoots, but the roast pork is riveting. When this toothsome, tender meat is on the table, I can focus on nothing else. Fortunately for me there's many ways to get a fix: I like it sliced over rice or skimming the surface of a voluptuous noodle soup. There's dozens of homemade noodles on the menu—thin or thick, pan-fried with seafood and various meats, or dropped into steaming broths. It is called Great NY *Noodle*town, after all. I can never resist a side order of mysteriously greaseless duck rolls and fried rice with sausage (I am my father's daughter). I got my mom into Noodletown, too. The lady was hooked on the salt-baked soft-shell crab, with plump, dewy meat just beneath a crunchy shell.

Cantonese is a seafood-rich cuisine—the fresher, the better. In fact, many Cantonese restaurants have fish tanks on the premises, so the fish can keep swimming until you order. Cantonese food tends to be light and mild—you'll rarely come across anything spicy. Sweetness is rare in Cantonese dishes—they stick to salty and tart flavors, using lots of garlic, green onions, ginger, and soy sauce in their cooking. Agriculture flourishes throughout Canton, and game is abundant, too, so sautéed vegetables and roasted meats are plentiful, in addition to seafood. Really, the only thing they don't have plenty of is rice, so they make noodles, dumplings, and pancakes instead. There's a wealth of slow-cooked soups and stews as well as congee (rice porridge), too.

Every city in the Canton region has its own specialties. Hong Kong is famous for roasted meats, noodles, and dim sum. Its trademark dishes are crispy, not soft, lo mein (which means "tossed noodles") topped with brown sauce, and Hong Kong–style soups—

slow-cooked broth served in a separate bowl from the meat or fish it was simmered with.

Oriental Garden, just a few blocks from Noodletown, takes the Cantonese notion of fresh fish to another level. The dining room's both chaotic and sterile: the tables are tightly packed together, decoration is minimal, and the menu is epic. It's easier just to order by pointing at the fish tanks filled with a kaleidoscope of live sea creatures. Oriental Garden's sea bass is a silken, ivory wonder, steamed with ginger and scallions and served whole. There are fist-size oysters, scallops in hot garlic sauce, chewy clams in a woodsy black bean sauce, and lobster pretty much any way you like it. My favorite lobster preparation comes glossed in XO sauce, a thick night-black sauce made with chile, garlic, dried scallops, and shrimp. And if you're in the mood to splurge, you can partake in a Cantonese delicacy of clean-tasting shark fin soup for $68.00 a bowl. (To me it's one of those "emperor's new clothes" dishes that sound decadent but taste like nothing at all.) The sautéed spinach with garlic and the crisp Chinese broccoli taste just as fresh as anything that swims on the menu.

Just one meal of authentic, Chinatown Cantonese food turned me into a believer, and I decided to eat my way through China. Still, I discovered dim sum, a staple Cantonese breakfast food, by accident, not intent. I'm way too old to stay up all night anymore, but once upon a time in the late 1990s—what feels like an eternity ago—I would on occasion see the sun rise before I saw my pillow. (Ah, the good old days.) I'd been frolicking around the city one summer night until the wee hours of the morning with two equally invincible friends. The evening started off innocently enough with dinner at some Italian spot in the West Village. But next thing I knew, it was nine in the morning, and I was still wearing a dress and heels. I was at that point where you realize how sorely overrated all-nighters are. My friends and I wandered down Elizabeth Street, deliriously tired and hungry, looking for something to eat. Our last slice of pizza had been untold hours earlier. My feet were about to give out on me when I noticed a Chinese family, and then another, and another disappearing through an unmarked door. I've always been unusually curious, not just hungry, so I followed them inside and then up a long escalator that spilled out into a massive room. I thought I might be hallucinating because it looked an awful lot like a casino. Blue and pink fluorescent lights pulsed overhead. I was certain I'd stumbled into an illegal gambling hall in Chinatown until I noticed a steaming cart, and then another, feverishly circling the room. It was a miraculous sight: more and more carts appeared, stacked high with bamboo steamers, the scent of sweet, freshly baked buns and rich meats in the air.

Dim sum at Jing Fong was pure serendipity. We were rushed to our table, handed long, detailed "order cards," and seated with strangers—as is commonplace in dim sum halls—who paid no attention to our smudged makeup and evening attire. We were all united in one mission: hailing carts, which was challenging, considering the mob of eager eaters. Forget the niceties; dim sum is a "take no prisoners" experience. Waving your hands to get a server's attention is totally acceptable and advised if you don't want to miss out on a rapidly moving target—I mean, cart—filled

---

• TASTY MORSEL •

*At dim sum restaurants, there are no menus, just order cards. Every time you get a dish, the server checks off the corresponding box on the card. Most cards are organized according to small, medium, and large dishes. At the end of the meal, a server or cashier tallies up the bill from your card.*

with snacks. I liken dim sum to a roving buffet that comes to you—the perfect breakfast for three exhausted women with aching feet.

Dim sum was made for people like me who would rather eat breakfast at eleven than first thing in the morning, and who crave both salty and sweet flavors at every meal. There are salty dim sum, like barbecue pork rolls (char siu cheung fun), and there are sweet dim sum, like egg custard. There are sticky rice bundles with an array of fillings, like shrimp or lotus root; outrageously fluffy steamed buns filled with everything from sweet red beans (dow sa bow) to meaty chunks of sausage (lat cheung bow); rice dishes flavored with curry or black bean sauce; noodles tangled around beef or crab; flavorful soups and plates piled with roast pork spareribs and fried squid. (Luckily I didn't then know there were upward of sixty kinds of dim sum floating around the room, or we never would've made it out of there.) I needed to strategize, so I ordered a pot of oolong tea, which is dim sum's raison d'être. Tea drinking—"yum cha" in Chinese—is a social ritual in China, replete with its own customs and traditions. In fact, dim sum were originally made to complement the yum cha experience. Without tea, there is no dim sum. We learned a lot by observing the strangers seated at our table. They taught us to open the lid of our teapot when we needed a refill and to tap the table with two fingers as a gesture of thanks.

It was a beautiful thing really, strangers bonded by sweet pork buns (cha siu bau), supple sheets of rice noodles as wide and flat as an eight-by-ten piece of paper, fried shrimp balls, and a slew of hand-pinched dumplings, some filled with beef, others with minced shrimp or pork or finely chopped vegetables, or some tasty combination of the above. The wrapper is a good litmus test of a dumpling: gummy, thick, or overly chewy are not qualities you want in a dumpling. Jing Fong's steamed shrimp har gow—pleated dumplings that look like little bonnets—were perfectly chewy; the wrappers are made from a combination of wheat starch and tapioca, so that they offer the perfect amount of resistance with each bite. The siu mai (also called shumai), purse-shaped dumplings that are pinched at the top but left unsealed, so that the meaty filling forms a golden crust at the top, were marvelously juicy, the rice paper wrappers taut and tender. But the best by far were the shrimp and chive dumplings, the pale pink stuffing flecked with green visible through the translucent wrapper. I wasn't brave enough to tempt the soy sauce chicken feet, but we gorged ourselves silly on wu tao go (sweet turnip cakes) and pai guck (steamed pork spareribs) with taro root, garlic, and red pepper. I was in heaven. And as soon as I made it home and fell into bed, I slept like a baby right through to Monday morning.

One Chinese breakfast staple down, but I still had yet to taste congee, also known as jook, so I went straight to the source: a Cantonese restaurant on the Lower East Side aptly named Congee Village. I've always loved hot breakfast cereals: oatmeal, Cream of Wheat, cream of rice, and grits, but rice porridge topped with pork and liver or fresh squid had never been part of my morning repertoire. Congee Village is one quirky-looking restaurant: the dining room's decked out in bamboo huts and hanging plastic vines to evoke a tropical village, but I think it looks like a kitschy tiki bar. The crowd's a motley mix of night crawlers, big families, and serious

• TASTY MORSEL •

Dim sum *means "touch your heart." The name comes from the emotional effect of eating such lovingly created and appetizing food—it's both a compliment to talented dim sum chefs and a good litmus test for how dim sum (and all food, for that matter) should make you feel.*

eaters intent on their steaming bowls. En route to our table, I noticed a plate of what looked like goose feet—with nothing attached to them. If I'd had a drink before dinner—in retrospect, I should have—I would've thought I was seeing things. But I was sober, and I have perfect vision. Needless to say, I was frightened of the meal to come. "I think I just saw someone eating goose webs. I didn't sign up for this," I whispered to my friend—the one who had coaxed me into going. "You wanted congee. I'm bringing you to the epicenter of Chinese rice porridge in New York," she reprimanded me. I felt like I was an unsuspecting contestant in a *Fear Factor* food challenge.

I had no idea the kind of extreme eating the Chinese were accustomed to, not to mention head-to-web eating. I received an eye-opening education that night. The sixteen-page menu was full of exotic dishes like turtle soup, snails with black bean sauce, and frogs with chives. But we came for congee, so that's what we focused on.

First we began with an order of pork congee and an order of duck and meatball congee. What arrived looked like two giant bowls of Cream of Wheat scattered with a fistful of fresh cilantro and green onions. The congee itself was marvelously thick and soothing, the perfect partner for the sweet strands of duck and succulent slivers of pork. The secret to congee's creaminess is that the rice is boiled at some length in a very large amount of water until the grains have broken down and released all of their glutinous starch. Even though we had eaten a copious amount of congee, we couldn't resist trying the braised sea cucumber with abalone sauce (perhaps the fortifying congee had restored some of our bravery). Not knowing what you're eating is sometimes a good thing. I assumed sea cucumber was a type of algae, the kind you find mingled in a seaweed salad at a Japanese restaurant, and that abalone was a kind of shellfish. Not exactly. Both crawl, if that gives you any indication of their character. Sea cucumber—a marine animal that indeed looks like a cucumber—doesn't have much flavor, just a pleasantly chewy texture that sponges up its sauce, which in this case was made from briny abalone, otherwise known as sea snails. The dish was a cool complement to the house special chicken, which was as crispy as any Peking duck I've eaten and heaped with browned garlic; it might just be the best thing on the menu.

## Shanghai Cuisine

I didn't find Shanghai cuisine. It found me. During the work-week I try my hardest not to travel far for lunch, or I'll end up spending the day in search of something exciting to eat, which means that by the time I get back to do a little work, it's already time for dinner. One day I was determined to get lunch within a five-block radius, so I headed to Fifty-sixth Street between Sixth and Seventh avenues. This isn't the loveliest block in the city, but because it's Midtown—land of cubicle dwellers galore—there are lots of decent lunch options, including Joe's Shanghai. I jumped at the chance to sneak in a little "research" during lunch. I had no personal guide, so I stood by the entrance and read the restaurant's many reviews posted along the wall, which all pointed in the direction of the Shanghai soup dumplings (xiao long bao). Unless they were referring to the kinds of dump-lings you find in wonton soup, I didn't think I had ever tried them. The menu featured two kinds of soup dumplings: straight pork or a mix of pork and crab, so I ordered one of each. (On the menu, they're referred to as "steamed buns," not dumplings, be-cause the dumpling wrapper is made from the same dough as steamed buns.) I was expecting two bowls of soup with a dumpling or two floating in each. What came to the table were two plates of pudgy dumplings that looked like they would burst at any second and a shallow bowl of vinegar—soy sauce with ginger. "Wait," I thought, "the soup is inside the dumpling?" They were mesmerizing. "How on earth do they get the broth in there?" I found myself wondering until the server interrupted my reverie and urged me to start eating the dumplings before they got cold. I was a little afraid to take the plunge, fearing that scalding hot liquid would flood my mouth. The server, noticing my nervousness, instructed me to poke a hole in the dumpling's thin skin with a chopstick, dip it in the sauce, and "eat quickly." That's what I did.

Let me tell you, soup dumplings are mysterious acts of god. Each one is a hypnotic revelation composed of breathtakingly thin wrappers, deeply flavorful liquid, and nibbles of rich meat. Years after that serendipitous lunch, I traveled to Los Angeles, where I made a pilgrimage to Arcadia, a suburb of Los Angeles that's a haven for phenomenal Chinese food and, more importantly, home to the only Din Tai Fung outpost in North America. (The original is located in the Taipei city in Taiwan.) Din Tai Fung is widely known among foodies as the holy grail of xiao long bao. Word of my expedition spread quickly among my friends, as tends to happen with food fanatics. Next thing I knew, we were a party of six.

Because Din Tai Fung's soup dumplings have inspired such a cult following, there's always a long line of waiting diners trailing out the restaurant's door. I passed the time pressed up against the glassed-in kitchen near the entrance, where an assembly line of cooks molds every single dumpling by hand, an enchanting sight that I could watch for hours on end. When we were finally seated, the server dropped off a pot of tea and an order pad, and then disappeared. There was some debate about what to order, and everyone was fighting for the pad. Arguments broke out about whether we should devote all our efforts to pork soup dumplings or venture into some of Din Tai Fung's other dishes. (I bet you can guess which way I leaned. Hey, the more, the merrier.)

Shanghai is also known for its steamed buns, pork pot stickers, and stir-fried dishes. The sauces are notably darker and sweeter than in Cantonese cooking, employing lots of soy, sugar, and alcohol. Seafood dishes are popular, particularly oysters, crabs, and seaweed. They're famous for "drunken chicken" cooked in spirits, "beggar's chicken" wrapped in lotus leaves and cooked in clay, as well as thick pan-fried noodles slathered in sesame sauce. Perhaps the most unique Shanghai contribution is the "Thousand-Year-Old Egg," an egg preserved in salt, lime, and calcium, and buried in the ground for twenty-eight days, which tastes curiously of cheese and ginger.

We ended up adding a side of electric green spinach, the mountain of crisp, sharply flavored leaves further sparked by golden garlic. I felt it my foodie duty to throw in an order of hot noodles coated in a luscious sesame-peanut sauce. I'm in awe of the Chinese finesse with dumplings, and they produce the same soft, stretchy quality in their noodles as well. And there's a proliferation of noodle dishes to choose from: chow fun, stir-fried wide, flat ribbons of rice noodles; lo mein, egg noodles "stirred" with various meats and vegetables (the same noodles stir-fried are called chow mein); and the aforementioned sesame noodles. As for the soup dumplings, they were dazzling works of art—precious pouches of deliciousness with perfect pleats—that came in a tall tin steamer, ten to an order. The broth was profoundly fragrant and the wrapper super thin.

> • **TASTY MORSEL** •
>
> *The secret to soup dumplings is that the meaty, brothy filling is actually made from squares of aspic that the dumpling skins are then wrapped around. The gelatinous squares of broth melt into a liquid as soon as the dumplings are steamed.*

## Szechuan Cuisine

On the way home from Din Tai Fung, I must've passed fifteen advertisements for "hot pots," a fiery mainstay of Szechuan (also spelled Sichuan) cooking that used to make the hair on the back of my neck stand up. See, I was blindsided by a hot pot after college, and I had been deathly afraid of all matters of the spicy Szechuan sort since. Long story short: a friend who had just spent the year in China wanted to show off his newfound food knowledge, so we went to Flushing, Queens, for dinner at a restaurant appropriately named Spicy & Tasty. Someone at the table likened a hot pot to a "Chinese fondue with a kick," so I ordered one. Now, I can hack kung pao chicken—easy on the POW—with its signature dice of fried chicken, peanuts, red chiles, and peppercorns. But kung pao chicken is like peewee soccer in the face of a major league hot pot. Our server should have handed me a release form with my hot pot, or at least posted a disclaimer on the menu that said, "Eat at your own risk," so I had some indication of the burn to come.

Hot pots are nothing like a typical cheese or chocolate fondue, and whoever says they are is not your friend. A hot pot is a deceptive dish: it's not as if they hand you a bowl piled with chiles. What's at the bottom of the pot is an oily, shallow pool that's technically a dipping sauce. Admittedly I dunked instead of dipped, but my so-called friend neglected to mention the Szechuan peppercorns that had been toasting in the oil or the potent dose of red chiles in it. The fiery combination is known as "mala sauce," which has a unique "spice-numbing" effect. Mala gets its tongue-tingling quality, or "ma," from the peppercorns and its fire, or "la," from fiery red chiles. Szechuan peppercorns are my Darth Vader, my Lex Luthor—the kind of fire-breathing spice that wildly exceeds my capacity. I had no feeling in my tongue for days past that hot pot incident. It's the tingly sensation fire-eaters are after when they go for Szechuan. Lesson learned: hot pots are not a beginner dish.

Despite its heat, Szechuan is the most widely eaten cuisine in China and is notoriously spicy and pungent. There is a method behind the madness: the Szechuan region is extremely humid, and the combination of chiles and peppercorns helps make you sweat, cooling the body off in the process. Szechuan cooking is known for its oily, hot taste and the presence of ginger, garlic, fermented soybeans, and soy sauce in many dishes. The Szechuan employ unique cooking methods, like pickling, tea-smoking, dry-braising, dry-frying, and twice-cooking meats. As a result, pork and beef tend to be soft and luscious, while vegetables tend to be crisp.

Hunan and Szechuan cuisines are like kissing cousins. Like Szechuan, Hunan also tends to be spicy. Most dishes are made with dried chile peppers, garlic, and shallots. You'll find lots of brown sauce and sweet and sour sauce dishes on Hunanese menus as well as rice and fish, which are abundant in this region. Their favorite cooking methods are braised, stewed, and double-cooked.

What I didn't know was that not all Szechuan food should come with a fire extinguisher. (Thank God.) I'm a foodie, and foodies don't like to feel defeated, so I decided it was time to give Szechuan another try. This time I brought a mala interpreter who wanted me to love Szechuan as much as she did. She took me to Grand Sichuan in Midtown Manhattan for lunch, and later that week we went back for dinner. She ordered for us, and I added, "Mild!" at the end of every dish. I discovered Szechuan's trademark pickled vegetables, tea-smoked duck, double-cooked pork, and righteously tender braised beef, as well as the comparatively cool heat of ma po tofu. I experienced the pungent, sour, sweet, salty, and hot flavors that embody Szechuan cooking, performing a number on your tongue in a single bite. I love pickled anything, and I especially loved the sweet and sour crunch that pickled vegetables brought to a sliced fish soup and even more to a traditional dish of dan dan noodles, which came tossed with pickled greens, ground pork, and an oily red sauce that became a recurring theme at the table. "See that?" my friend warned, pointing to the oily pool forming at the bottom of the plate. "That's mala, so be careful." "But it's mild mala, right?" I asked. "Yes," she answered. My first bite was baby-size as I nervously assessed the strands of thin, slicked noodles, bits of pork, and one lone pickled green in my mouth. It wasn't mild, but the heat was tempered by the salty, sweet, and sour crunch of the pickled greens, the succulence of the pork, and the soft, soothing noodles. And that was the exact moment when I conquered my fear of mala and made my way into ma po tofu (also called mapo dofu.)

Ma po tofu is one of the most complex and interesting tofu dishes I've tasted—creamy cubes of tofu scattered with crumbled pork, red chiles, and musky, fermented black beans in that ubiquitous oily red sauce I was slowly starting to embrace. Seeing as I was now a duck convert-cum-fanatic, I insisted on ordering the tea-smoked duck, which was not at all like Peking duck. It was elegant; the skin was not as crisp as Peking duck, but the meat was moister than any I had tried, with an intense smokiness that would've gone well with an aged red wine. We had twice-cooked pork (boiled, then wok-fried), nearly as creamy as the tofu, and dry-sautéed string beans, incredibly blistery and crunchy.

The Chinese aren't habitual dessert eaters. Their idea of a sweet ending is fresh fruit, which explains the customary plate of orange wedges next to the check. The more elaborate confections are made for special occasions and holidays, like my favorite, Eight

Treasure Rice Pudding—a milky rice pudding laden with dates, red beans, almonds, and maraschino cherries—made for New Year's, or Exchange Moon Cakes—small cakes filled with a salted duck yolk and lotus seed paste—made for the Mid-Autumn Festival, which celebrates the lunar cycle. I do love the egg custard tarts and sweet, red-bean-stuffed sesame buns served at dim sum. The best way to go are the shaved ices covered with those addictively chewy tapioca pearls you'll also find floating in bubble teas.

## Table Setting and Modern Manners

The Chinese dinner table is pretty straightforward. Most of the time you'll find a napkin and chopsticks. It's more likely you'll find teacups rather than water glasses on the table, especially at dim sum parlors, where water is typically served by request only. I asked for a knife once, and the server acted as if he hadn't heard me. So I asked again, and he sent the owner over to tell me, "No knives." "That's strange," I said, "How come?" "No knives," he responded and turned and walked away. The Chinese think of knives as weapons, not table utensils, which is probably why everything's diced or minced into little pieces. (For the record, I did need a knife.) But you can ask for a fork, and you'll likely be happily obliged (and you can use its edge to cut with, should you need to). The only thing you shouldn't cut are noodles. It's bad luck to cut noodles because they symbolize longevity. Cut your noodles and you'll have a shorter life. Enough said.

As with most Asian chopstick cultures, it's impolite to gesture with, chew on, or wave your chopsticks. Sticking them straight up in something indicates death rituals, so I'd advise against that. And don't use them to stab a piece of meat. That was my second mistake after I was refused a knife. Boy, did I get a dirty look, though

I'd consider that one a misdemeanor—the kind of look you'd get if you stuck chopsticks up your nose to imitate a walrus. (I've had some bad dates.) You can, however, laugh and converse as loudly as you'd like at the dinner table. In fact it's quite flattering to the chef and the owner because noise and crowds are telltale signs of a good restaurant. To the Chinese, quiet, empty restaurants are red flags. Instead, look for busy, boisterous ones. "Man man chi!"

# Mastering a Restaurant

The art of dining out involves more choreography than you might think, both for the restaurant staff and for diners. In an ideal world, everyone would be welcoming and dinner would be perfect. You'd be whisked to the best table in the house, enjoy delicious food and flawless service, and get a goodie bag on your way out the door.

That hardly ever happens in real life or in a restaurant. People linger at their table longer than predicted. The kitchen gets backed up, or it's a server's first night, or the chef got sick and a line cook had to step in. Mistakes happen all the time. But there are just as many opportunities to ensure a better night, a better table, better service, and increase the likelihood of a great dinner as there are unexpected kinks in service.

The way you treat people matters. "Nice begets nice," Drew Nieporent says, and he should know; he's been a successful restaurateur for twenty-five years. Hostility and aggression aren't productive measures. Most of the time they work against you. I've lost my patience. I've demanded a table and gotten one . . . right next to the kitchen door. When you're hostile, it puts the staff on the defensive and fosters a negative relationship, not a positive one. You want the best experience, not the worst. What goes around comes around. You piss them off, and they'll piss you off. You want a table right away, you might get one, but I'll bet my ass you're not getting a good one. Drew's advice: "If it's understaffed and I can't get someone's attention, I get out. It also doesn't bode well when there's a crowd around the hostess station or there's an argument in front of the hostess stand."

Do your homework. Certain restaurants are better suited to certain occasions. If you're going to propose, you want it to be perfect. You want to find the ideal setting—the perfect sunset, a romantic fireplace, waterfront view, or the perfect dessert. It's no different when you go to a business dinner. The stakes aren't quite as high, but you don't want to negotiate a deal over long-stemmed roses and candlelight. You want great wine, action, and attention. If it's a meet-the-parents brunch, you don't want to pick someplace loud and sceney. You want to be taken seriously by your potential future in-laws.

In other words, you're not always at the mercy of a restaurant. It's up to you to be proactive. If your date doesn't eat meat, don't pick a steakhouse. If you're having dinner with your grandparents, don't pick a sushi restaurant that only serves omakase. Most restaurants have Web sites, and there are lots of food blogs and online magazines with photos of the interior and food, so you know what you're getting into. Look at pictures of the dining room online and make sure the atmosphere suits the occasion. Don't take a meat-and-potatoes guy to a fussy restaurant with precious plates.

And don't forget to make reservations—especially if you're dining out with people you don't know well, or whom you wish to impress. If you do want to chance a walk-in table or you're heading to a place that doesn't take reservations, there are little things you can do to help your cause. Get there early. Most of us don't want to be the only ones in the restaurant or eat the early bird special, but you'll have a better chance of getting a table. If you're attempting a walk-in table, dress to fit the part—dress to fit in, but not so much so that you blend in. Make sure you stand out just enough so that you look like you'd be an asset in the dining room. As superficial as it sounds, restaurants like to fill their seats with attractive guests because it tends to draw regulars with money who just want to sit in a room with pretty people. Be flexible or at least act like you're flexible. If you're chancing a walk-in, you'll have better luck with a two-top table, not six. The smaller your party, the more likely you are to get a table, and the friendlier you seem, the more they'll want to accommodate you. It's much harder to say no to a nice person than it is to a grouchy one.

When it comes to making reservations, there's no surefire formula for getting a table. Every restaurant has its own policies and politics. Some restaurants reserve all prime-time tables for friends or VIPs. Others are democratic. Some accept reservations only via e-mail or through a Web system like OpenTable. Some have listed phone numbers *and* unlisted VIP numbers. Some like to leave half the tables available for walk-ins, while others fill every seat with reservation requests. Regardless, there are many ways to increase your likelihood of getting in the door.

Always remember: the reservationist is more important than the chef until you've been seated at a table. Be assertive, but not demanding. It may be a phone conversation, but reservationists can still read a person by the tone of voice and how they ask. Are they pushy, polite? Do they mean business? I'm all too familiar with the reservation game. I spend hours making reservations for review dinners. I don't visit a restaurant once. I visit every one three to five times, so I've become all too familiar with the system. Do you know how hard it is to get a prime-time reservation at Babbo? And it's just as impossible at the new, "it" restaurant with a big-name chef. I've had to simultaneously call restaurants from three different phones to get through.

Nobody's better at building chic, impossible-to-get-a-reservation restaurants than Keith McNally. Just look at his body of work—Balthazar, Pastis, Pulino's, Schiller's Liquor Bar, and Pravda. I'm a veteran of the reservation game, and I had to eat the early bird special at McNally's revival of Minetta Tavern. It had been open just a week, and the only reservations available were for six-thirty or ten. I chose six to avoid "hanger." (Hanger is what happens to people when they get so hungry they become angry and irritable until they're fed. It happens to the best of us.) But if I had known some inside secrets, I could've had a prime-time table. Now I do. I talked to Keith McNally. "The very first person of the day who calls for a reservation at Minetta Tavern gets whatever he or she asks for. That's a rule." "Being pleasant on the telephone helps," McNally also says. "Even if we're full and the customer isn't a regular, the reservationist almost always finds room for someone who's pleasant or funny. However, if you're pleasant *and* funny, you're guaranteed a table."

Some restaurateurs advise you to call early in the morning. "It doesn't matter whether you're looking for a new reservation a month from now or one for tonight. People cancel or don't confirm reservations. A lot of restaurants leave a few tables unreserved for last-minute calls or walk-ins. It's fine to put your name on a wait list. We really do call people off the wait list when people cancel last minute," Jimmy Bradley, owner of The Red Cat and The Harrison asserts. Others say you should call around 5:00 P.M. that day. "That's when everyone cancels," Drew Nieporent says. It's worth a shot.

Never tell a lie. If you don't know the owner or chef, don't pretend you do. Jimmy Bradley says, "I have people call and say they know James, the chef. My staff knows I don't go by James. Dead giveaway." And ask for the time slot you wish to dine at. When you don't specify an ideal time, you probably won't be offered a prime time. Restaurants tend to save those time slots for customers who request one. I've tested this little theory myself. When Daniel Boulud's DBGB Kitchen and Bar first opened, I called and asked for a table on the following Tuesday evening. The first time I called I asked for a reservation for a party of three on Tuesday evening but didn't specify a time. They told me they could do a six-thirty or a nine-thirty. "You don't have anything between seven and nine?" I asked. "Oh, sure. We can do eight," she said. If I hadn't asked, I would've eaten the early bird special or the late-night one (nine-thirty is too late for me at least). Then I had a friend call her back twenty minutes later and request Tuesday evening at eight, and that's what she got.

Often a reservationist will bend the rules or meet you halfway. If you're having dinner with someone who's getting a babysitter, you should explain the situation, and the reservationist may accommodate you. Sometimes their hands are tied. If there's an eight-thirty and you're looking to dine at eight, have a drink at the bar, and look at the menu. Cocktails are a great way to pass time and foster patience. By the time you're seated, you'll be a cocktail in and know what you want for dinner. Most people do just this for the first thirty minutes at their table anyway.

If the restaurant's booked up, ask if there's a cancellation or wait list. Take an earlier time and check back the night before or the morning of your reservation. Restaurants usually call to confirm reservations the day before. Shit happens. People get sick or go out of town for work and have to cancel a reservation. When that happens, the first thing a reservationist does is go to their wait list, and suddenly you've got a table.

It's never easy to get the bartender's attention at a crowded bar, but there are ways to cut down your wait time and make friends with the bartender. Waving your hands around wildly is not one of them. You're likely to be served last. I've been that annoying girl desperate for a drink, and I've overheard the bartender curse me out under his breath. I've seen a bartender intentionally ignore another patron, and I've been ignored many times.

Be kind and smile. Say please and thank you. If you have your money in your hand, you're showing you're not going to dilly-dally. You're ready to order and make a quick transaction. Don't throw a fit if they don't have your favorite scotch behind the bar. That gets you nowhere. Ask the bartender, aka barkeep, what he recommends instead. These aren't just bartenders. They're experts whose muses are spirits, bitters, and fresh-squeezed juices.

Why order a cosmopolitan or a Red Bull and Coke when there are so many great cocktail menus these days? Skilled bartenders are reinventing classics like the dark and stormy or the mint julep. They're creating new ones with homemade bitters and house-infused spirits. They're throwing out the simple syrup and triple sec, using muddled berries, fresh cilantro, lemongrass, and basil. There are also wonderful new wines and beers from all over the world—everywhere from Turkey to Africa.

Order something you've never had before. Start with an alcohol you're familiar with. If you're not a bourbon drinker, you might want to skip the bourbon cocktail. If you like tequila, go with the tequila or the mescal drink. Baby steps lead to great discoveries. I never knew I liked whiskey until I tried bourbon. Then I worked my way back to Japanese whiskeys at Char No. 4—located in Carroll Gardens, Brooklyn—a whiskey shrine stocked with more than four hundred whiskeys from all over the world. Whatever you do, don't drink too much before dinner. After a few drinks, everything starts to taste the same.

## BECOME FRIENDS WITH THE HOST

Smile when you approach the host's stand. Being a host at a crowded restaurant is a little like being a gate agent on an oversold flight or driving a car with twelve kids who all keep asking, "How much longer? Are we there yet?"

Restaurants seldom seat guests just to shut them up. They're used to hungry, impatient customers who'll do or say anything to be seated, so pushiness usually backfires. Instead ask how their day is or if it's always this crowded at the restaurant. Make a joke. Try something like "I wouldn't want to be you right now." The host usually appreciates your empathy and does what they can to help you to your table. Anyone who's understanding about the situation is rewarded for it.

Check in with the host as soon as you arrive. Even if your party's not complete, let them know you're there so they can check on the status of your table and get the ball rolling. You don't want them to think they're "stood up" and give away your table. I can't tell you how many times I've been stuck in traffic and found my friend sitting at the bar, figuring we'd check in when I arrived, our table gone.

## GETTING THE BEST TABLE

The best way to get a great table is to call in advance. You're much more likely to get a good table when you make a specific request when making your reservation. Don't outright demand "the best table in the house." Request an intimate table, something not near the kitchen door or the bathroom. If it's a date or a special occasion, tell the reservationist. If your dinner partner speaks softly or is hard of hearing, explain the situation when you make the reservation. Tell the host quietly that you have a friend who speaks very softly and you don't want him to miss out on a great restaurant just because of acoustics. It never hurts to ask.

Jimmy Bradley's advice: go to the restaurant to scout out your favorite table, then ask someone there the number of the table. Most of the time, a hostess doesn't have the authority to assign you a table, but she can make a note of your request in the computer. When you check in, politely remind the hostess about your request and assess the situation.

If you're unhappy with your table, say so before sitting at it. It's more difficult to move you after you've undone a napkin or drunk from a water glass. If they tell you that you'll have to wait for another table, that's your call. In my experience, I'm always happier when I choose to wait for a better table after getting stuck with an awful one.

If there's no possibility of a table change or they're not budging, order a drink and forget about it. I got stuck at table 39 on every one of my review visits to Monkey Bar, Graydon Carter's new incarnation of an old New York institution. Have you ever been to a wedding and picked up your place card, only to find out you're at the kids' table with your back to the dance floor? That's table 39, on the edge of Siberia, crammed up next to the servers' station. Jerry Seinfeld, Katie Couric, and Hugh Grant all dined on the balcony, of course. The real mission of a place like Monkey Bar isn't serving food. It's serving up a scene. When I asked to move, the manager said the tables were "all preassigned by the owners." Preassigned, like on an airplane? I didn't throw a fit or act like a diva. I took a deep breath, made a mental note, and ordered a glass of wine. The food was subpar, but the scene was worth a visit, and I wrote exactly that in my review.

## BECOMING FRIENDS WITH THE SERVER

Don't underestimate the relationship between you and your server. Your server wields a lot of power during dinner. Unless you're looking to get super-slow service and no attention, be friendly. Servers want to help people who are courteous. Sure, they'd like a big tip, but that's not their only motivation. You'd be surprised how many servers, who have no ownership in a spot, take pride in the food. They memorize every ingredient in every dish and every special, because they stand behind the chef and the food. Hopefully, that's the server you get.

My favorite way to win over an unreceptive server is to ask them what they recommend, what their favorite things on the menu are. It shows you respect their opinion. Even a server who's in it for the paycheck will likely change his tune. When you care about other people, they take care of you. Keith McNally suggests, "Always ask the server what on the menu he *wouldn't* recommend. If he doesn't recommend anything not to eat, then I wouldn't trust him."

If your server's not interested in being friends, show him you mean business and expect a good meal. This isn't something you explain to your server. You demonstrate you know the subject matter, that you're well versed in the art of dining out and cuisines. When push comes to shove, I'll order something really regional or obscure, just to prove I mean business. I can't tell you how many times a server's changed his tune after I ordered something unusual. Servers respect knowledgeable customers, so be informed or go ahead and fake it with tons of confidence.

# · 3 ·

# Cuban Cuisine

*His limes were gently squeezed with his
fingers lest even a drop of the bitter oil from
the peel get into the drink; the cocktails
were mixed (but not overmixed). . . . The
stinging cold drink was strained through
a fine sieve into the glass so that not one
tiny piece of ice remained in it. No smallest
detail was overlooked in achieving the
flawless perfection of the drink.*

DAVID EMBURY ON CONSTANTINO RIBALAIGUA
IN *THE FINE ART OF MIXING DRINKS*

For many years, my primary association with Cuban food was cocktails, specifically the mojito. (That should tell you a lot more about me than about Cuban food.) I know Ernest Hemingway loved daiquiris, but I can't think of anything I'd rather drink more on a hot summer day than an ice-cold mojito fragrant with fresh mint. It even smells like summer. To me a mojito is like a little Caribbean island in a tall glass, a bubbly combination of white rum, lime juice, club soda, a dash of sugar, and muddled mint. When you can't hop a plane for a tropical getaway, a mojito is about as good as it gets. The more mojitos I drank, the more demanding I became about their quality. And, well . . . that's how I discovered Cuban cuisine. If anyone would know how to make a flawless mojito, I reasoned, it would be the Cubans.

So I'm not ashamed to admit that I roped a blind date into meeting me at Victor's Café in the heart of New York's Theater District. I figured if I didn't like the guy, at least I'd get a great mojito out of it. The Theater District is the ideal location for this festive eatery, which is decorated with potted palm trees, colorful Cuban artwork, and woven palm fronds swaying from the ceiling. Salsa music plays in the background. It feels like dinner theater, except that the main attraction is food . . . and mojitos, of course. We started in the Cuba Lounge, where we sat along a wood bar and ordered cocktails. I got a mojito and he ordered a traditional lime daiquiri. (I used to confuse a daiquiri with that frozen drink dispensed from a commercial machine, but the original daiquiri featured three simple ingredients: rum, lime juice, and sugarcane.) Victor's Café makes a mean mojito with just the right balance of tartness and sweetness, and my date's daiquiri was nearly as good—a classic blend of lime juice, white rum, sugar, and shaved ice. (Of course I tasted his!)

Our date was going swimmingly enough, so we moved into the dining room for dinner. Though I can't remember my date's name for the life of me, I do remember what we had for dinner. (What? I'm a foodie.) We never made it to a second date, but we did share a mind-blowing roasted suckling pig—the lechón asado—that I'll

### • TASTY MORSEL •

*Not only was Hemingway a famous writer, but he was also an infamous boozer. In the two decades that he lived in Cuba, he became a regular at El Floridita, a bar known as the birthplace of the daiquiri. "Papa" Hemingway preferred his daiquiris stiff and made without sugar, so Constantino Ribalaigua, El Floridita's bartender, created the Papa Doble, a double daiquiri made with rum, lime, grapefruit juice, and a few drops of maraschino liqueur.*

never forget. A forty-eight-hour marinade of sour orange, lime juice, garlic, and cumin teases the sweetness and subtleties from the pork, and the results are intoxicating. You could get high off the incredibly garlicky aroma wafting up from the meat. If you want to sample the representative foods of Cuba on a single plate, then the lechón asado is the dish to order. It's traditionally served with arroz moro, also called Moros y Cristianos (mixed black beans and rice, laced with mojo), and boiled yuca smothered in garlicky mojo, a highly aromatic sauce made with *lots* of garlic, olive oil, cumin, pepper, and orange or lime juice.

That same citrus-infused, tender roast pork is the star of the Cubano—the Cuban sandwich that, alongside cigars and mojitos, is one of Cuba's most popular exports. The Cubano is an ingenious marriage of thinly sliced ham, roast pork, pickles, Swiss cheese, and mustard all loaded onto fresh, crusty Cuban bread, then pressed on a plancha. If it's not properly pressed, it's not a Cubano. That's what mingles all the flavors into one glorious bocadillo (sandwich) and ensures there's a little of everything in each bite. There's serious debate over what exactly constitutes a true Cubano; some insist it must be made with Cuban bread, while others think a French baguette is a respectable substitute. But whatever its provenance, the key to the bread is a crusty exterior and tender, textured interior. Where condiments are concerned, eaters and experts are unified against lettuce, tomato, and mayonnaise. They'll happily add mayonnaise, lettuce, and other condiments to other Cuban bocadillos, but not to the Cubano, the pinnacle of all bocadillos. (In the mood for a sweeter Cubano? Try a medianoche—a Cubano made with sweet egg bread instead of a crusty Cuban roll—if you can find one. The closest I've come to a medianoche in New York is the Cubano Cristo at Carteles, a café in the East Village. Carteles's version is essentially a Cubano dipped in sweet egg and deep-fried, like a hybrid of a Cubano and a Monte Cristo.)

You can get a great Cubano at Café Cortadito, a quaint eatery on the edge of the East Village. Their gooey rendition, dubbed the Cubanito, comes with savory shavings of ham, pork, pickles, Swiss cheese, mustard, and a crunchy stash of mariquitas (fried green plantain chips). It's not the most traditional version, but you certainly won't hear me complaining about the mariquitas. The walls at Café Cortadito are a sunny yellow, ceiling fans spin lazily overhead, and on a summer night, the storefront windows are flung open onto the balmy streets. The owners aren't Cuban (they're El Salvadoran and Ecuadoran), but you'd never know it from the cooking. They're a husband and wife team: Patricia Valencia runs the front of the house, and I'm convinced Ricardo Arias, Café Cortadito's chef, is summoning some feisty grandma in old Havana with serious cooking skills, which explains why another classic Cuban meat dish named ropa vieja is excellent there. Arias, who also cooked at Victor's Café for sixteen years, braises flank steak into submission, shreds it into supple strands, and stews it in savory-sweet criollo, a Creole-style sauce made from green peppers, onions, garlic, and tomatoes. (The Cubans borrow many dishes and sauces not only from Spain but also from the Caribbean.) Ropa vieja translates as "old clothes," because the shredded meat is supposed to resemble frayed garments, but I think whoever named the dish was just trying to keep everyone away from his plate. Most Cubans use ropa vieja as a litmus test of a great chef. "It's a classic dish that defines a cook's style," Arias says. It's pretty hard not to get hooked on this twice-cooked tangle of tender meat in a tangy tomato sauce. Or on his vaca frita, braised and seared skirt steak with lime. The crispy, tangy shreds of steak are ridiculously flavorful in their own right, but he ups the ante by smothering them in a mix of mojo and criollo sauces—which makes a dish that means "fried cow" seem downright decadent.

Here in New York there's a chain called Sophie's that everyone loves to hate. It has a remarkably extensive Cuban menu with many traditional bocadillos, including one of my favorites, the pernil especial, a lusty combination of roast pork shoulder (that's the "pernil"), onions, sweet plantains, mayonnaise, and a feisty green sauce spiked with jalapeños. Really, it's a tie between the pernil especial and the bistec (steak) bocadillo topped with lettuce, tomato, mayonnaise, and . . . fried potato sticks. (You gotta love the Cuban attention to crunch.) I used to walk right by Sophie's without so much as a backward glance. The gloomy, cafeteria-style counter service evoked unpleasant memories of my high school lunchroom. And how could the food be any good in a Midtown lunchrush spot that lines you up, plops food in a plastic container and spits you right back out the door? It was the flimsy paper menu that finally lured me into Sophie's Cuban Cuisine—renamed Tina's Cuban Cuisine—in the first place. (I don't know why Sophie's disowned this outpost, but I'm staying loyal to it.) I mindlessly grabbed one from the entrance and kept walking. I got to the corner of Fifty-sixth Street and Sixth, happened to read the words "fried sweet plantains" (maduros) and "arroz moro" (beans and rice), and turned right back around. You don't walk away from freshly fried plantains or arroz moro.

Beans, rice, and plantains are the "holy trinity" of Cuban food. Arroz moro is not nearly as simple as beans and white rice. It's a fully realized, fully flavored dish in its own right. Like almost everything else in Cuban cooking, arroz moro is sauced with sofrito—a highly aromatic sauté of green peppers, garlic, onions, cumin, oregano, and olive oil—which animates the ingredients, making ordinary beans and white rice seem like no fun at all. Congri is arroz moro made with red beans instead of black beans. Yellow rice is also commonly used in Cuban cooking and is yet more evidence of Spain's culinary influence on the island. One of the best ways to experience yellow rice is in arroz con pollo, a wonderfully homey dish that mixes buttery yellow rice with juicy shreds of chicken.

Apart from breakfast, savory (unripe/green) and sweet (ripe/yellow) plantains in some form—tostones, plátanos fritos, or

maduros—are served at every Cuban meal. I've had a thing for
savory plantains since I was young. Our housekeeper, Cookie (her
real name was Orrie, but everyone called her Cookie), used to fry
up plantains (tostones) for herself as a snack. I had no interest in
her green plantains when they sat on the kitchen counter, but once
they hit the sizzling oil and she started seasoning, I'd appear out of
nowhere. (It was not unlike a dog begging at the dinner table. I still
have no shame when it comes to food.) Finally she'd give in and
fork up a salty, smashed coin, then wrap her arms tightly around
her plate to discourage greedy children from reaching in while
she watched her shows. Don't think I didn't try. I wouldn't have
done that for a potato. If I had my way, we'd all be eating plantains
instead of potatoes. (I hope I didn't just alienate the entire state
of Idaho in one starchy swoop.) I had no idea that what I'd been
snacking on since I was seven was called tostones, but I can understand why they're a staple of Cuban cooking. Though the plantain
is technically a fruit with a striking resemblance to a banana, it
tastes more like a starchy vegetable than it does a banana.

Cubans use plantains in as many ways as Americans use potatoes. We eat potato chips; they eat green plantain chips (mari-

quitas). We eat French fries; they eat savory green tostones. But potatoes don't ripen; they just grow "eyes." When plantains ripen, they turn a brownish yellow hue and become very sweet. Sliced and fried, as maduros, they're a sticky, caramelized treat. Boiled and mashed, they're called fufu. I'm not debating the creamy merits of mashed potatoes, but restaurants should make room on their menus for fufu, too. Not only is fufu fun to say, but it's got plenty of body and texture—a delightfully thick, sweet mash that balances out the succulent fattiness of the many roast and fried pork dishes Cuba's famous for. Fufu often comes topped with chicharrones— fried pork rinds or chicken skin—edible tools for scooping. Then there's yuca—aka cassava—another starchy vegetable that's even denser and starchier than plantains. It doesn't bring much to the table in the way of flavor, but its coarse, comforting texture makes yuca a great canvas for soaking up Cuba's many-flavored sauces. The menu at Victor's Café is studded with yuca—boiled and doused in mojo, molded into turnovers, or fried into crispy golden fingers perfect for dipping in coriander sauce.

But the Cubans have nothing against potatoes. In fact, papas rellenas, fried potato fritters stuffed with picadillo (a savory mix of ground meat, sofrito, tomatoes, peppers, olives, and capers), are one of the most popular Cuban tapitas (appetizers). Picadillo also gets stuffed inside peppers or rolled into croquetas, little logs of minced meat, battered in bread crumbs, and deep-fried. When I feel like grazing, I head to Victor's Café and wander the tapitas, where I can choose from smoked ham croquetas, picadillo-stuffed red peppers, pork tamales, and mini–Cuban hamburgers topped with fries and onions. One of my favorites is an empanada (a deep-fried turnover in the shape of a half moon) filled with sofrito-sauced lobster— the pastry shell is made from yuca.

The only drawback to conducting an impromptu tapitas tasting is missing out on the bounty of tropical salads, grilled meats, soothing stews, and seafood entrees. I don't know if you've ever experienced what I like to call "order regret" or "order envy," but I can't stand watching a dish go by that's not coming my way. When I see a plate of pollo manigua pass me by at Victor's Café, my first thought is to wonder how I can get the lucky recipient to give me a bite. If you need to renew your faith in chicken, just try the pollo manigua—also known as pollo al estilo "aljibe"— which must mean born-again chicken (actually, it means "in the style of a fountain," which doesn't exactly clarify things). This spirited breast of chicken, marinated in citrus juice, comes topped with a vibrant tropical salad of watercress, avocado, and tomatoes. I get just as jealous of neighboring tables enjoying their plantain-encrusted red snapper, sautéed shrimp in Creole sauce, and even a watercress salad with avocados and chiles in mango vinaigrette. (I'm only human.) And that's just at Victor's Café.

At Café Cortadito the menu features a tropical salad with mixed greens, roasted peppers, pears, and heart of palm, and another with tropical cheese (a fresh white cheese popular in the Caribbean), avocado, and pineapple. Café Cortadito is like a mini–Cuban steak-house that grills a perfect steak with a side of chimichurri sauce (a zesty parsley sauce originally from Argentina but used throughout Latin America and the Caribbean). Meaty, charred pork chops hint at orange and lime; roast chicken resonates with citrus and garlic; and even fried steak gets splashed with lime juice. Cuba's hearty stews combine their many styles of beans and rice with their bounty of grilled meats and fish. I've never seen a better selection of Cuban stews in New York than at Tina's (formerly known as Sophie's). On Mondays, Wednesdays, and Fridays, Tina's serves ox-tail stew and goat stew, while the picadillo beef stew—which has raisins and plantains in it—is, fortunately, on the menu Mondays and Thursdays. I love the way the chewy raisins play against the briny olives and starchy nibbles of plantain. But if you're looking for heat, you won't find much in Cuban cooking. Hot and spicy is not really in their vocabulary. One of the spiciest things they eat is a Cuban hamburger (Frita Cubana), a spiced meat patty topped with onions and fried potatoes (papas fritas), and sometimes mojo.

Cuba isn't known for its desserts. And in my opinion, a well-made cocktail is the best ending to a great Cuban meal, followed by a strong café Cubano (a shot of espresso mixed with demerara sugar) and a hand-rolled cigar. (Unless it's smuggled into the country, that cigar is unlikely to be truly Cuban, but hey, expert cigar rollers often are.) If you're dying for dessert, though, the Cubans do make a fine flan (egg custard), especially coconut flan wreathed in freshly shredded coconut. Coconut is one of the most popular ingredients in Cuban sweets, like coconut ice cream (helado) and candies. Many of the desserts you'll see in a Cuban restaurant, like pastel tres leches (three-milk cake), arrived there via other cultures (in that case, Mexico). And, in a way, Cuba is a melting pot: a variety of peoples and nations have influenced Cuban culture and its cooking, including the Canary Islands and neighboring Caribbean islands, and even Africans and Chinese laborers who were moved to Cuba through the years (because of Spanish and Portuguese colonization in those places). From all these vastly distinct influences, Cuba has managed to create its own unique cuisine.

## Table Setting and Modern Manners

The Cuban dinner table is an informal and social place. Diners greet one another with hugs and handshakes and share food, so they traditionally order family style and encourage you to do the same. They treat yuca fries, croquetas, and mariquitas like finger food. For most everything else, they follow standard fork-knife-spoon procedure. And they booze at lunch. (How great is that?) As they say in Cuba, "Buen provecho!"

# · 4 ·

# French Cuisine

*There is no such thing as a pretty good omelette.*

FRENCH PROVERB

Balthazar, the ever-popular brasserie in ever-trendy SoHo, has been in business for over thirteen years, and it's still just as difficult to get a dinner reservation there as it was the day it opened. In New York City, the standard-bearer of "been there, done that" culture, this is no mean feat. I think the setting has a lot to do with it. Balthazar looks like a classic Parisian-style brasserie, right down to the archetypal tightly packed tables, glossy red banquettes, zinc bar, and weathered brass trimmings. Ceiling fans twirl overhead, and mirrors line the saffron yellow walls, tilted slightly downward, maximizing guests' ability to "see and be seen." I don't blame everyone for wanting to dine in such a timelessly chic room. And really, that's half the fun of brasserie and bistro dining.

And Balthazar just gets better with age. The steak tartare is just as silky and superbly flavored as ever. I owe a debt of gratitude to the French for gifting the world with delicate, spreadable raw steak. The secret to Balthazar's tartare is filet mignon, which I don't care for grilled, but minced and mingled with a vivacious slew of ingredients—capers, cornichons, onions, parsley, sherry vinegar, mayonnaise, Dijon, Worcestershire and Tabasco sauce, anchovies, and egg yolks—it becomes a revelatory experience of velveteen meatiness. If you count steak tartare as a spread (I do!), you could practically make a meal of Balthazar's opulent spreads alone: order the chicken liver and foie gras mousse with red onion confit, and the brandade de morue—a garlicky puree of salt cod, cream, olive oil, and potato—and you're good to go.

OK, the steak au poivre (coated in black peppercorns) is mandatory, though. This pepper-crusted steak doused in a cognac-cream sauce is a required initiation into bistro cuisine's rich meats and sauces. Or find someone, anyone, with whom to share a côte de boeuf—a perfectly seared bone-in rib eye steak, finished in the oven—served with Roquefort sauce or a red wine reduction. You'll quickly discover, whether at Balthazar or at any other brasserie or bistro, that the French are extremely liberal in their use of butter, milk, cream, oil, and egg yolks. They have a talent for creating sumptuous sauces out of mayonnaise. But French mayonnaise is a distant cousin of good old American Hellmann's. French mayonnaise is made from freshly whipped egg yolks and olive oil. Add a little vinegar, fresh herbs, and a pronounced dose of tarragon and you have béarnaise sauce. Béarnaise typically accompanies steak frites, asparagus, and many fish dishes. Aioli, French mayonnaise blended with garlic, is often called the "butter of France" and is one of their favorite condiments for fries, fish, or vegetables. If you haven't dipped your French fries in rich and creamy aioli, I highly recommend it! Tartar sauce—a piquant blend of mayo, hard-boiled eggs, herbs, pickles, capers, and diced onions—is, no surprise, also French in origin.

I don't understand why the French aren't fat. It defies all logic. These people eat cheese, bread, butter, and creamy sauces all day—and don't even get me started on the inordinate amount of wine they drink. It's annoying. I read Mireille Guiliano's *French Women Don't Get Fat* and I still don't get it. They're insatiable. Even sole, a notably slender fish, takes a dip in flour before it's panfried in butter and sent out to be filleted tableside—that's the classic dish sole meunière. The first time I saw a fish filleted in a restaurant dining room, I leaned over to my father and whispered, "Shouldn't the waiter do that in the kitchen? Gross!" Grinning, my dad answered, "It's part of the show." I grew out of "gross," but I still don't need my fish deboned at the table. In fact, I'd rather eat the skin and pick it apart myself. The French "meunière" everything, from scallops to chicken; "au poivre" everything, from salmon to lamb; and "à l' orange" everything, from lamb to that slender sole they're so fond of. When you think about it, it's not terribly difficult to speak "menu French." Once you've tried steak au poivre, you know what to expect from any dish deemed "au poivre."

Truth be told, I did get a lot of practice learning "menu French" at Balthazar. Not long after I first moved to New York, I dated a man who lived just down the street from Balthazar. When he'd head off to work, I'd head down the block for breakfast. Balthazar has its own bakery (you can stop in there to pick up sensational breads and pastries to take home), and in the mornings, you can wander in for espresso and read the paper virtually undisturbed for hours if you feel like it. I'd cozy up to a cup of coffee and a brioche—a sort of flaky, sweet pastry and fluffy bread in one, no jam or butter required.

If I was in a salty mood, I'd order an omelet aux fines herbes (anything described as "aux fines herbes" means it is seasoned with freshly chopped herbs, usually a combination of chervil, chives, parsley, and tarragon) and a café au lait (equal parts coffee and milk), so I could really get into character. (In real life, I like my coffee black.) You haven't really tasted an omelet until you've had one cooked by a Frenchman. There is a tangible difference. The French just have a way with slow-cooking eggs on a low flame so as to preserve the eggy nuances. They're also famous for baking satiny egg pies with buttery crusts, the beloved quiche. Eggs, cream, and milk are required to make the rich custard filling of a quiche, but the rest—ham, mushrooms, cheese, maybe—is up to the whim of the chef. Quiche lorraine, laced with bacon and onions (and often Gruyère or Swiss cheese) and seasoned with nutmeg, is the most iconic preparation of quiche.

You know how kids like to play "let's pretend," as in, "let's play cops and robbers" or "let's play house"? Well, I'd pretend that I lived in Paris and it was breakfast time. On weekends, my boyfriend and I would go together for brunch, which meant one thing: I had someone to share the breadbasket with—and that's all that I cared about. Balthazar's breadbasket comes piled with brioche, pain au chocolat (chocolate croissantlike pastry), and a pudgy sticky bun. My boyfriend considered himself a connoisseur of pain au chocolat, rating them wherever we'd go. Were they frozen? Was the chocolate dark enough or rich enough? Was it freshly baked and rolled on the premises? Was it too dense, too flaky, chocolate-challenged? I loved his passion. Sometimes I'd go twice in one day, once in the morning by myself, and again when he got home from work, though I kept that to myself. It was my secret Parisian breakfast life, and I'm quite sure he wouldn't have approved of the mornings I dillydallied in that golden yellow room.

When we went for dinner, my personal pain-au-chocolat critic would order a martini, loosen his tie, and settle into some steak tartare, followed by steak au poivre. (The man was a carnivore, what can I say?) Sometimes I'd convince him to share oysters or a salad with me. I made a habit of the grilled brook trout (with beautiful grill marks and crispy skin) resting on a spinach, walnut, and lentil salad. It was a simple yet elegant dish; the crowning touch was a sweet drizzle of aged balsamic vinegar. (It's still on the menu, and it's still just as good.) But I never stayed loyal to any one dish for too long. I discovered escargots en persillade, baked snails, and how good these chewy mollusks taste when drenched in butter, garlic, and parsley. I ate succulent duck confit, a classic French preparation of duck leg cooked in its own, marvelous fat and chicken paillard— a breast pounded to exquisite thinness—topped with a fistful of France's go-to green, frisée. The pain-au-chocolat critic and I are no more, but I'll always have Paris and Balthazar. C'est la vie.

And if I'm feeling too sentimental to indulge in a night at Balthazar, I can always stop

> **• TASTY MORSEL •**
>
> *What Americans call French toast isn't actually French per se. Many cultures around the world serve stale bread soaked in milk or eggs, which is then panfried, as a way to prevent waste and stretch limited resources. The American version takes its name from an Albany, New York, restaurateur, Joseph French, who popularized the dish in the United States in the late eighteenth century. The French call their version pain perdu, which means "lost bread," as in "waste" bread. (I call it sublime.)*

by its sister restaurant, Pastis. Owner Keith McNally is a British restaurateur—and a very charming one at that—in love with French bistro and brasserie culture. He dubs Pastis a bistro, not a brasserie, since it's open fewer hours a day than Balthazar and has a slightly more intimate, neighborhood feel. For the sake of simplicity and our sanity, let's agree to think of bistros and brasseries as basically interchangeable—at least on American soil. Just remember that a brasserie is open longer hours than a bistro and is more casual than a bistro.

Walk by Pastis on a warm night, and it's something to see. The doors are flung open and a gentle buzz and golden light spill out onto the cobbled streets of the Meatpacking District. The tables alongside the sidewalk—and inside for that matter—are forever occupied with diners grazing on lemony roast chicken, grilled lamb chops, and bowls of French onion soup with its famously gooey lid of Gruyère cheese. Break through the Gruyère seal and you'll discover a hunk of bread basking in beef and onion stock, mingling with caramelized onion ringlets. Onion soup gratinée is often misunderstood: it's nothing like the dried mix used to make dips, nor does it bear any resemblance to anything you might have had the misfortune of eating in the school cafeteria. Here's the thing about French onion soup: if it sits too long, the cheese hardens and the bread below gets soggy. But when it's done well and delivered swiftly, it's a pretty terrific soup, and Pastis is a pretty exciting place to experience it.

Bistro cooking is home cooking for the urban set. For the French, the bistro, culturally, is somewhat akin to a very fancy diner, in terms of ubiquity and reliability. But bistro food is an art form that the French take as seriously as fine dining. The menu varies very little from establishment to establishment. A diner without pancakes, grilled cheese, and milk shakes isn't a diner. It's the same with any bistro. You can expect steak tartare, steak au poivre, and a frisée salad scattered with smoky chunks of lardons (fried pork fat). Fixtures like moules frites (mussels in an herbaceous broth, served with a cone of bistro fries) and salad Niçoise (a composed salad of greens, tuna, hard-boiled egg, new potatoes, olives, and French green beans—haricots verts) are practically mandatory. You can count on croissants at breakfast and a croque monsieur—grilled cheese with ham—for lunch. The croque madame, which is a croque monsieur topped with a sunny-side-up egg (and proof that French food doesn't always have to be fancy), often makes an appearance, too.

But I'd have to say that France's signature—pencil-thin pommes frites—are the universal symbol of bistros and brasseries everywhere. The French have been eating deep-fried slivers of potatoes since the late 1830s, so they're well schooled on the subject. I imagine the Eiffel Tower trembles whenever "French fries" and "McDonald's" are uttered in the same breath. Pommes frites are the perfect litmus test of any bistro worthy of the name. They should be sufficiently salty, crispy on the outside and soft on the inside, made from fresh potatoes, and preferably served in a paper cone. You won't see thick-cut, steak-fry-style pommes frites at bistros, and the presence of ketchup is frowned upon (though many stateside bistros do have it on hand if you ask). Most French diners don't dip pommes frites in any kind of sauce, but when they do, it's usually simple mayonnaise or aioli.

At the Midtown outpost of Le Relais de Venise L'Entrecôte, a popular French bistro chain that opened its first location in Paris in 1959, they serve one entree and one entree only: steak frites. Imagine my initial displeasure when my waitress, dressed in a black and white barmaid's costume—excuse me, I mean uniform—informed me that there was no menu and just one offering. (Though honestly, her outfit alone was worth the $24.00 price of admission.) Those twenty-four dollars get you a ho-hum salad in a standard mustard vinaigrette, an average sirloin steak, and possibly some of the best pommes frites in town, served with an insanely addictive steak sauce, the recipe for which is top secret. I lie awake at night thinking about those fries and that sauce. No one knows the recipe, but there's talk of butter, cream, mustard, spices, and chicken liver. Dip anything you can in it. I would've dipped my profiteroles in it had they not swiped my sauce to make room for coffee.

The French go mad for all sorts of potato dishes, and they have one for nearly every occasion. There's pommes soufflés—round, fried potato puffs—better suited to hefty meats than skinny frites because the soufflés have more surface area to soak up meaty juices. For refined spuds, the French skip the fryer, turning to baked, cream-bathed inventions, like gratin dauphinois, thinly sliced potatoes layered with cream, nutmeg, and a touch of garlic. Though Minetta Tavern—another genius McNally joint—isn't exclusively French, the menu flirts with French preparations, and the best dishes are all "Pommes" of some sort or another. Their Pommes Anna—a baked layer cake of thinly sliced potatoes and butter—is far more delicious than it should be, and so are their pommes frites. At my last supper, I'd want one of the side dishes to be Minetta's Aligot—a divinely gooey purée of melted cheese curds, garlic, cream, and velvety potatoes. Or better yet, the poulet fermier rôti, wonderfully moist roast chicken served on a bed of Pommes Aligot.

Strangely, my first real experience with French food was not casual bistro or brasserie cooking. In fact it was about as fancy as it gets. When I was fourteen years old, my family and I went on a summer vacation to Monte Carlo. It was the most lavish vacation we'd ever taken, or would ever take. Everything about Monte Carlo left an indelible impression on me. The twisty streets climbing the hills of the practically vertical city-state. The grand old hotels and casinos. (My mother preferred the humble slot machines to the gaming tables.) Most of the beaches were rocky, pebble-strewn coves completely unlike the sandy stretches of the Jersey shore. Flip-flops were a no-go—I'd stub my toes every time I tried wearing them—and yet the women of Monaco seemed totally at ease navigating the beaches in killer heels. But I think what will likely stay with me the longest is my memory of the dinner we ate at Le Louis XV, Alain Ducasse's temple of French haute cuisine in the Hôtel de Paris.

Le Louis XV stunned me; it is, to this day, one of the most opulent, palatial settings I've dined in, and the meal I ate there remains one of the single most exquisite meals of my life. The bread trolley, with its cloth-lined baskets of semolina rolls, rustic wheat breads, and baguettes flecked with ripe Niçoise olives, chewy bits of figs and walnuts, was a magnificent Parisian bakery on wheels. I can't recall all of the dishes I ate that night—there was a transcendent flurry of them—but I can't forget the ingredients, because it was as if I were eating them for the first time. I was fourteen years old: I thought a tomato was, well, just a tomato until I tasted the astoundingly sweet summer tomatoes of Monaco at Le Louis XV. And I discovered the subtle nuances of sea bass, a firm and yet delicately flavored filet, which was served with supremely tender artichokes in an intensely aromatic olive oil.

The menu featured Provençal-style French cooking, which tends to be lighter and fresher than traditional French food. Olive oil is more common than butter in Provençal-style cuisine. Provence capitalizes on the wealth of fresh vegetables, herbs, olives, and other fruits that grow on the land as well as the fish that swim in their coastal waters. And so did Ducasse. The menu was abundant with just-caught crustaceans, ripe, seasonal fruits, and freshly clipped herbs. But nothing brands itself in my memory quite like Ducasse's Provençal Simmered Vegetables. The flavors were all so sharp and pure; it was like tasting each vegetable for the first time. I wasn't the type of kid that refused to eat her vegetables or camouflaged them with ketchup, but I had never truly contemplated the complexity of a carrot, zucchini, or eggplant before. And, of course, I can't forget the chocolate croustillant (a crispy pastry) we ate for dessert either. It was the most beautiful dessert I'd ever seen or tasted, a glossy, dark-chocolate-covered biscuit layered with hazelnuts and wondrously crispy pastry dough.

I fell head over heels for Le Louis XV. For the first time, it wasn't just about the food for me. I was in love with the entire evening—from the moment we set foot into that gorgeous room, with its glittery crystal chandeliers, painted ceiling, bread and cheese trolleys, to the complimentary macarons and madeleines at the end. It was so romantic; I never wanted to leave.

Maybe that's why when it comes to romance, I can't separate seduction from food. The French are masters of the dinner table seduction. In a great French restaurant, I'll let the bubbly and caviar go straight to my head, happily losing my inhibitions, indulging in course after course of delicate fish, rich meats, and voluptuous sauces, that all climax with a divine chocolate soufflé.

Part of what makes such an evening feel so grand is how perfectly choreographed the service—not to mention the meal—is guaranteed to be. In an haute French restaurant, every staff member has a formal title—the waiter is a "chef du rang"; the manager "le directeur"—and a regimented set of duties to perform. They're all acrobats who effortlessly balance loaded trays, gliding gracefully through the dining room. They take their roles (and the food) very seriously. (And they don't even want to be actors!) The fancier the restaurant, the bigger perfectionists they are. Everything matters: the napkin, the knife, whether the server places the plate in front of you from the left or the right, what your server is wearing, and even what you're wearing matters. And the food ought to look as beautiful as it tastes. The attention to detail can get a touch extreme. I've been offered my choice of ten knives for a steak and twelve pens to sign the bill. (I have a hard enough time deciding what to order. Any pen will do.)

Unlike Americans and Italians, the urban French rarely eat or entertain at home. (Martha Stewart would have to go on unemployment.) That's my kind of country: I could spend my life at the table. At a French restaurant, the food receives the same regal treatment as the guests. You'd never catch the French putting everything on the table at once and saying, "Dig in," or "Mangia!" That's not their style at all—it may be homey and charming, but it's not particularly romantic. A fancy French dinner is a slow seduction: a canapé crowned with caviar; a consommé or a velouté topped with crab; roasted meat scattered with truffles. There's a rhythm and a reason for the sequence of things: fish before meat, cheese before chocolate, the right wine with every course. And there's a crowning touch on each plate—a dab of caviar, crème fraîche (thin sour cream), or perhaps gold flakes to seal the deal.

Thankfully you don't have to jet off to Paris or Monte Carlo to experience that kind of service and food. You can dine in the lap of French luxury right in Midtown Manhattan. Visit Daniel and you might sink your fork into a velvety duck terrine with apple slivers, pistachios, and raisins, or a crisp-skinned roasted squab, decadently stuffed with foie gras (fattened duck or goose liver) and truffles—the kind of dish that convinces you there is heaven on earth. Or you can head west to Jean-Georges and dine on a sumptuous foie gras brulée with spiced fig jam and toasted brioche. Nowadays Jean-Georges may dabble in haute and nouvelle Asian and Daniel Boulud in foie-gras-plumped burgers and charcuterie, but when it comes to the classic dishes of France, even these lauded chefs don't mess with tradition.

There's exactly one way to make a proper steak au poivre, béchamel sauce, or a steak tartare. Tamper with a time-honored recipe in France, and it's off to the guillotine for you. The French often act like they invented food. They treat classic cookbooks like the Bible; altering one of Escoffier's recipes is like messing with scripture. Often called "the king of chefs and the chef of kings," Georges Auguste Escoffier shaped modern French cooking. He refined and simplified the elaborate French cuisine of the nineteenth century, emphasizing the beauty and simplicity of dishes made from fewer ingredients. Along the way, he invented new dishes, which are now considered classics, like peach melba (poached peaches with raspberry sauce over vanilla ice cream). Most importantly he documented his techniques and recipes—many of which are still used today—and codified modern French cuisine. If you want to know how to make a chicken consommé or a basic cream sauce, you'll find the recipe in his book, *Le Guide Culinaire*. Taillevent's recipes are centuries older than Escoffier's. Taillevent cooked for King Charles V in the fourteenth century. He introduced exotic spices to the French pantry and wrote *Le Viandier*, a cookbook that's still referenced today.

In France, you don't challenge the sacred sauces and stocks. Quel sacrilège! Nope, the French cook the classics by the rules. Try to tell that to a curious American who's prone to testing boundaries and asking too many questions. "Why can't you use oil instead of butter? Why can't I use white wine for coq au vin instead of red?" Actually you can, but it's not traditional. Coq au vin is a rustic dish—originally a rooster stewed in red wine with lardons, mushrooms, onions, and garlic—created in the countryside. Without getting into much graphic detail, a rooster needs to be cooked for a long period of time in order to break down all that yummy connective tissue. These days, most chefs use chicken instead of rooster and some use white wine. Red wine does the trick. I had coq au vin at Bar Boulud with chicken so tender and richly flavored with red wine that I wouldn't tamper with the recipe either. And how can you improve on a classic bouillabaisse? Dipping your spoon into this zesty, saffron-scented fish stew—teeming with plump mussels, crab, firm cod, or halibut—is like dipping your spoon in the sea. There are all sorts of debates on the kind and number of fish and shellfish that should be in a bouillabaisse, as well as the seasonings. And many other cultures, like the

Greeks and the Italians, claim to have created the first fish stew, too. What makes a bouillabaisse so unique is the intensely flavorful stock, made with saffron, fennel, olive oil, orange zest, onions, and tomatoes. (Some chefs add white wine or Pernod, an anise-scented liquor, to the broth.) A bouillabaisse should have at least four or five kinds of fish, a mix of both shellfish and seafood. It's traditionally served with a garlicky rouille—a blend of olive oil, egg yolk, garlic, pepper, and chiles—with toasted bread. Scores of hallmark sauces have stood the test of time as well, like béchamel—made with scalded milk, flour, and butter—a creamy white sauce that's poured over everything from meats to vegetables. Mornay sauce is béchamel with grated cheese, and bordelaise sauce is pure brown bliss: a blend of red wine, beef stock, bone marrow, and shallots. But some traditions have changed, and restaurants are changing with them, even the old French institutions.

Fast forward to 2010: I wore jeans to Le Cirque, the world-famous French restaurant in Manhattan. My friend wore jeans and sneakers, and no one batted an eyelash, not even Sirio Maccioni, who looked right at us with indifference. Sirio Maccioni is Le Cirque's owner, the man who wrote the playbook on working a dining room and keeping the rich and famous happy. These days Sirio patrols his domain from a table near the door. Across from Sirio's front desk is a pop-up bookshop where you can buy a copy of the Le Cirque cookbook, *Sirio: The Story of My Life and Le Cirque* (the English or Italian version). Maccioni's story is an interesting one: he was born in Italy and got his start in Europe at a time when most restaurants were run in the French manner and everyone who worked in them was required to speak French. He learned to cook in France and eventually made his way to New York, where he opened his own French restaurant. With Le Cirque he introduced opulence and French service to the New York dining scene. HBO even produced a documentary called *Le*

*Cirque: A Table in Heaven*, but it really tells the story of the old Le Cirque. I ate dinner at the new Le Cirque.

This is the third incarnation of Le Cirque, adorned with a gold, cloth-trimmed ceiling—reminiscent of a circus tent—lacquered ebony wall paneling, blue-and-gold-striped banquettes, and a glittery glass wine tower in the center of it all. There's still a jacket policy—tie optional—in the dining room, still silver sneeze lids over the plates, tableside theatrics, and a tasting menu. And there's still a secret menu that only insiders know about with pasta primavera and roast chicken for two. But the Maccioni family turned the café into a lounge where you can kick back in your jeans and sneakers while ordering a glass of wine and mini-cheeseburgers from the à la carte menu. The dessert menu is the same in the lounge as it is in the dining room, but all you need to know is this: Le Cirque makes the best crème brûlée in the city. You don't even have to take a bite to judge the merits of this cream custard. Just do the "click, click" test, tapping the caramelized seal with the edge of your spoon. If it cracks, it's too thin. Tap it again with a bit of force. If it doesn't crack, it's too thick. Le Cirque's crème brûlée is perfect, and the recipe's right there on the plate. Oh, by the way, don't try the jeans-and-sneakers bit in the main dining room. It works only in the lounge.

Places like Le Cirque are increasingly rare here in New York. There are only a few pillars of French fine dining left in the city, and almost no newcomers. Eleven Madison Park is the exquisite exception. For many years it was a reliable (but unexciting) American restaurant. Then chef Daniel Humm arrived on the scene, revamped the kitchen, and transformed the restaurant into a French temple gastronomique. The restaurateur Danny Meyer has built an empire of successful restaurants, but Eleven Madison Park is the feather in his cap. You won't even want to wear jeans in this gorgeous setting with its soaring ceilings, marble floors, and sweeping view of Madison Square Park. And the food is just as magnificent and luxurious as the restaurant itself.

If you're going to splurge, Eleven Madison Park is the place to do it. Humm's meticulous foams, reductions, and sauces—many of which are poured tableside—are thrilling. He makes classic French dishes seem new and exciting, such as foie gras mousse dabbed with rhubarb foam, which shares the same plate with a foie gras terrine, garnished with tart rhubarb, pickled ramps, and celery—a delightfully dizzying dish. A simple drizzle of olive oil and balsamic vinegar works wonders to sharpen every flavor in an appetizer of gnocchi mingled with shrimp, calamari, and candied ribbons of Meyer lemon. The entire meal is a stunning balancing act of voluptuous and delicate flavors. One night I had glistening halibut with a curl of sweet crayfish, the next pork belly garnished with mint, and on another occasion tuna tartare finished with avocado cream. The evening ends with a "chocolate peanut butter palette" that tastes like a sophisticated riff on a crunchy candy bar, along with homemade chocolates.

Aside from a few French institutions, there isn't a huge difference between haute and everyday French cuisine nowadays. You're just as likely to find pig's trotter on a menu at either kind of restaurant. The fundamental distinction is preparation and presentation. Both schools of cooking revere the fine art of cheese making and charcuterie. Charcuterie refers to the universe of cured, salted, and smoked meats. When the French do something, they do it to the fullest. Have you seen their vast selection of charcuterie? You could get lost among all the sausages, pâtés, terrines, and mousses. The motives of all great charcuterie traditions are ultimately the same: survival and preservation. It's as simple as that. Back in the day, you couldn't run out to Sears and buy a fridge that would keep your freshly hunted and hard-earned meat from spoiling. Smoking, salting, and curing meats meant they could be stored for much longer periods of time. Originally charcuterie was only made from pork. A single pig was so valuable—and meat so hard to come by—that no one could afford to waste any bits of it, so everything—liver, hearts, kidneys, you name it—was preserved, with spices, nuts, and fruit added to make it all as palatable as possible. Voilà, rillettes, pâtés, and sausages were born. The French may be infamously snobbish, but they're also brave diners.

Who would have thought that fattened duck liver and goose liver would become luxury items? They're both potential foie gras in the making. *Foie gras,* which means "fat liver," is a pâté made from fattened duck or goose liver. (Goose liver is a little more expensive than duck, so it's less commonly used.) The type of foie gras depends on the percent of liver in it. Some are 100 percent liver, others are mixed with seasonings, like cognac or mushrooms. My favorite way to eat foie gras is seared and served warm with quince or some other fruit preserve to offset a bit of the melt-in-your-mouth fat. Most of the time, warm preparations are 100 percent liver.

Cold foie gras is molded into terrines or pâtés, like the ones you find at Pastis or Balthazar, and mixed with other meats or seasonings, like truffles, mushrooms, prunes, or brandy. The difference between a pâté and a terrine is mostly texture. Pâtés are made with finely ground foie gras that's smooth and spreadable. A terrine, on the other hand, is made with chopped foie gras, which makes it more coarse, and cooked in a terrine pan. Terrines are often pressed, so they're denser than your average pâté. The ingredients are up to the charcutier (that's French for the person who prepares it). At a restaurant, you can't read the back of a box and get a full rundown of the ingredients. (And you probably don't want to know the nutritional values on the deliciously fattening food you'll be eating at a French restaurant!) Likewise, there's no fine print on a menu. But when it comes to deciding what kind of charcuterie to order, texture is often more important than the ingredients. You know your tongue: does it like the feel of light, fluffy spreads or coarse, thick ones? Because that's going to determine whether you're the mousse or terrine type. The silkiest and lightest of them all is always going to be a mousse. If you want a little more substance, but still smooth and spreadable, try a pâté. And definitely sample some sausages.

I never thought of myself as the sausage type until I tried a boudin blanc (white sausage made with pork and chicken). The only French-style sausages I knew were saucisses de Frankfurt, the skinny boiled hot dogs you get at ball games or from street carts. The French eat theirs with a fork and knife and a glass of Riesling. At Bar Boulud on the Upper West Side, the boudin blanc looks and tastes nothing like a hot dog. For starters, it's laced with truffles. Even if it weren't, it would win accolades for its thickness and juiciness alone. There's also a boudin noir on the menu, made with beef blood, pork, and onions, and served over celery root and roasted apples. It's really, really rich. Bar Boulud is chef Daniel Boulud's answer to Manhattanites' demands for more casual French wine bars, and his personal homage to all things cured, spiced, smoked, and ground.

Boulud's talent for producing outstanding French cuisine is matched by his restaurants' equally impeccable service. At Daniel (his haute flagship), servers glide gracefully through the dining room. At Bar Boulud, they frantically weave through the narrow quarters, crowded with oenophiles, locals, and Boulud devotees. Guests swarm the hostess stand, eager to feast on the vast array of charcuterie displayed in the glass counter that runs the length of the one-hundred-seat space. With its blond wood accents and arched ceiling, Bar Boulud evokes a wine cellar, and there's a splendid list of robust reds to match the robust charcuterie. The menu boasts a stunning roster of pâtés and terrines, all made by Bar

Boulud's in-house charcutier, Sylvain Gasdon. Chicken liver and cognac impart a rustic sweetness to the "pâté grand-mère," while truffle juice, foie gras, and port lend a seductive luxuriousness to the "pâté grand-père." The terrines look like savory mosaics, and just a nibble of any of them will instantly transport you to the French countryside.

As if the French haven't conquered enough culinary territory, they are also, arguably, the finest cheese makers in the world. Ugh. They remind me of that perfect girl (or guy) in high school you hated for their lack of flaws. Perfectly soft, stinky cheeses are a French specialty. Oh, and they make the most crusty baguettes and gorgeous wines to eat them with. I adore Roquefort (sheep's milk blue cheese) in all its pungent glory crumbled on a bistro salad. And I admire how creamy and spreadable Brie (unpasteurized cow's milk cheese) can be, how delicate and supple Camembert (cow's milk cheese) is, and how tasty the rinds are. Fresh cheeses, like ricotta or goat cheese, have no rind at all. Only aged cheeses have rinds, which seal in the flavor and moisture of the cheese. The rind is a natural shell that develops on the outside of cheese as it ages. With few exceptions—wax and cloth—all rinds are edible. And some are divine, especially French rinds. (Some rinds taste even more delicious than the cheese itself.) Some have washed rinds (washed with wine, beer, or brine), others have soft, thick, bloomy rinds (sprayed with mold), while still others have hard natural rinds that form as it ages. Brie and Camembert have bloomy rinds and a velvety texture. Stinky cheeses, like Roquefort, typically have fragrant washed rinds. The easiest way to tell one rind from another is by color: bloomy rinds are white, and washed rinds are a reddish color.

Unfortunately we eat only a few great French cheeses, with the volume set on low. You can't get truly stinky Brie in America, because unpasteurized cheese isn't legal here. Most of us wouldn't even know that good Brie ought to be stinky in the first place. "Brie is for people who don't like cheese," a foodie friend of mine says. "Or at least American Brie." That's true, but it's still a good beginner cheese—eating the rind takes some getting used to, so this inoffensive cheese is as good a place as any to start. But there are hundreds of others you can enjoy on American soil. Over fifty years ago French president Charles de Gaulle joked, "How can you govern a country with 246 varieties of cheese?" There are now over 1,000 French cheeses—and counting. There's mild, blue, sharp, soft, semisoft, semihard, sheep, cow, goat, and washed rind, for starters. It's not as complicated as it sounds: mild cheeses are mildly flavored or mildly fragrant, and often both. Sharp cheeses are strongly flavored or strongly fragrant, and often both. And the softer the cheese, the more spreadable it is. The harder it is, the harder it is to spread. (You'll need a knife to slice it.) Soft doesn't necessarily mean mild. Roquefort, a stinky blue cheese, is soft and sharply flavored. Blue cheeses like Roquefort have mold added to them, which gives them those blue/green streaks you often see. Their flavor is distinctive and complex. Some cheeses are nutty or fruity, runny or hard, and the possibilities are endless. You could eat nothing but cheese, bread, and wine and die happy.

Cheese is so important in French cuisine that it gets its own course in the meal. Unlike in America, where we often serve cheese and crackers as an appetizer, the French save cheese for after dinner, just before dessert. That takes some getting used to, but it's a nice transition between rich meats and sauces to rich desserts. I've had the cheese course at lots of fine French institutions, and the best serve them runny and at room temperature. Too cold, and the essence of the cheese is crippled.

But to really eat French cheese well, make an evening of it. Or better yet, visit one of Terrance Brennan's restaurants. This is a man with a serious fromage fetish. Not many brasseries have their own cheese cave, especially in the middle of Manhattan. Not only does Brennan's restaurant Artisanal have its own cheese cave, but you can even dine in it, surrounded by smelly cheeses from all over the world. Cheese plates, scattered with fresh grapes, candied walnuts, and fig and other fruit pastes, rest on many of the tables. There's wine and cheese pairings and pungent cheese fondues served with chorizo and saucisson for dipping. The lactose intolerant need not apply.

> • TASTY MORSEL •
>
> *A well-cooked cheese fondue should have a crust at the bottom, called "le religieuse," that tastes like a cracker. It can and should be lifted out of the pan and eaten.*

Which brings me back to the mystery of how the French stay so svelte . . . I mean, these are a people with a dedicated cheese course in their meal structure. And I guess it would be small consolation if dinner ended with cheese. No such luck. Dessert is a very big deal to the French, and good thing. Dessert would be much less extraordinary without their many contributions. They gave us the soufflé, a minor culinary miracle. How can something so light and fluffy taste so rich? It's a bewitching dessert—a cross between a cake and a custard made with a base of sugar and eggs—that goes from the oven straight to your plate. Pierce the swollen crust with your spoon and it deflates, yours for the taking. The classic French soufflés are chocolate and Grand Marnier (a cognac and bitter orange liqueur), and they're both heavenly.

And nobody makes better tarts than the French. I'm not referring just to the tarte tatin, that archetypal and marvelous tart with candied edges and caramelized apples. There are almost as many French tarts as there are cheeses. Wander into any patisserie (bakery) and you'll see an ever-changing menu of tarts. If you have time, linger over a slice of strawberry and rhubarb tart at Balthazar, or get to go a piece of apricot frangipane (a creamy almond filling), mixed berry, or lemon soufflé tart from the bakery next door. Unlike a pie, a tart has only a bottom crust—it's like a pie with the top down. And how it looks is just as important as how it tastes; every single berry and apple sliver in a tart is beautifully arranged. (I'm proud to be an American and all, but we're not as concerned with looks as the French are. We'll happily toss a bunch of sliced apples into a crust, seal it with a second layer of crust, and top our slices with a spray of whipped cream. The French make artfully flaky tarts with immaculately arranged apple slices and a thick cloud of crème fraîche on top, none of this light whipped cream nonsense.)

Walk by any patisserie and admire the freshly baked artwork in the window: round chocolate tarts with perfectly shaped crusts, crowned with sliced strawberries and a sprig of fresh mint, raspberry and almond tarts paved in slivered almonds and plump raspberries in the shape of a flower. More rustic, free-form tarts are called galettes—they look like little fruit-filled wallets. Financiers are dainty tea cakes with a notably crispy crust and a soft interior. You may already be acquainted with the madeleine, the financier's kissing cousin, with its beautiful shell shape and buttery, cakey interior. Just one taste of a madeleine inspired Marcel Proust's epic six-part novel *In Search of Lost Time*—which is about three thousand pages pages long! I should disclose my distaste for profiteroles and éclairs because I don't like choux pastry dough. It's the same pastry dough used for cream puffs—with a thin crust on the outside and a hollowed-out interior. In my opinion, the crust is too chewy, and there's too much air and not enough dough inside to make it worth my while. (I'm glad I got that off my chest.) Since a profiterole is hollowed out and then stuffed with cream, the crust is all that's left. You might not know it by name, but you'd recognize it. An éclair is that hot-dog-shaped pastry filled with cream and coated in chocolate icing. That's not my guy either, but let me know what you think. You're a critic, too.

Americans have the chocolate chip cookie; the French have the macaron. Macarons are elegant, meringue sandwich cookies with a rich filling, often displayed in glass cases. There's a pastel-colored sea of macarons at Bouchon Bakery in Midtown, which come in lots of flavors: espresso, vanilla, pistachio, raspberry, and many others, depending on the whims of the bakers. Any macaron worth its name should be crunchy on the outside, moist on the inside. The finest melt on your tongue like a communion wafer. A meringue is a wonderfully light, sweet, and ever-so-crunchy invention, made with just egg whites, ground almonds, and sugar. There are complicated meringue cakes, like the dacquoise, a layer cake of almond meringue and whipped cream or butter cream. Minetta Tavern makes a fabulous chocolate dacquoise with chocolate ganache and hazelnut meringue. There's even a fancy ice cream cake called a Vacherin, with meringue rings (the shape of doughnuts), cream, and fruit. (A Vacherin is also a type of runny, rich cow's milk cheese made in France and Switzerland only in the winter.)

There's pastry beyond meringue, like the mille-feuille (known as the Napoleon in the United States), a layer cake of puff pastry and crème pattissière—the name translates as "a thousand leaves." Volumes could be written on French pastry, like the baba au rhum, a rich yeast cake saturated in liquor (usually rum) and topped with pastry cream. There are too many incredible desserts to wax rhapsodic about all of them, but I hold a special place in my heart for cherry clafoutis—or any fruit clafoutis at all. The clafoutis is a curious creation, not quite a custard or a cake, but an exceptionally moist hybrid of the two.

## Table Setting and Modern Manners

First of all, there's no such thing as "fashionably late." It's considered rude, especially at a restaurant. If you're running late for your reservation, call ahead and let them know you're running a few minutes behind. And although the French don't care for being fashionably late, they are fashionable eaters. They dress for the occasion. Just look around Balthazar, Pastis, or your local bustling bistro, and you'll see a lot of well-dressed diners. But once you're there, feel free to linger, to really take in and appreciate your meal.

I've never gotten used to using the tablecloth as my bread plate. Plenty of cultures do it, but it still feels awkward to me. I feel like a child in a high chair who throws her plate on the floor, then eats right off the table. It's fun and all, but it's not a pretty sight in a restaurant. But the French don't mind it one bit, especially at brasseries and bistros. First, look for a bread plate and take it as a hint. If there's no bread plate on the table, go for it. However, they are less liberal about how you eat that piece of bread than they are about where you put it. The French follow the "tear as you go" bread policy, so tear off only as much as you can swallow in one bite, then repeat as needed, and butter as you go. That doesn't mean reaching for the breadbasket every time you want a bite. Tear off a big piece to keep in front of you.

Follow standard protocol when it comes to dinner table manners: no elbows on the table, napkin on the lap, the usual please-and-thank-yous, and utensils vertically placed together on the plate when you're finished. Salt and pepper aren't joined at the hip, so you can pass them separately. The French do talk less when there is food on the table to give food the respect it deserves, and they don't approve of ice in wine.

The French are famous for their wines and fanatics about them. When in France, or a French restaurant, drink French wines. Most are named after the region they're produced in. Real

Champagne is made in Champagne, France. Sancerre wines are all from Sancerre, and Burgundy is from Burgundy. I recommend letting the sommelier guide you through the menu. The French are one of the biggest wine producers in the world, so it gets complicated. Whatever you settle on, hold your glass by the stem. I've seen plenty of people freeze up when it comes time to pick up the salad fork or the soup spoon (myself included). The fancier you go, the more forks and knives you'll find in front of you. It can be very intimidating, but it doesn't have to be. There's a trick. No matter where you're dining, the utensils are laid out in the order you'll use them. Start on the outside and work in. The butter knife is often laid across the bread plate, and the dessert spoon is often placed above its plate. Bon appétit!

# Why Manners Matter

**F**orget Emily Post. I'm pretty sure she never used a cell phone or checked her e-mail. She wrote *Etiquette: The Blue Book of Social Usage,* her famous manual of appropriate behavior for every social situation, in 1922, long before credit cards or gender equality came into the picture. She was a socialite who hosted dinner parties and attended galas; restaurants were not her domain. I'm betting she never had a blind date take her to a Chinese buffet or a husband who texted at the table.

Even the most updated version of Emily Post's blue book advises you to "keep your elbows at your side. Never make noises when eating." That sounds like no fun at all to me. This isn't crime and punishment. It's dinner. You're not supposed to suffer through a meal; you're supposed to enjoy it. Obviously you don't want to jab the diner next to you in the ribs with your elbow or have an orgasm at the table, but pleasurable little peeps are entirely acceptable and rather flattering to a chef.

We all want to make a good impression—to get the job or a kiss good night, or even better, an invite upstairs. You might be a great catch or have a great résumé, but if you use your fingers instead of your fork or blow your nose in your napkin, that will be what people remember about you. And, more important, no one will want to dine with you again. I've eaten in more than my fair share of restaurants and witnessed many faux pas. I've been guilty of a few dinner table fouls myself, so I know there are a few major dos and don'ts that can make or break a meal. For instance, I love eating ice cream or peanut butter straight from the container, but that's something you ought to do alone in your pajamas in the privacy of your own kitchen. If I stick my spoon in your soup without asking, you're going to be unhappy. If I put my feet up on the table, the waitstaff, the chef, and my dinner companions will all be unhappy with me. At a restaurant, we might be paying customers, but we're also guests in the chef's "house." As much as I'd love to, I can't go into the kitchen and snack on anything in the fridge. Then again, I don't have to cook, and that is much more compelling. My only job is deciding what to order and being a good guest.

I've heard about "the good old days" when a man picked a woman up at her house, rang the doorbell, and waited patiently while she finished getting ready. These days your date might keep the car running and honk to let you know he or she has arrived—if they don't just meet you at the restaurant. People used to say grace before dinner. Now, I'm not rallying for grace before dinner, but it did force people to take a minute to think about their food before digging in. Slowing down, paying attention, and taking the time to really notice what you're eating and who you're with—whether you're thanking God, your mother, or the chef, or just admiring the flatware—makes you appreciate the food in front of you and your company that much more enjoyable.

In many ways, dining out is not just about food but also about ritual and ceremony—dressing up, being escorted to your table, ordering a glass of wine, leisurely perusing the menu, and savoring every bite. Have you noticed how most restaurants don't offer you bread until after you order? It's not because they think you might devour the breadbasket and split. They want you to be hungry when you read the menu. They don't want to ruin the seduction of dinner with a breadbasket binge. If you're a singer, you want someone to buy your album. If you're a chef, you want someone to eat your art and make noise about it. Likewise, if you go to dinner with someone, you want to share a meal with them. The ceremony of dinner doesn't involve instant messaging or your BlackBerry. What happened to talking to the person sitting across the table, not the person who just e-mailed you a photo of his King Charles spaniel?

Sure, there's alcohol, but manners are an even more effective social lubricant. They're also an integral part of the ceremony. After all, dining out is inherently social: if you don't wait for your companion's meal to arrive before you begin eating, you might as well have gone to dinner by yourself. Even if you do go to dinner by yourself, there are still others around you who are paying for the pleasure of the restaurant experience, which includes the ambience—and ambience relies on an implicit pact between the diner and the restaurant to observe certain codes of conduct.

# · 5 ·

# Greek Cuisine

*We should look for someone with whom to
eat and drink before looking for something
to eat and drink, for dining alone is leading
the life of a lion or wolf.*

EPICURUS

As silly as it sounds, before I actually visited Greece, I imagined it was always summer there. The photos I'd seen were all of sun-splashed islands with whitewashed houses climbing their cliff sides. Whenever I went for Greek food, I always ordered summery foods: I'd start with a bowl of grassy olives; warm, dill-scented pita with garlic-infused spreads; tender, char-grilled calamari; and fresh fish, presented whole and crowned with just-snipped herbs. When a friend and I finally traveled to Greece, it was late fall, apparently right around the time the cool weather sets in. It was a brisk November day when we touched down in Athens, and as soon as I stepped out into the chilly air, I realized I wouldn't be needing the bikinis I'd packed. Well, if I wasn't going to get a tan, I wanted to at least eat well.

Our first night in Athens, I ordered all my usual favorites: roasted beets slicked with olive oil, fried zucchini chips, terrifically vinegary octopus, and a salty block of feta flecked with oregano, but I couldn't find a Greek salad anywhere on the menu. I knew this lettuce-less salad sometimes went by other aliases, like "peasant salad" or "village salad," so I expanded my search, but still no luck. By the time we got to the island of Mykonos, I was consumed with the mysterious disappearance of my beloved Greek salad. Our first night on the island, in a local taverna, I interrogated the waitress. She had no idea what I was asking for, never mind what I was saying, so she sent the owner over to field my question. "Greek salad," I said slowly, then began listing the ingredients. "It has cucumber, feta, olives, onions, green peppers, and tomato——." "Ahh," he jumped in. "Horiatiki salata. Tomatoes aren't in season. We have others you will like." Of course, it was winter. Oops. And I was doubly embarrassed it had never dawned on me that "Greek salad" isn't even the salad's real name. It's what Americans call it, which is a lot like my father asking for "more Spanish soup" every time we had dinner at the Spanish Tavern. Spain has more than one soup, and Greece has plenty of salads.

It was oddly liberating, calling off my search for a Greek salad and surrendering to the seasons. It got surprisingly nippy at night, and because most hotels and hostels aren't heated, I slept in my jacket and began to crave warm, filling foods. I had never paid much attention to macaronia (pasta) dishes. (Technically, macaronia refers to short pasta tubes, like the ones you find in macaroni and cheese, but most Greek restaurants in America refer to pasta at large as macaronia or makaronia.) At home when I craved pasta, I went for Italian. And though I don't mind lasagna, I usually opt for pasta that's lighter and brighter, like spaghetti carbonara. But the Greeks devised my dream lasagne. Imagine macaronia (short tubes of pasta) layered with beef ragu and luscious béchamel sauce, perfumed with a potent dose of cinnamon, nutmeg, and cloves, and that's pastitsio. I'd been skipping over not just pastitsio, but the entire macaronia selection in favor of octopus, feta, and the same old dishes since childhood. How could this have happened? I grew up in a food-focused family and yet, the closest I'd come to Greek comfort food was that familiarly flaky, phyllo-crusted spinach and feta pie called spanakopita. After that first pastitsio experience, I wanted to dabble in other kinds of pasta, like sheep's milk dumplings, which tasted like sweet, ethereal gnocchi, rice-size orzo pilaf, and spaghetti topped with kima—a ground beef sauce—which recalled Bolognese sauce, only thicker. I tasted soft hilopite noodles—tiny, square noodles rich with egg yolks—bathing in a beef and tomato ragu. And I cozied up to a classic casserole called moussaka, which is all you really need on a cold, quiet night during Greece's off-season. I know a casserole doesn't exactly sound sexy, but this one was, a voluptuous layering of eggplant, ground meat sauce, and béchamel. I took full advantage of the wintry weather, sampling savory stews, redolent with cinnamon and cloves, including the classic beef stifado, simmering with beef, onions, tomatoes, red wine vinegar, and cinnamon, which made the beef stew my mom made when I was a kid seem downright dull. I loved the way the sweet spices invigorated the rich cuts of beef and made a hearty stew taste somehow delicate.

After we had eaten our way through Mykonos, my friend and I took a boat over to Paros, a teeny island where a mutual college friend was studying for six months. There was one restaurant on the entire island and no hot water. I didn't mind the outdoor shower's frigid water. I just didn't shower for four days. But for someone who's made it her life mission to eat at new restaurants nightly, the notion of one lone restaurant was challenging. My travel companion didn't seem to mind this one-restaurant island a bit. She didn't care that much about variety and food. Nope, she had just one request everywhere we ate: no oil or butter. She was going through one of those "fat-phobic" phases. She even typed

up the translation for "no oil or butter" for every country we visited and carried it in her bag at all times. (True story.) As long
as my food came the way the chef intended, I didn't mind. The
dining room was cozy, plainly outfitted with a smattering of wood
tables, and the menu was short and sweet. As soon as my friend
made her fat-free request, our host got nervous. I don't blame
him. Who wants to piss off the chef of the only restaurant on an
island where you have to live for two more months? Our server
seemed indifferent to her request, which naturally made my "no
oil or butter" friend nervous as well. Before I realized what she
was doing, she had snuck into the kitchen. By the time I got to her,
she had already gotten to the chef.

Of course, there was olive oil in his hand. You don't ask a
Greek chef to forsake his olive oil. That's like asking a painter to
give up his paintbrush or a pastry chef not to use butter or sugar.
The Greeks consume more olive oil than any other country and
produce some of the finest olive oil in the world. The majority
of it is extra virgin olive oil, the most refined variety with no
more than 8 percent free fatty acid. (It's like that china you save
for special occasions.) It has a fantastically fruity aroma and a
greenish hue, a perfect dipping oil for fresh bread or to use in
salad dressings. If there's a shallow bowl of green, Greek extra
virgin on the table, consider it your duty to meditate on its ex-
ceptional fragrance and flavor. The Greeks are also known for
their olives grown specifically for eating, not for pressing into
oil. In fact the most widely consumed olives in the world are
Greek kalamata olives. They're dark purple olives shaped like
large almonds with a rich, fruity flavor. There are over 140 mil-
lion olive trees growing in Greece, and more than 100 kinds of
olives growing on them: some are picked when they're fully ripe
and have turned black, while others are plucked from the trees
prematurely, while they're still green.

The Greek islands are flush with olive and lemon trees, and they're both put to good use. Lamb, pork, beef, and even rabbit are seasoned with plenty of olive oil and lemon before cooking. While I was there I discovered how lemon perks up pork shanks and intensifies the flavor of lamb chops. I was already familiar with the lemony marvel of avgolemono soup, a bright, velvety egg-lemon soup flavored with chicken stock, dill, and rice, but I didn't know that the Greeks also made an egg-lemon sauce by the same name. Anything blessed by avgolemono sauce should be devoured on sight. (Lamb fricasse comes to mind.) What I love most about Greek food is its unique combination of flavors. You don't often see lamb and cheese consorting on a single plate, but lamb chops crowned with feta is a signature Greek move. Most countries are wary to let cheese and fish get too close, but the Greeks don't think twice about stuffing cheese inside octopus or calamari. And they have a knack for transforming meat ragouts and rich pastas into vibrant dishes bright with a dash of cloves, nutmeg, and cinnamon. What's traditional to them often tastes brave and unexpected to newcomers. These bold combinations and aromatic ingredients embody the ethos of Greek cooking. But they don't overseason, oversauce, or overspice. The spiciest dish I've eaten is

> • TASTY MORSEL •
>
> *The word* oregano *derives from the Greek* oros, *meaning "mountain or hill," and* ganos, *meaning "brightness or joy." In Greek mythology, Aphrodite, the goddess of love, created oregano as a symbol of happiness and grew it in her garden on Mount Olympus. At traditional Greek weddings, the bride and groom are crowned with wreaths of oregano.*

keftedes, a meze of meatballs in tomato sauce dosed with cumin.
In the scheme of spicy, it doesn't rank very high.

Greek food is highly fragrant food. If you had to choose one
herb to define a cuisine, the herb for Greek food would be oregano.
You can't miss its sweet smell in salads, soups, meats, and meze.
Aside from their oregano obsession, they season with lots of dill,
parsley, mint, basil, bay leaves, sage, rosemary, and thyme, as well
as garlic and capers. You'll see dill-flavored breads and salads,
parsley-flecked fish, minted meatballs, thyme-infused honey, and
caper salads. Apart from a few desserts, nothing leaves the kitchen
without a little lemon and olive oil.

Many native Greeks are farmers, herders, and fishermen.
(They invented fish stew way before the Italians and the French.)
Naturally, they want to show off the freshness of their catch—
the size, color, and shininess of the skin. That's why Greek restaurants often display fish on ice in the dining room. I like to call
it the "let it be" approach to cooking. They want you to experience the brininess of sardines, so they grill them and let them
be. There might be parsley, garlic, or lemon to illuminate the
flavors, but nothing else is added to get in the way. Order grilled
octopus or whole fish and you'll taste the char of the grill and the
unencumbered nuances of the fish. Olive oil, lemon, and oodles
of oregano are part of the package. That's what makes it Greek:
they add a few of their signature seasonings and let it be. What
makes potatoes and wild greens (horta) Greek is a little olive oil
and lemon. What makes beets Greek is a little olive oil and vinegar, or oftentimes, skordalia. Skordalia is a thick potato puree
loaded with garlic, which is served alongside or tossed with beets,
and on its own as a meze.


Mezedes (aka mezethes)—the plural form of meze—are the
Greek equivalent of tapas. They're little bites meant for graz-

ing and sharing any time of day. You don't keep skordalia all to
yourself. For starters, it's too garlicky, but mainly, it's very unmeze-
like to hog. And no one notices garlic breath when everyone has
it! I follow a feisty scoop of skordalia smeared on pita with a scoop
of cooling tzatziki—a tangy sheep's milk yogurt dip with cucumber, garlic, mint, and fresh dill. Then I head to taramosalata territory. Some people read "fish roe" and pass. Please don't: This is
briny Greek caviar whipped up with olive oil into a lemony, cor-
al-colored mousse. Dab a little on pita and you have a Greek
blini (a whole lot cheaper than a Russian blini). As with skordalia, I follow taramosalata with a scoop of not-quite-as-garlicky
tzatziki. The holy trinity of Greek dips is skordalia, tzatziki, and
taramosalata, though I hestitate to call them dips, because most
dips don't demand this much respect or attention. Some foodists
might argue that chickpea puree (revithia), better known as
hummus, and roasted eggplant puree (melitzanosalata) are both
holier than skordalia or taramosalata. I beg to differ: you can
order hummus or roasted eggplant in plenty of Middle Eastern
restaurants, but not taramosalata and skordalia. And as for tzatzi-

• TASTY MORSEL •

*The word* opa *is a jubilant affirmation of life's joys, often associated with dancing and celebrating. Smashing
a plate is a welcoming gesture, like saying, "No wor-
ries. Have fun, dance, drink. Live a little this evening."
But just because your waiter smashes a few plates
doesn't mean you should follow his lead. They're his
plates, not yours.*

ki, you'll find yogurt dip in Lebanese or Turkish joints, but no one makes thicker, tangier sheep's milk yogurt than the Greeks. End of story. Of course if someone ordered hummus or roasted eggplant, I'd swipe a pita triangle through both, too. I just wouldn't choose them over the meze holy trinity. Just like Spanish tapas, meze were originally created to complement wine and Greek spirits, particularly ouzo (an anise-scented liqueur). If I lived in Greece, I'd become more social all in the name of meze. They're not complex nibbles, but they are vividly flavored and unique.

Where food is concerned, I like to think I have my priorities straight. I can order grilled calamari or a grilled whole fish at almost any seafood restaurant, but I can only find true meze at a Greek restaurant—and that includes Greek cheese. Greece is celebrated for a number of its tangy goat's and sheep's milk cheeses, many of which are served as meze with pita or a crusty loaf of bread. Where else but a Greek restaurant can you order fried cheese (saganaki) doused in brandy or ouzo and set ablaze at the table? This isn't just an excuse to shout "Opa!" or smash a plate. It's gooey greatness. Any cheese that melts is potential saganaki material. In Greece I learned that "saganaki" doesn't mean always fried cheese, nor does it even indicate a specific type of cheese. It actually refers to the little frying pan in which the cheese is cooked, and anything cooked in such a pan is dubbed saganaki. Kasseri, graviera, and halloumi cheese are all served saganaki style. Feta gets most of the fanfare among Greek cheeses, but when it comes to fried or grilled cheese, I prefer the meaty texture and tang of halloumi (a marvelous blend of sheep and goat's milk) and the bubbly crust that forms on the outside as it cooks.

I love the salty, crumbly character of feta sprinkled with olive oil and fresh oregano; the cream-cheese-like texture of manouri cheese for spreading on fresh-baked pitas; the rich nuttiness of graviera grated over lamb ragu; and the stringy texture of kasseri stuffed inside ravioli. But my favorite is the grilled halloumi, splashed with Greek grappa, and a scattering of sautéed grapes at Pylos, a meze mecca in the East Village. The dining room at Pylos is adorned with whitewashed walls, plush throw pillows, and over a thousand clay pots dangling from the ceiling. If you didn't know better, you'd think you were in Greece. There's an all-Greek wine list and close to twenty mezedes on the menu, which makes it nearly impossible to dip your toe in the rest of the menu. There's piles of fried, paper-thin eggplant and zucchini chips with tzatziki, earthy gigante beans baked in a tomato-dill sauce, grilled sardines with garlic and parsley, meatballs (keftedes), a fine spanakopita, and freshly stuffed grape leaves (dolmades) filled with raisins, pine nuts, and rice with a side of dill-inflected yogurt sauce.

Mezedes are a window into the soul of Greek cuisine. After all, the Greeks make cheeses and wines, herd sheep and goats, press olives, catch fish, and grow vegetables and fragrant herbs. They sip ouzo and graze on cabbage salads, peppers, or eggplant filled with ground meat, rice, and dill—any stuffed vegetable is labeled dolmades—and spiced sausages. Molyvos in Midtown makes the juiciest, sweet-smelling Greek sausages (loukaniko) in the city—a mix of ground lamb and pork, heavily perfumed with orange peel, fennel, and coriander. And it's just as hard to top their dolmades, made with a lusty blend of ground pork, lamb, beef, and rice, tightly wrapped in cabbage leaves with a terrific garlic yogurt dipping sauce. Molyvos also has an impressive selection of ouzo to pair with all of the homey dishes on the menu.

Ouzo—a clear, anise-flavored liqueur—is Greece's national drink. Just as Champagne is produced exclusively in the Champagne region of France, ouzo is produced exclusively in Greece. From what I can tell, any occasion is a good occasion to drink ouzo—before dinner, after dinner, midday, and definitely with meze. But it's very strong, so drink it slowly, and with lots of meze, or you'll be in bed before dessert. (I once drank it too quickly. I sadly missed out on baklava and woke up with a wicked hangover.) You can water it down, the way the Greeks do; just remember that ouzo naturally clouds up when you add water or ice, so don't send a cloudy glass back. Ouzo is usually served in a shot glass for sipping, not for downing in one swift swallow. If you're not a fan of licorice, you won't be a fan of ouzo. On occasion you may come across another anise-scented liqueur called raki, which is native to Crete, the most populated Greek island. Apparently the Cretans don't consider themselves Greek—they treat raki as their national drink—and they like their liqueur even stronger than ouzo. So if you order raki instead of ouzo, add more water to it and drink even more slowly. (Raki is also the national drink of Turkey, so many menus will offer Turkish raki as well.) I enjoy alcohol, but I'd rather eat my ouzo. Molyvos spikes their halloumi saganaki with ouzo. The licorice flavor mellows out when you heat ouzo, and it lends a fresh flavor to the bubbling cheese or anything else it's splashed on. Sometimes I picture the chef pouring a glass of ouzo for himself before he spills a little into the saganaki pan.

> ## • TASTY MORSEL •
>
> *It's widely accepted that the best ouzo is from the island of Lesbos (or Lesvos), the center of ouzo production in Greece. The epicenter of ouzo on Lesbos is the town of Plomari, home to the Barbayannis Ouzo distillery—where they've been making exceptional ouzo for over 140 years . . . and the recipe is still a secret!*

In Greece you can while away a sunny, or in my case, a brisk, not-so-sunny afternoon in the off-season at an ouzeria, which are devoted solely to the enjoyment of ouzo and a smattering of meze. We don't have many, if any, ouzerias in America, but we do have "estiatorios" with glimmering seafood displayed on beds of shaved ice and formal fare. Up until I visited Greece, I ate most of my Greek meals in estiatorios. Then I discovered Greece's "tavernas" and stateside tavernas, like Pylos and Molyvos, that specialize in hearty, rustic cooking. They don't have seafood displays, and their focus isn't fish. Their menus are peppered with braised, roasted, ground, and grilled meats, rich ragus, sauces, and stews. Michael Psilakis—the chef of Kefi, a taverna located on the Upper West Side of Manhattan—is a master of the lusty flavors that embody Greek home cooking. I'll eat shank of anything he's braising—it's usually lamb shank—as long as there's plenty of orzo pasta on the plate to soak up all the gamey juices. And the man can do no wrong by macaronia either. His braised rabbit mingled with hilopite noodles, salty nuggets of graviera cheese, and a whisper of cinnamon is a sublime revelation. His sheep's milk ravioli bask in a sage-scented pool of brown butter, and his keftedes (meatballs) are lavished with a tomato sauce swimming with whole garlic cloves and olives. Psilakis excels at comfort foods and fast foods, like lamb burgers topped with manouri cheese and juicy pork souvlaki served on a grilled pita with creamy gobs of tzatziki. Souvlaki is skewered fast food. It's a cube of meat or meaty fish—swordfish, lamb, chicken, or steak—threaded onto a stick and grilled. Sometimes it's all-meat, and other times, it's meat interspersed with eggplant, zucchini, onion, or tomato. Souvlaki traditionally comes on a warm pita with tzatziki sauce. People sometimes confuse souvlaki with gyros, but I quickly learned otherwise in Greece. Have you ever seen a vertical spit-roaster stacked with pork or lamb slowly twirling round? That makes gyros, and the meat is never cut 'til you order. Only then does the chef shave off a few slices, dripping with fat, and tuck it into grilled pita with lettuce, tomatoes, onions, and tzatziki.

Just down the street from Molyvos is Estiatorio Milos, one of the most beautiful and expensive Greek seafood restaurants in the country. There's white gauzy curtains anchored by garlic bulbs, soaring ceilings, and white sun umbrellas scattered around the room. The fish on the ice display should be insured. There's freshly flown-in porgy, shimmery red mullets, scallops the diameter of bracelets, branzino, snapper, and if you're there on a good night, langoustines. I've never had more perfectly charred octopus, fresher fish, or thicker, homemade Greek yogurt drizzled with thyme-infused honey for dessert. But if you don't want to mortgage your house for a meal at Milos, head to Astoria, Queens. Astoria is famous for its large Greek community and has a wealth of Greek restaurants to feed them all. In my experience, the key to finding the best Greek restaurants anywhere in the country is locating the Greek churches and scoping out their neighborhoods. That's how I found all of my favorite Greek restaurants in Los Angeles. A little something I also learned: if there's no menu at these family-style restaurants, chances are you're in good hands. Now I'm a menu girl, so I felt helpless the first time I dined at Elias Corner. There's no menu, but the glass case at the entrance is a visual menu of sorts, where you can pick your main course and leave the rest to your server. Everything's excellent, especially the astoundingly tender grilled octopus, fried calamari, and salty fried bits of whitebait. Their char-grilled whole fish is almost as good as the fish at Milos at a quarter of the price. Elias Corner doesn't do dessert. They want your table back, so wander down the street to a local bakery for baklava and another glass of ouzo.

• • •

I know it was close-minded of me, but I never considered the possibility of Greek desserts beyond baklava. Most of the restaurants I'd visited had the requisite sticky-sweet baklava and a few unidentifiable slices of cake that they toted over to the table on a tray. I always chose the path of least resistance and ordered the baklava. There's a fine line between good and bad Greek baklava, and you never can tell which one is sitting in front of you. It's hard to find the right ratio of chopped nuts to honey to phyllo, and some chefs overdo the honey, and you end up with a gloppy, wet mess. Stale baklava is the worst because it loses its flakiness and collapses onto the layers below.

It wasn't until an afternoon in Astoria, Queens, that I found life beyond baklava. On the way back to the train that takes you from Astoria to Manhattan, I strolled by a Greek bakery where the hypnotic aroma of nuts and honey wafted from the entrance. Inside there was a glass counter piled with an assortment of almond, cinnamon, and olive oil cookies. Right next to it was a fogged-up case with honey-drenched walnut cake, slightly sour yogurt cheesecake, and a semolina cake, soaked in olive oil and syrup, which the woman behind the counter described as halva. (I had a bite of all of the above.) The halva I was familiar with was a nutty sesame halva, molded from crushed sesame butter and syrup, but Greek halva refers to any dense confection sweetened with simple syrup. After regular visits to Elias Corner, I'd stop in for coffee and kataifi, a close cousin of baklava that reminds me of a square of extra-large shredded wheat. Instead of layered phyllo pastry, the nuts, honey, and spices are wrapped in a crunchy tangle of kataifi dough. Sometimes a simple bowl of Greek yogurt with thyme-infused honey or fresh fruit is the most satisfying end to a Greek meal—unless there are loukoumades on the menu. Then all bets are off. Loukoumades look like Dunkin' Donuts munchkins, but these fried puffs of dough are crispy and warm, drizzled with honey and cinnamon. There

are plenty of good Greek bakeries in Astoria, Southern California, Atlanta, and Greektown, Chicago, where you can sample
the scope of traditional desserts with a foamy cold frappe (foam-
covered iced coffee drink) or a strong, unfiltered cup of Greek
coffee to dip them in.

The first time I had a cup of Greek coffee was in college, and
I spent the night jittery and wide awake in my freshman dorm
room. Like most college kids, I dabbled in men and marijuana . . .
and meze. I spent my first two years of college at Duke and ate at
least two meals a week at Nikos Taverna, a Greek restaurant in
Durham. The chef, George Kastanias, got me through my freshman year. I lived in a jail-cell-size dorm room stacked with plastic
crates and snacked on Cap'n Crunch. Dinner at Niko's soothed me.
The dining room was warm, and George's food was the closest
thing I had to home cooking. When I studied, I got stressed, and
when I get stressed, I eat. I spent most of midterms eating my
weight in meze. In fact it was at Nikos that I first got attached to
Greek salad. Many years after my trip to Greece, and after I had
eaten my way through Greek in New York, I went to back to Durham and revisited Nikos. I ordered everything I had overlooked in
college: I had the chicken stifado, pastitsio, spiced sausages, and, of
course, a Greek salad. (I couldn't resist.)

## Table Settings and Modern Manners

If you want to eat like you're Greek, then the first cardinal rule
is to share. The biggest crime you can commit in a Greek restaurant is not sharing, because Greek food is inherently social. Meze
are the Greek excuse to socialize and drink ouzo. It doesn't matter
who ordered the taramosalata and who got the Greek salad. Once
they're on the table, they're communal property. The only crime

you can commit with meze is to hover over one or keep it right in front of you. The right place for meze is the middle of the table, so everyone can swipe a grilled pita triangle through the spreads. Salads, sides, and fried cheese are for sharing, too. As they say in Greece, "Kali orexi!"

· 6 ·

# Indian Cuisine

I feared Indian cooking for years. I mistakenly thought of the entire cuisine as fire-breathing, artery-clogging food that made your clothes smell. My family never ate it growing up, so I assumed there must be something wrong with it. We loved to eat, but not once did we go out for Indian or bring home takeout. I'm not sure what my parents were thinking. Everyone's parents make mistakes, but this was a big one. Huge. I had no idea how much I'd adore Indian food. I liked it even before I knew I did. All the signs were there: I delighted in freshly baked flatbreads, especially the kind with doughy bubbles. And I wasn't one of those kids who hated vegetables, either. I loved okra, eggplant, cauliflower, spinach, and peas—staple ingredients in the repertoire of Indian dishes. Parents of vegetable-loathing children might want to take their kids for Indian. I've seen packs of carnivores voluntarily order spinach dumplings in yogurt, okra with dried mango, coconut-dusted green beans, and a hundred other tasty unions of various vegetables. They make such smooth, smoky baingan bharta (mashed, spiced eggplant) and a many-flavored—sweet, spicy, and sour—chana masala (spiced chickpeas). And I *wish* my mom had made me eat cauliflower and peas simmered in coconut milk. I can't get enough of this traditional dish!

And Indian rice is a lot more exciting than the plain white rice my mom used as a plate filler. I wish she would have added nuts and raisins to it, or, better yet, switched it out for the aromatic basmati rice that makes biryanis (rice casseroles) and pilaus (rice pilafs) so distinctive. For the longest time, I couldn't understand the difference between a biryani and a pilau. The answer, I discovered, is not very much: they're both highly seasoned rice dishes made with lots of spices and flavorful broth. Biryanis, which are eaten as a main dish, are oven baked and always made with fragrant basmati rice layered with meat; while pilaus are stir-fried, moister, and are served as a side dish. I never knew how fragrant and flavorful baked rice could be until I tried a chicken biryani, moistened with savory chicken broth, redolent with saffron and cinnamon, and studded with raisins, almonds, and translucent bits of onion. Because biryani is not stirred, you often stumble upon a fantastically crusty nibble of basmati rice here and there, a lot like the toasty socarrat in Spanish paella. Pilau, on the other hand, is moist throughout because it's constantly stirred. Vegetable pilau (or any pilau really) is the Indian version of fried rice, spiced with cumin, cardamom, and black pepper, laced with carrots, peas, raisins, and walnuts. (Some can be downright spicy, so ask your server just how spicy it is.) Almost no Indian meal is complete without homey dal, the traditional Indian dish of dried lentils, peas, or other split legumes, usually served as a soup, gently spiced and eaten with flatbread. We ate plenty of beans and lentils growing up, too; I loved lentil soup on snow days! What was the issue? Did my parents have a bad experience with Indian food, or were there just no Indian restaurants in New Jersey? (There were.)

My mom would've been crazy for paneer. The woman was

addicted to farmer cheese, a white, unaged cheese stuffed inside blintzes or pierogi. Paneer is also a fresh, unaged cheese, but it's been curdled in lemon or vinegar, which makes it even softer and fresher-tasting than the store-bought farmer cheese I grew up eating. The first paneer I tasted was in mattar paneer, a rich curry dish tangy with paneer and peas. I'd also been missing out on saag paneer, pillows of paneer combined with delicately spiced spinach; and paneer makhani, paneer in a creamy tomato sauce. Just the other day, I had the most amazing paneer lababdar, paneer in a fenugreek, tomato, and onion sauce, at Tamarind, a popular Indian restaurant in Manhattan's Flatiron District. I mopped up all the sauce or, as the Indians call it, gravy, with warm, garlicky naan (pitalike flatbread). It wasn't the best thing I ate that night, but that's only because my meal featured such a standout lineup of dishes.

I probably ate enough for two in one sitting at Tamarind, but how could I resist? There were grilled scallops dabbed with coconut mint sauce, and tantalizing grilled lamb patties (shami kabab) garnished with a sneaky coriander–green chile chutney that by all rights should have been too spicy for me, but I couldn't stop eating. I subdued every feisty bite with naan dipped in cooling cucumber-yogurt sauce (kheera raita), then got right back in the game. There was also okra simmered in a dried mango and browned onion sauce, along with murg lajawab, chicken in a fragrant tomato onion sauce, heavy on the coriander. That too was excellent, but even that wasn't the best part of the meal. The highlight was a sea bass special, marinated in yogurt and cooked in the tandoor oven. It was miraculously moist, served in fenugreek-laden tomato gravy—the kind of dish that brands itself in your memory and you never see sea bass the same again. (Sigh.)

Magical things happen in the tandoor clay oven. There's no other way to explain such achingly tender and succulent chicken or such delicate fish with crispy skin. I want to get a tandoor for my apartment, but it would take up too much space. I'm not sure what happens inside the tandoor, but what emerges is thrilling, like fat shrimp tenderized by a yogurt, garlic, ginger, and lemon marinade. Unlike thick Greek yogurt, Indian yogurt is thin, so it's easily soaked up by anything marinating in it. Tandoori chicken is a terrific example. It's a team effort: the yogurt moistens the meat and the tandoor seals in the flavors. Chefs take a lot of pride in their tandoor offerings, so it's a good bet that those are some of the kitchen's finest moments.

One of the most beloved Indian dishes, chicken tikka, is kissed by the tandoor. I don't speak Hindi, so the only word I understand is chicken. That's another reason I avoided Indian food for so long. How could I order if I didn't understand what my choices were? But after eating Indian a few times, I started paying attention to repetition on Indian menus (the first step in learning any "restaurant's language"). Anything "tikka" is cooked in the tandoor and then cut into bite-size pieces or chunks. Interestingly, chicken tikka masala, one of the most popular dishes at Indian restaurants in America, isn't truly Indian. Tikka *is* an Indian preparation, and so is masala—which means "mixture," typically a spice mixture used in curry. But combining them in one dish isn't a traditional Indian foodway. Chicken tikka masala is Indian by way of Britain. Because of Great Britain's historical colonial relationship to India, the two cultures have experienced a lot of cross-pollination. When chicken tikka made its way to the Britain, English diners—accustomed to heavily sauced foods—added curry sauce to it, and chicken tikka masala was born. (*Masala* also means "gravy.") Chicken tikka masala is made with garam masala, a hot, but not at all scorching, spice blend. The heat in garam masala often comes from cinnamon, cloves, cardamom, ginger, mace, and nutmeg. What pulls the dish together is a creamy tomato gravy. "I thought you didn't like curry?" my friend said after I added it to our order one night several years ago. "I don't," I responded, then asked, "It's curry?" "Uh-huh," she said. She had every right to smirk. This was early in my journey into Indian cuisine. Maybe I didn't know what curry really was, or I hadn't been paying attention to what I was eating. Or maybe I liked Indian food. I thought that curry was a type of spice—one that was fiery—but I was so wrong.

*Curry* actually means nothing more than "cooked in liquid"—any liquid—typically coconut milk, tomatoes, or yogurt. That blew my mind. By that definition, tomato sauce, garlic sauce, salsa verde, and mole are all types of curries. I'd been eating curries my whole life and I didn't even realize it. That night at Tamarind I studied my chicken tikka masala carefully, inhaling all the potent aromas wafting up from the plate. Then I took a bite: every spice was intense but carefully in balance with the others. Spice is the heart and soul of Indian food. And they're not all fiery, far from it. Some spices are actually sweet, like cinnamon and cloves. The level of heat in a curry all depends on what you order. Some of the milder curries, like korma, are yogurt based. The richness of butter and cream in aptly named silky "butter curries"—also called makhani curry—offsets the bulk of the heat. Goan curry will be somewhat spicy and sweet, because it's made with tamarind and red chiles (as well as ginger, garlic, and coconut milk). Anything vindaloo—a sour, vinegar-based curry—is going

> • TASTY MORSEL •
>
> *The oldest continuously operating Indian restaurant in the United Kingdom is Veeraswamy, on Regent Street in London's West End. Opened in 1926 by Edward Palmer, the great-grandson of an English soldier and an Indian princess, it has hosted luminaries from Winston Churchill to Charlie Chaplin.*

to rank high on the spicy scale because it's spiked with fresh chiles.

Interestingly most of the Indian food we eat in the United States is North Indian. India is an enormous country with an incredibly culturally diverse population and equally diverse food traditions. But because many of the earliest Indian immigrants to the United Kingdom were from the Punjab region, in India's northwest corner, much of the food we think of as "Indian" represents North Indian traditions. Tandoori chicken, biryanis, and makhani curry are all Punjabi dishes. And much of Punjabi cuisine reflects the influence of the Muslim Mughals, who ruled a huge swath of India from the sixteenth century through the mid-nineteenth century. The Mughals introduced many Middle Eastern and Persian elements into Indian culture, which is why dishes like rice pilaf, koftas—the same spiced ground meatballs the Lebanese, Turks, and Israelis eat—and kababs are common features on Indian menus. (Though Indians typically de-skewer before serving, unless you order "seekh kabab"—*seekh* means "stick," indicating the kabab will be served on its skewer.) The Mughals also introduced Punjabis to lamb rogan josh, a rich, brick-red curry with red chiles and braised lamb. The aroma of lamb rogan josh is seductive enough to lure anyone to the table, fragrant with garlic, ginger, cloves, cinnamon, black cardamom, paprika, and of course, chile pepper.

One of the reasons for North Indian cuisine's popularity outside of South Asia might just be its array of delicious flatbreads. I have a serious weakness for freshly baked bread, second only to my peanut butter problem, so Indian cuisine is dangerous territory. Fortunately for me (though unfortunately for my waistline), there are tons of great Indian restaurants in New York where I can deliberate over my favorite flatbreads. Popular naan (you can even buy it prepackaged at Trader Joe's now) is just one kind of Indian flatbread. This leavened, white flour bread is cooked in the tandoor—thrown against the hot oven's wall, where it sticks and then bakes. Naan is surprisingly similar to pizza dough in appearance, texture, and flavor. I know Indian and Italian cooking seem drastically different from each other, but they share similarities. Naan and pizza dough are both leavened breads—kneaded until they're smooth and elastic—riddled with bubbles of trapped air and pocked with golden scorch marks from the oven. Sprinkle naan with olive oil and rosemary, and you have rosemary naan. Sprinkle pizza with rosemary and olive oil and you have salsa bianca. And kulcha—stuffed naan—filled with ground lamb, or with garlic and cheese, bears a striking resemblance to a calzone.

Many Indian flatbreads aren't made in the tandoor—some of them are cooked on a griddle or even deep-fried. (Deep. Fried. Bread. Need I say more?) Bhatura, made with extra-fine flour, yogurt, and ghee (clarified butter), is a fluffy deep-fried flatbread traditionally served with spiced chickpeas (chole). Simple, straightforward roti, on the other hand, is the pure, unleavened Indian flatbread (and rotis are also eaten everywhere from Thailand to the West Indies), cooked on a griddle and delicious slathered in curry, topped with vegetables, or eaten plain. Earthy chapatis are rotis made with whole wheat flour, and parathas are layered rotis, cooked with ghee (clarified butter). I'm crazy about parathas stuffed with paneer. (I once watched someone make a one-hundred-layer paratha on YouTube. That's a one-hundred-layer edible plate you can smear with chutney or fold around whatever's sitting on the table.) We have South Indian cuisine to thank for dosas. Made from rice and lentil flour (two common staples in South Indian cooking), dosas look like crepes and taste like heaven—and for a texture addict, they're fantastic: one side is fried until crispy golden brown, while the flip side remains pliant and tender. In India, a meal without naan, dosas, or roti is like eating without a plate. It doesn't happen.

The dearly departed Tabla was one of my favorite places to sample the spectrum of Indian flatbreads. The moment you entered this sleek two-story restaurant along Manhattan's Madison Square Park, you felt like you'd stepped into a Salvador Dalí painting. Colorful mosaics adorned the walls, and a winding redwood staircase lead to a lofted dining room with a viewing balcony of the bread bar below. The best seats in the house were all bar stools overlooking the tandoors, griddles, and roti chefs at the bread bar. (Can you tell how much I miss Tabla?)

It was the perfect setting for chef Floyd Cardoz's modern, and often whimsical, interpretation of his native cuisine. For Cardoz, India arrives by way of the Greenmarket with bacon or ramp-stuffed naan, peanut-chipotle raita, and Meyer lemon chutney. But he didn't ignore tradition entirely: I was surprised to learn crab cakes are popular on the coast of India and was blown away by Cardoz's mash-up of this American *and* Goan classic. Spiced cakes of sweet crab nestled on a crispy lentil wafer (papadum) alongside a sweet and sour tamarind chutney. But the Goan guacamole, dusted with cumin seeds and served with lotus root chips, is his fabulous invention. His chicken pakoras were accompanied by a zesty cashew and mint chutney. These deep-fried battered fritters remind me of Japanese tempura—it's the batter (in this case, made from seasoned chickpea flour), not the filling, that makes a fritter a pakora. Pakoras belong to a much larger community of Indian fried snacks, of which samosas enjoy the most renown in America.

I'd heard fanatics praise these fried triangular turnovers, but I never quite got the allure until I tried the down-and-dirty version available at inexpensive cab stands, no-frills eateries, and take-away spots (which makes sense—samosas are a simple, hearty street food meant to fill you up and get you through the day). My favorite kind of samosa is the super-straightforward potato and pea version, sprinkled with yogurt, onions, and hot sauce. (I'm a bit of a wimp with the hot sauce, though.) If an Indian restaurant makes good potato and pea samosas—crispy and golden without being too greasy, the potato filling moist, not crumbly and dry, and the peas tender but not mushy, it's a good bet the rest of the food will be great, too. Potatoes turn up in all sorts of snacks, including aloo tikki, a fried potato cake reminiscent of a chubby latke, and as fillings in savory crepe-style dosas, which are often eaten as snacks. At N.Y. Dosas, a food cart that parks on the border of Washington Square Park, South Indian expats and hungry NYU students alike line up for chef/owner Thiru Kumar's dosas filled with curried potatoes and served with coconut chutney. (He also makes a mean samosa.) I think Indian snacks—called chaat—are best eaten at bare-bones joints and carts just like this one, where the focus isn't on complex curries or other labor-intensive dishes, but on simple and tasty finger foods.

*Chaat,* which in Hindi means "to taste," is a little like Indian fast food—small dishes of finger food that Indians traditionally eat between meals. Most chaat begins with some form of fried dough, which is then mixed with other ingredients—the key to good chaat is a mix of flavors and texture: crunchy, crispy, flaky, and soft, salty, sour, and sweet. The most popular chaat in India is probably pani puri, small, hollow rounds of fried dough filled with water, potatoes, chickpeas, and spices. You're supposed to eat an entire pani puri in one swift bite—it releases an unforgettable gush of flavor (kind of like Chinese soup dumplings). And forget salt and pepper—a respectable chaat spot will offer chaat masala for sprinkling—a traditional spice mix made from red chile powder, black salt, dried mango, coriander, cumin, and black peppercorns. Chaat is almost always served with the same trio of condiments— sweet-sour tamarind sauce, cool yogurt, and fresh cilantro—as well as a variety of chutneys, which range from sweet to savory.

• • •

Indian desserts are simple and sweet. That's a good thing, considering how rich and full-bodied the savory dishes are. They're worth trying, unless you can't have milk. In that case, you're out of luck, though most menus feature a conciliatory fruit sorbet or fruit salad. Indian desserts tend to be refreshingly cool complements to all of the spiced curries and gravies. Kulfi is India's answer to ice cream. To me kulfi tastes more like an exotic frozen custard, perfumed with cardamom and studded with raw pistachios. That's the most traditional version of kulfi, but others are flavored with mango, almonds, or saffron instead. In most cultures, saffron appears in the savory section of the menu, but saffron can go sweet or savory in Indian cooking. Saffron turns up on many sweet occasions, including in a classic dessert called rasmalai. Rasmalai are paneer dumplings, soaked in sweet cream that's scented with saffron or cardamom. There's saffron-spiced shrikhand, strained yogurt, and even saffron-spiced cheesecake. They also eat a sweet rice pudding, called kheer, which is flavored with cardamom. One of the only desserts that doesn't have cardamom or saffron in it is halwa (not to be confused with halva), composed of grated carrots stewing in condensed milk, and scattered with nuts and raisins. Sometimes I finish a meal with a tall glass of lassi, a drinkable yogurt. Fruit lassis are both tart and sweet, a great introduction to this traditional drink. But I encourage you to try a salty lassi at least once; its unusual flavor comes from toasted cumin and lemon juice. Chai—milky black tea, sweetened with sugar and spiced with cardamom, cloves, cinnamon, and ginger—is practically mandatory.

## Table Setting and Modern Manners

No need for a plate when you can place everything on top of your flatbread. I realized early on that this maxim really only applies to chutneys and gravies, not salads or lamb chops. Anything you'd eat with a fork or a spoon in another culture is appropriate here. Since naan is integral to every meal, washing your hands is very important. Upscale establishments offer guests a wet towel or a finger bowl with lemon to clean hands at the start and finish of a meal. You don't really want to rip off a piece of paratha with dirty hands. *Ripping* is the operative word here. Roti is one those "rip as you go" foods. It's tradition to eat only with your right hand. The left is for holding your glass and transferring food from shared plates to your own. I'm a lefty, so this doesn't really work for me. Thankfully, it's not a hard-and-fast rule in America, so I can go left if I like. Like most other cultures, chewing with your mouth open or stuffing too much into your mouth at once is poor form. Also you don't need to sample everything at the table or finish everything on your plate, for that matter. Leaving a little food on your plate is a sign that you're full and is not insulting in the slightest.

# Dinner Table Crimes and Misdemeanors

## CELL PHONES AND BLACKBERRIES

**W**hat if instead of a coat check, there was a mandatory BlackBerry and cell phone check at the entrance of every restaurant? Ahhh, the collective dining room would be such a peaceful place. People would get anxious and angry at first, but they'd quickly adapt. (We humans always do.) Now, that's a touch drastic, though it does sound paradisiacal to me. Instead I think we should all enforce a rule: no cell phones or BlackBerrys on the table. Either electronic device on the table signals to your dinner companion that you're not fully present. And kindly turn your ringer off; everyone in the restaurant doesn't need to hear the latest ring tone you downloaded. It's jarring and disruptive—half the reason we eat out is to enjoy a particular atmosphere or ambience we can't get at home. If you're expecting an important phone call or need to be reachable, set your phone to vibrate and keep it on yourself somewhere discreet. If you really need to take a call, please step away from your table—go outside, really—to have the conversation, especially in a restaurant of tightly packed tables. We all lose awareness of how loudly we're speaking when we're on our phones, especially in settings with a lot of ambient noise. It's inconsiderate not only to the people you're with, but also to the other diners, who didn't choose to go out with you. I once endured listening to a woman at a table next to me describe her recent gynecological exam over her cell phone. (Who knows who she was talking to!) And there's nothing sadder than seeing a couple out to dinner who are both texting other people throughout the meal.

## DRESSING UP OR DOWN

Up until the end of the twentieth century, going out to eat at a restaurant was a formal affair, and people dressed for the occasion. Women bought new dresses and wore hats. Men wore suits, ties, even tuxedos. The wealthiest dined at places like Le Cirque. Institutions like the 21 Club continue to embrace old-school traditions. When I order steak tartare at the 21 Club, a tuxedoed server still rolls out the steak tartare cart, asks me how I like it, and prepares it in the dining room. When I eat with a regular, I get a tour of the illustrious wine cellar. When I eat with other everybodies like myself, I eat in the nosebleed section of the dining room. But these days the dining room looks dramatically different, and so do the diners. There's a new generation of notably laid-back eaters and chefs, who prefer dressed down to dressed up. For the most part, suits and skirts are a thing of the past. Even great warhorses like the 21 Club have had to alter their dress codes to stay alive. The 21 Club has loosened its tie policy, though jackets are apparently still required. (My friend took his jacket off, and a few minutes later, the maître d' picked it up and helped him put it back on.)

But you should still try your best to dress the part, both for your comfort and in order to maximize the full experience. There's a good reason most people don't show up to church in a bikini or do housework in a suit and tie. Likewise, you don't want to go to an In-N-Out Burger in a ball gown (unless you're Hilary Swank and just won an Oscar) or to Le Cirque in sweatpants. When in doubt, call ahead and ask the hostess. The Web is very helpful in this department. Look online at the menu, the prices, and any photos of the interior.

And unless you're going to a hamburger joint, please leave your baseball cap at home. My thirty-year-old brother still wears a baseball hat when he dines out at night. Some hosts will ask him to take it off, others don't bother. But I swear he's lost a girl-friend or two because he dressed like a boy, instead of a grown man.

## PUNCTUALITY

This is a huge peeve of mine. Be on time. Showing up late shows disrespect for your companion's time, not to mention you're disrupting the flow of the reservation schedule for the night. For instance, if I'm late for my 7:00 P.M. reservation and you have a 9:00 P.M. reservation at the same table, you're going to end up waiting for me to get up. I can't imagine you'll be pleased, and I don't blame you. I'm not perfect. I've run late for reservations. (I'm not trying to point fingers, but traffic in New York is awful!) The best thing to do is call your dinner date as well as the restaurant to let them know. Besides, you might just end up losing your table. Some restaurants only hold reservations for fifteen minutes. If you show up late and they seat you, or you order thirty minutes after you sit down, you'll get stuck in "gridlock." Your server isn't trying to rush you when he asks for the third time if you're ready to order. He knows when the kitchen's going to get backed up, and he doesn't want you to be a victim of the crunch.

## SILVERWARE

**T**his is where it gets a little complicated, but there's no need to panic. It's only dinner, after all, not nuclear physics. Whether it's a formal restaurant or a casual one, every restaurant has their own style of table setting. Some restaurants keep it simple, and some give you five forks. There's no clear-cut rules, so my philosophy is simple: work from the outside in. In this rule, the fork farthest to your left always pairs with the appetizer. If it's an itty-bitty baby fork, it either pairs with your amuse-bouche or seafood. The itty-bitty knife on the bread plate is the butter knife. The knife farthest out is meant for the appetizer. If there's no butter knife in sight, it can be used for both. The big spoon is the soup spoon. Often restaurants don't put a soup spoon on the table unless you order soup. (Less silverware to clean in the kitchen.) Steak knives aren't usually put on the table setting unless you order steak or you're at a steakhouse. If you order a steak and your server forgets to bring you a steak knife, just ask for one. Otherwise you'll have a hell of a time cutting your meat.

And about those knives: don't lick your knife, no matter how tempting. This isn't the Big Apple circus, and you could get hurt. Also, please don't use a knife as a mirror. A knife is for cutting food, not applying lip gloss. If you need to freshen your lipstick or check your teeth for wayward greens, excuse yourself and do it in the restroom. When you've finished your entrée, lay your fork and knife across the plate (this is a good signal to the server to remove your plate), not on the table.

## SHARING

I strongly encourage passing. If you weren't supposed to share, every table would be a table for one. The general rule is to pass everything to the right. When in doubt, go right—bread, butter, steak, you name it. In passing meat, always pass the knife or serving fork with its dish. (The critic Gael Greene taught me that one night at dinner, and I've never made that mistake again.) The steak knife stays with the steak. Any knife you use has the flavor of the meat or fish on it and should accompany its original dish around the table.

## NAPKINS

Did you know that, up through the 1950s, napkins had buttonholes in them, so men could attach them to their dress shirts? Let's hope that trend doesn't come back in style. Restaurants wanted guests to enjoy their food and not worry about soiling their clothes. Unless you want to look like Fred Flintstone or Archie Bunker, don't tuck your napkin into your collar. It looks ridiculous.

Put your napkin on your lap as soon as you sit. This misdemeanor is becoming an epidemic, and here's what happens: if you leave your napkin on the table you make it difficult for the server to place your appetizer down because your napkin is in the way. Put your napkin on your lap and stay a while.

If you visit the restroom during dinner, place your napkin on your chair, not the table. This borders on a felony, as it's impolite to toss a soiled napkin on the table while others are still eating or even between courses. At the end of the meal when the check's paid and you're ready to leave, then you can put your napkin on the table, right in front of your place setting. Please don't place your used napkin on the plate itself.

And never blow your nose in your napkin. Ever. Doing so is

rude to your table companions, as well as to the people sitting near you, not to mention unsanitary. If it requires more than a subtle dab, politely excuse yourself to the restroom and use a tissue.

## EATING WITH YOUR HANDS

**E**ating with your hands, when appropriate, is one of the many joys of eating. Some things are meant to be eaten with your hands—French fries, pizza, tacos. If you're unsure, look for utensils and at fellow diners. It varies significantly from one dish and culture to another. The Japanese traditionally eat sushi with their hands. So can you. In Indian cuisine, flatbread often functions as a plate. So pile all of your food on your bread, pick up your plate, and eat it. For simplicity's sake, European cultures generally favor utensils. Southeast Asian cultures favor hands. East Asian cultures generally use chopsticks, but it depends on the food and the meal.

# · 7 ·

# Italian Cuisine

*Everything you see I owe to pasta.*

SOPHIA LOREN

H ere in Manhattan, there are almost as many pizza joints as there are ATMs. And there are over two thousand Italian restaurants in the city at large. I know because I'm trying to eat my way through the list of 'em. If you travel almost anywhere in the world, you're bound to find an Italian restaurant—from Israel to Japan, Alaska to India. It's an extremely lovable cuisine. As my sister says, "What's not to love about tomato sauce, cheese, and dough?" Pizza and pasta alone are pretty compelling reasons for the worldwide popularity of Italian food, but those two barely scratch the surface of all this cuisine has to offer an eater.

And yet when it comes to Italian, we tend to think we're experts on the subject. How many meals have you eaten in an Italian restaurant in your lifetime? Probably tons. But how many times have you looked at the pasta selection and stuck with the spaghetti pomodoro or Bolognese, instead of choosing something unfamiliar like puttanesca—even though you've likely seen it on the menu a thousand times? (Puttanesca is worth trying! It's a highly aromatic and robust tomato-based sauce, flavored with capers, olives, anchovies, red pepper flakes, and plenty of garlic.) Well, guilty as charged. Until the age of ten, I only ordered spaghetti and meatballs. My sister refused to eat anything but pasta with butter, even in Italy.

Then there's the guy who always orders pasta carbonara. Now ask him, what's in carbonara sauce? There's a good chance he hasn't got a clue. (Carbonara is a blend of eggs, guanciale—unsmoked Italian bacon—Parmesan and pepper.) We all do it. Most people wouldn't admit it, but half the time we don't know what we're eating, what we ordered, or what we might be missing out on, just because we're too embarrassed to ask our server or too lazy to look it up. I used to think all Italian restaurants were red-sauce joints with checkered tablecloths, cheap red wine, and softball-size meatballs. Until the night my parents took me to a restaurant that—gasp!—didn't serve spaghetti and meatballs. I was nine years old and I wanted my usual spaghetti and meatballs. When I opened the menu, they were nowhere to be found. What kind of Italian restaurant doesn't have spaghetti and meatballs? How could my parents make us eat dinner at this place? "It must be a mistake. They just forgot to write it on the menu," I thought. Of course, it wasn't a mistake—and I was not a happy camper. I made my dad promise he'd take us for pizza after we left.

Then our food arrived. That night I discovered northern Italian cooking: risotto with wild mushrooms, polenta, fonduta, and osso bucco. I was reluctant at first. What was Italian food without pasta underneath a blanket of tomato sauce? But my mom swore I'd like polenta (boiled ground cornmeal). "It's sort of a cross between Cream of Wheat and Cream of Rice," she said. That just made it sound boring, like something I'd eat for breakfast topped with brown sugar and cinnamon. Let me tell you, polenta is no morning gruel. It has a texture similar to grits, only much nuttier, with a lot more give. I loved it. Of course, the intoxicating Parmesan sauce it was bathing in didn't hurt either. It was soothing yet refined—the kind of dish you want to eat in the privacy of your own kitchen in your pajamas—and so was the fonduta. I'd tasted fondue, but never Italian fonduta—a warm, luscious combination of fontina, milk, egg yolks, and, if you're lucky, white truffles. My mother likened risotto to "soupy rice," which in my opinion is a gross injustice. The only rice I was familiar with at the time was the bland, boiled Minute rice my mom used to shovel onto our plates at dinner. Risotto requires an Italian short-grained rice—Arborio, Carnaroli, or Vialone Nano—that, as it's slow cooked, releases much more starch than long-grained rice, with luscious results. Making great risotto is an art. First, Italian chefs toast the riso (rice) itself in butter, then slowly cook it in a broth of their choosing, and finally add seasonings and other ingredients. The wild mushroom risotto was crazy creamy, spiked with sharp Gorgonzola (blue cheese), and studded with wild mushrooms.

My father ordered chicken marsala (sautéed in a fortified red wine sauce) for himself and an osso buco (braised veal shank) "for the table," which, of course, meant he couldn't decide between the two entrées, so he ordered both. When the osso buco arrived, he forgot all about his chicken marsala. It was a beautifully braised veal shank, served on the bone, simmered in white wine, tomatoes, carrots, and herbs. Osso buco brings new meaning to the phrase "fall off the bone." One poke with your fork and the meat slips right off the bone and into the sumptuous sauce pooling beneath it. In Italian, osso buco loosely translates as "bone with a hole"—the veal cut is a cross section of the shank bone, which means you can literally suck out its marrow. And you should! It's to die for slathered on the nearest piece of bread. I imagined a king and queen might take comfort in a meal like this. (I would if I were in their shoes.)

There are so many great Italian dishes, why order your "usual" all the time? There are over 350 varieties of pasta alone. How could you possibly know every one? Though no one can say for sure who first invented the noodle, Marco Polo definitely did not introduce it to Europe—despite the popular myth that he returned to Italy from his journey to China noodles in tow. Marco Polo traveled to China in 1295, and Italians were eating noodles long before that. And the Chinese weren't even the only non-Europeans who ate noodles regularly—so did Egyptians, Greeks, and Arabs. Most food historians believe that the Arabs brought pasta to Italy during the Arab invasion of Sicily in the eighth century. If you look at Sicilian pasta dishes, you'll notice Arab influences and ingredients, such as cinnamon, eggplant, and raisins.

Why were noodles so popular, particularly in Italy? Four reasons. First, dried pasta was really, really cheap. After all, it was just flour and water. Second, it could be stored for two years at a time without degrading in quality. Third, it was very filling. Four, it was nutritious. But it wasn't always so easy to make pasta. In Italian, *maccheroni* (from which the general term for pasta, macaroni, comes) means "to knead forcefully," and it lived up to its name. Up through the eighteenth century, it was so difficult to knead pasta dough that men would sit on benches and mix the dough with their feet. (And eat it with their hands.) Once the dough was kneaded, it had to be extruded by pushing it through a die, a task so physically demanding it required the strength of two men or one horse. That's what you call a labor of love.

When Ferdinand II, the king of Naples, fell in love with pasta in the early 1700s, everything changed. He demanded that an inventor named Cesare Spadaccini find an easier and more civilized method for producing pasta. It took Spadaccini a year, but he came up with a mechanical man complete with bronze feet—the first pasta-making machine. Since kings didn't eat with their hands, Spadaccini also invented a fork with four short prongs. In 1740,

Paolo Adami opened the first pasta factory in Venice, and by 1785, there were 280 pasta shops in Naples.

Italians *love* pasta. They eat sixty-two pounds of it per person a year—Americans eat twenty by comparison. There's even a patron saint of pasta makers, Saint Stephen, who was found dead in a kneading trough. That love of pasta has led to such a proliferation of varieties that no one could be expected to know them all. (What would be the fun of that anyway? This way, there's always something new to discover.) I mean, do you know your tagliolini from your tagliatelle, your gnocchi from your gnudi? Can you tell the difference between agnolotti and tortellini? Believe me, you're not alone. So let's start with the basics. In Italian, *pasta* means "dough." There are two fundamental types of pasta, fresh and dried. Dry pasta is always made with durum semolina flour and water. In Italy, it's actually a law: if it's not 100 percent semolina flour and water, it's not dried pasta. Dried pasta is molded into a shape, then boiled and dried for storing, while fresh pasta is molded into a shape, then boiled and served while it's still soft. On the other hand, fresh pasta can be made with semolina flour or several other types of flour mixed with water, and sometimes eggs, oil, or salt as well.

> • TASTY MORSEL •
>
> *Gnocchi aren't technically pasta. They're dumplings, made of potato and flour, semolina, or ricotta. They can be baked or boiled and served, like pasta, with sauce. Gnudi are kissing cousins of gnocchi— ricotta dumplings, which are Tuscan in origin and typically made with much less flour.*

Honestly, I always assumed fresh pasta was better than dried. I was the girl who never ate day-old bread or vegetables from the freezer, but those rules don't apply to pasta. Dried pasta is supposed to be firm, so it can stand up to the weight of chunky or meaty sauces. And semolina flour is coarse, which is ideal for grabbing onto sauce. Dried pasta is created with the sauce in mind, which is the reason it comes in so many splendid shapes, sizes, and textures. There is a method to pasta's numerous and often curious shapes and sizes. You can think of pasta as a canvas: different sauces need different canvases to shine. For instance, the traditional conchiglie or shell shape is a perfect example. Its bowl-like shape ingeniously traps sauce inside it. The exterior of the shell is often ridged to grab onto both light and heavy sauces. Unlike a shell, pasta tubes are hollow, cylindrical-shaped noodles. A tube can be short or long, fat or thin, with pointed or blunt ends, and a smooth or ridged exterior. Small tubes don't have enough width in the center to trap chunky sauces, but the big tubes do, and the smaller ones are great for catching cream or butter sauces. There are all sorts of shapes and sizes of dried pasta: long strands, hollow strands, ribbon or flat-cut noodles, tubes, stuffed shapes, tiny shapes, and odd shapes.

Fresh pastas tend to be softer and more delicate than dried pasta. They're better suited to stuffed pastas, like ravioli, and light sauces. The focus of fresh pasta is often the stuffing inside the ravioli or the freshly made pasta itself, not the sauce.

There are machine-made pastas and handmade pastas: some pasta is kneaded and rolled into sheets by machine, while some is kneaded by hand and rolled out with a rolling pin. If you see "hand-rolled" pasta on the menu, it means they made their pasta the old-fashioned way. Hand-rolled usually implies that the noodles have been cut by hand with a knife or another tool, but more complicated shapes are usually created with extrusion molds. (When a chef wants to make homemade rigatoni, there's no way he can create perfectly even ridges and equally sized tubes without a mold. So he pushes his dough through an extrusion mold, and out the other end come his perfectly ridged tubes. The Italians prefer copper extrusion molds to steel molds because steel produces smooth pasta, which doesn't grab onto sauce as well.)

A chef aspires to serve all of his pastas al dente—meaning "to the tooth"—because perfectly cooked pasta should offer a slight resistance when bitten. Al dente ain't negotiable by Italian standards. Tender but not chewy. Resistant but not chalky. You can still taste the texture of the pasta. Limp, overcooked pasta is a no-no in the Italian kitchen. It's the equivalent of boiling pasta to death: you kill the texture and the shape in the process. What makes a pasta like cavatelli so distinctive is its small, curled shape. Cavatelli bears a striking resemblance to a teeny hot dog bun. Its rolled-in edges are like the rim of a bowl, excellent for trapping sauce. When I was growing up, my mom used to make cavatelli with broccoli, olive oil, Parmesan, and garlic. I loved trying to curl back the rolled edges with my tongue, and in the process, discovering a toasted sliver of garlic or nibble of Parmesan trapped on the surface of the little "hot dog bun." My mother never made pasta by hand or by machine, for that matter, but she had a knack for pairing the right shape with just the right sauce. She also made orecchiette, but she served this little, ear-shaped pasta in a chunky tomato sauce fresh from a gourmet Italian grocery. (We're not Italian. What do you expect?) Orecchiette is an interesting pasta to nibble on because it's thinner and softer at its center, thicker and chewier at the edges. Bucatini, on the other hand, is nothing like orecchiette, cavatelli, or any other small pasta. Bucatini is a type of noodle, but it's unique because it literally looks like a thick straw. It's hollow in the center yet incredibly dense and chewy. Perhaps the most classic rendition of this hollowed-out spaghetti noodle is bucatini all'Amatriciana. I could eat these strong, bouncy noodles in any sauce (or even naked), but slathered in Amatriciana sauce—made with smoky bits of guanciale, tomatoes, garlic, onions, and Parmesan—is the way to go.

Whoever came up with all the eccentric pasta shapes and names had quite an imagination. One of my favorites is strozzapreti, which is Italian for "priest strangler." Someone took a look at this hand-rolled noodle—the long version of cavatelli—and thought it looked like something you might use to choke a priest. (Wishful thinking.) There's an adorable hat-shaped pasta called cappelletti; long strands as thin as an "angel's hair"; or a pennelike tube folded to form a triangle named trenne. Sometimes you can't appreciate a noodle or shape until it's paired with the perfect sauce. I used to think fusilli (which means twisted) was a silly pasta shape. In fact I ordered the fusilli at Marea—one of the best Italian restaurants in Manhattan—despite the fusilli. (I was in it for the accompanying bone marrow and red-wine-braised octopus.) I had always assumed the corkscrew shape was purely a device created to get children to eat their dinner. Boy, was I wrong. The corkscrew trapped all the heavenly bone marrow and red wine flavors along its ridges, which run the length of the fusilli. A shape can make a world of difference. Case in point: tagliolini, tagliatelle, and tagliarini. All three are egg noodles originally created in the Emilia-Romagna region of Italy and derived from the Italian word *tagliare*, meaning "to cut." Tagliatelle are long, flat noodles similar to fettuccine noodles, except tagliatelle are thicker and usually made with eggs. (Only fresh fettuccine is made with eggs.) Tagliatelle is often served in a Bolognese sauce (a hearty ragu made with beef, pancetta, chopped vegetables, and a touch of tomatoes). Tagliolini—long cylindrical noodles, thinner than flat tagliatelle noodles—work best in cream sauces, like vodka sauce (vodka-spiked cream sauce). Tagliarini—long, flat noodles that are thinner than tagliatelle—work best in a light vegetable sauce or pesto, a sauce that's very dear to my heart. Pesto is a marvelously herbaceous sauce, made with basil, crushed garlic, parsley, pine nuts, Parmesan and olive oil. I think just about anything tastes better with vibrantly flavored pesto.

I haven't even mentioned the stuffed pastas, which are just as terrific. There are square, puffy pillows of ravioli made with two thin sheets of pasta, and often filled with soft, subtly sweet ricotta cheese (fresh whey cheese). There's delicate agnolotti, made with just one sheet of pasta that's folded over the stuffing and pinched shut, or small, ring-shaped tortellini. Tortelloni are simply larger rings, but I think both tortellini and tortelloni look more like belly buttons than rings. (I suppose pasta is in the eye of the beholder.) Any pasta that ends in *ini*, like tortellini, is a smaller or thinner version of a particular shape. Likewise, any pasta that ends in *oni*, like tortelloni, is a larger or thicker version of that same shape.

In a serious Italian restaurant, pasta is its own course, often listed as a primo—a midcourse served after the antipasti and the appetizers—not as a secondo, a main course. (My mom used to serve pasta as a side, which would be frowned upon by most Italians.) If you find yourself in a restaurant where you can mix-and-match a pasta shape and a sauce, head for the door. That's a very bad sign. An earnest chef serves the pasta exactly as he believes you should eat it. The chef picks the best canvas—with the ideal shape and texture—to complement his sauce. If the server offers pepper or cheese, the chef has given his blessing. If you are not offered cheese or pepper, then that's the way you ought to eat the pasta—or at least try to eat it. A really serious Italian restaurant won't even put salt or pepper on the table. And no substitutions. In a restaurant, trust the chef's instincts. We're not standing behind the stove, so leave the decision making to the kitchen. If the wild boar ragu (yummy!) comes with pappardelle (a wide ribbon-cut noodle), I beg you not to ask for angel hair instead. It's insulting and a bad idea. Angel hair won't survive the weight of wild boar, and it certainly won't service the sauce. If the ravioli comes "alla" vodka, don't ask for it "alla" puttanesca, unless you'd also like the chef to spit in your food. *Alla* is an Italian preposition that translates to "in the style of," and is traditionally used to describe any type of sauce or preparation. For example, ravioli alla vodka is menu-speak for "ravioli in the style of vodka sauce."

After all, the heart of all Italian cooking is sauce. It's the character of the sauce, not the pasta, that distinguishes one chef from another. As with pasta, there are countless variations on sauce. Tomato sauce is just the beginning. And tomatoes didn't even come into play in Italian sauces until the eighteenth century. The Spaniards brought tomatoes from the Americas back to Europe in the sixteenth century, but most Europeans thought tomatoes were poisonous and avoided them like the plague. Here's how the whole poison rumor got started: the tomato is a member of the nightshade family, some of which happen to be poisonous, so it was really guilt by association. And it didn't help matters that an Italian herbalist named Pietro Mattioli classified them as poisonous in 1544. (We all make mistakes, but that was a big one.) Instead the Italians ate pasta dressed in olive oil, cream, garlic, oregano, pine nuts, or nothing at all. The first recorded recipe with tomatoes was published in Naples in 1692, but it took a while for most Italians to get over the poison rumor and take the leap. When they finally did, in the mid-1700s, they never looked back.

When pairing pastas with sauces, trust your instincts. Pretend you're the chef: close your eyes and imagine the texture of the noodle on your tongue. Pasta is all about architecture. The bigger the canvas, the more it can hold. Meat sauces or chunky sauces need surface area, something for the sauce to cling to. Tubular and ridged pasta like rigatoni work best with chunky sauces, and so do ribbon-cut noodles. A lusty meat sauce like Bolognese needs pasta with surface area, like wide, flat ribbons of pappardelle. Serving Bolognese or any other type of ragu on vermicelli noodles would be like drawing a big painting on a tiny canvas. Not a good idea. Thin, delicate pasta goes best with thin, light sauces. Sauce shouldn't overwhelm the pasta. It should coat it, complement it, but not take over the dish. If your pasta arrives drowning in sauce, tell the server you ordered pasta, not soup.

Despite the wide variety of sauces, there are four basic ingredients that Italians use as the foundation for almost all of their sauces: olive oil, tomatoes, butter, and cream. In the north, where tomatoes are scarce, sauces are traditionally made with butter or cream. In the south, where olives and tomatoes are plentiful, butter- and cream-based sauces are rare. Both wine and ragu sauces vary from region to region. Sauce often takes its name from its town of origin, like Livornese, Sorrentino, and Siciliana sauces. Livornese sauce contains tomatoes, onions, garlic, capers, and black olives, so whenever you see Livornese on a menu, you know what you're getting. And if you spot any dish alla Siciliana, you're getting eggplant, tomatoes, basil, and either mozzarella or ricotta.

In Italy, sauce isn't just for pasta. Arrabiata sauce—a spicy marinara sauce laced with red pepper flakes—traditionally served with spaghetti, also graces seafood, as in shrimp and lobster alla arrabiata. (I like the best of both worlds—lobster in spaghetti alla arrabiata.) Arrabiata is great for eaters who like a little spice, but if you don't, you can always order marinara, which forms the base of arrabiata—minus the chile flakes. Marinara translates to "mariner's style sauce," and apparently the Italian sailors liked their tomato sauce with garlic, onions, and parsley. Not with seafood. My family was drawn to any sauce that involved tomatoes, especially dosed with garlic. Thankfully my insatiable curiosity trumped my tomato fetish, and I started experimenting with tomato-less sauce. If it hadn't, I never would've discovered agrodolce sauce. Like many Asian cultures, Italy has its own sweet ("dolce") and sour ("agro") sauce. Italy's version is traditionally made with vinegar and sugar, and thought to be another by-product of the Arab invasion of Sicily. I've had lamb in agrodolce,

• TASTY MORSEL •

*Puttanesca sauce has a rather racy history. Puttanesca is derived from the word puttana, which in Italian means "whore"—anything "alla puttanesca" translates to "in the style of a whore." (Yep.) Keep in mind, there are several different theories, but most food scholars believe puttanesca sauce got its name from Italian prostitutes, who grabbed whatever was in the pantry—anchovies, olives, capers, garlic, chile pepper flakes, and tomatoes—and whipped up this robust sauce as a quick meal that would see them through long hours of work.*

pork in agrodolce, but my favorite was actually a simple bowl of cauliflower agrodolce.

There's a universe of deeply flavored sauces far beyond tomato sauce, like vongole. Vongole is a classic Italian clam sauce that comes two very different ways: vongole bianco (white clam sauce) and vongole rosso (red clam sauce). Considering my affection for tomatoes, you might think I'd side with vongole rosso, but I'm surprisingly in the vongole bianco camp. Vongole bianco, made with olive oil, garlic, red pepper flakes, and parsley, highlights the clams and evokes the brininess of the sea. Vongole rosso, made with garlic, olive oil, parsley, red pepper flakes, and tomatoes, is tasty, too, but it's less about the vongole and more about the ensemble of flavors. Some chefs add white wine to vongole bianco and red wine to vongole rosso to give it more body, but it's not the old-school Italian way to prepare it. I'm also crazy about bagna cauda, which is Italian for "hot bath." (I'd like to take a long, hot bath in this silky sauce.) Bagna cauda is really more like a briny fondue than a sauce—a combination of olive oil, butter, garlic, and anchovies—often served with crudités for dipping. (It's a whole lot better than French onion dip.) Bagna cauda's extremely versatile: you can use it as a dip, slathered on bread, or toss your pasta with it. If only all pastas were as sultry as the lobster ravioli alla bagna cauda at Marea: impossibly delicate lobster raviolis anointed with bagna cauda, and garnished with orange beads of trout roe.

Until 1861 Italy wasn't even a united country. It was a collection of five major city-states that consisted of hundreds of towns and villages. Residents of these city-states ate according to the local climate and geography. In the north, they ate wild game, rice, and polenta. In the south, they ate fish, pasta, and tomato sauce. Romans, Tuscans, Venetians, and Sardinians all have their own culinary traditions, to name just a few. But all twenty regions of Italy are united by the striking simplicity and generosity of their cooking. Italian restaurants specializing in regional cuisine are growing more plentiful every day. Some may be more formal ristorantes, others casual trattorias or rustic pizzerias. But no matter the type of restaurant you're in—and whether it specializes in food from Puglia or Naples—the old cliché "When in Rome . . ." is a good credo to eat by. When in Bologna (or a Bolognese restaurant), eat tagliatelle Bolognese. When in Sicily (or a Sicilian joint), try anything agrodolce or pasta con sarde (with sardines). When in a Tuscan restaurant, order ribollita (vegetable and bread soup) and bistecca alla fiorentina (a grilled Florentine-style T-bone steak, marinated in olive oil, garlic and lemon).

When in a Roman restaurant, you might want to order the spaghetti cacio e pepe (pecorino Romano and black pepper sauce) because it's a true Roman specialty. So is lamb scottadito, which is Italian for "burnt fingers," so named because these grilled lamb chops—marinated in olive oil, garlic, black pepper, and rosemary—are so irresistible that you'll be hard-pressed to restrain yourself from eating them before they've had a chance to cool. Rome is also known for its fried zucchini blossoms, stuffed with a gooey, salty mix of mozzarella and anchovies, and Roman-style pizzas.

Whatever you do, skip the same old, same old. And order anything with rabbit. "Rabbit is the chicken of Italy," says Riccardo Buitino, the chef and owner of Emporio. Shelves stocked with wine bottles line the subway-tiled walls, and brown butcher paper squares serve as place mats in this laid-back trattoria in downtown Manhattan. The carciofi alla guidea—Jewish ghetto-style artichokes, which are twice-fried and served with a lemon wedge—are a Roman specialty that the chef prepares perfectly. He's also a surprisingly talented pizzaiolo (a pizza chef), which makes Emporio a Roman pizzeria with a lot of other good food on

> **• TASTY MORSEL •**
>
> *Always classic margherita pizza takes its name from Margherita di Savoia, queen to King Umberto I, the ruler of Italy from 1878 to 1900. While the king and queen were on holiday in Naples in 1889, Naples's most famous pizzaiolo, Raffaele Esposito, whipped up three pies to celebrate their visit. Esposito topped one pie with mozzarella, basil, and tomatoes, an edible tribute to the Italian flag. The queen liked the patriotic pizza the best, so Esposito named it after her and the margherita pizza was born.*

the menu. Rome is famous for its pies with wafer-thin crusts and toppings like anchovies, mozzarella, and rosemary. My favorite pie at Emporio is topped with guanciale, kale, and homemade pecorino cream.

Pizzas have been eaten in some form or another in Italy since A.D. 1000. What is pizza really? It's basically just another version of flatbread—a cheap, edible plate. Pizza began life as inexpensive street food for peasants, who ate it for breakfast, lunch, or dinner. In Naples, considered the true home of pizza, street vendors sold it by the slice, pie, or pound, dishing it out from portable tin ovens. In 1830, the very first pizzeria, Antica Pizzeria Port D'Alba, opened its doors in Naples, and it is still serving pies to this day. Naples is the home of the original and archetypal pie, but there are several different species of slices. There are Neapolitan and Roman and Sicilian pizzas. Neapolitan pies have thin crusts with thick, doughy edges. Roman pies have wafer-thin crusts with thin, crispy edges. Sicilian pies have terrifically thick crusts—one inch thick to be exact—and come sliced in squares. And of course I can't neglect New York–style pies, which have thin crusts and bubbly, chewy edges.

Nowadays you can find great pizza at fancy joints and dingy dives alike. One of the most famous no-frills joint is Di Fara pizzeria in Brooklyn, where Domenico DeMarco stands behind the counter preparing one pie at a time. He spreads a thin layer of tomato sauce on the dough, which he then tops with three kinds of hand-grated cheese. As each pie exits the oven, he clips fresh basil over it. There are long waits, no seats, and no smiles at Di Fara—proof that we'll do anything for a great slice. Perhaps the secret to his pies is premium ingredients, which are all imported from Italy: San Marzano tomatoes, extra virgin olive oil, buffalo mozzarella, aged mozzarella, and Parmigiano-Reggiano cheese. Except for the oregano and basil. Those come from Israel. (Interesting, no?) If you're a pizza freak, Di Fara is the holy land. The pies are phenomenal. The bubbly, charred crust is chewy at the edges and crispy at the center. It's a perfect union of tangy, subtly spiced sauce and soothing cheese. (I get hungry just thinking about it.)

There are pilgrimage parlors like Di Fara. There are late-night craving parlors, like Joe's in the Village, and there are civilized dinner parlors, like Pizzeria Mozza in Los Angeles. The pies there are divinely pillowy puffs scattered with new and Old World toppings. And then there are places that specialize in over-the-top toppings, like Nino's Bellissima in New York, which sells a thousand-dollar pie topped with lobster tail, caviar, and crème fraîche. The Italians didn't intend for pizza to have opulent toppings, and personally, I don't think caviar tastes great on pizza. Pizza is a simple, essential pleasure, and pimped-out pies strike me as silly.

No matter what kind of pie you're eating, use your hands. No knives or forks. If it arrives unsliced, grab a knife or a pizza cutter, slice it yourself, and dole it out with your hands. Don't get me wrong. Pizza is a serious endeavor. There are Web sites devoted to rating and debating all the aspects that make up the perfect pie: sauce, crust, cheese, toppings, and the ratio of one to the other. There are people who travel the world tasting pies from every touted pizzeria. Pizza is so much more than just tomato sauce, dough, and mozzarella cheese. There are white pies (sauce-less pies) like the quattro formaggio, made with four types of cheese, each with its own distinct personality. The only cheese you can count on making an appearance is mozzarella; the other three depend on the pizzaiolo. Each one has their unique blend of cheeses, which is what makes quattro formaggio so interesting to eat. Hey, you might not even miss the sauce. Quattro staggioni, which is Italian for "four seasons," is a seasonal interpretation of the pie. The pizza is blanketed with tomato sauce and cheese, and then divided into four distinct topping quadrants: one topped with artichokes, one topped with mushrooms, one with cooked ham, and another with olives. (But the four ingredients often vary, depending on the region, season, and restaurant.) One of my favorite pizzas is the classic pizza alla Neapolitana, scattered with tomato sauce, mozzarella, anchovies, and oodles of garlic. Nowadays pizzaiolos create their own crispy-crusted pies, topped with everything from speck (smoked, dry-cured ham), pineapple, and jalapeño to egg, guanciale, and escarole. Those are just a few inspired combinations I'm wild about at Pizzeria Mozza. In fact, Nancy Silverton, Mozza's pizzaiola, devised my all-time favorite pie: squash blossoms, burrata (creamy, fresh cheese made with mozzarella and cream), and tomato sauce. It's just four ingredients, including the outstandingly chewy crust, and it's out of this world.

The best pizza is very simple and highlights just a few perfect ingredients. And really, that's Italian cuisine in a nutshell. Think about the polenta I ate that spaghetti-and-meatball-bereft night—plain old boiled cornmeal mixed with milk and Parmesan cheese. And spaghetti pomodoro is nothing more than pasta, olive oil, and tomatoes (and maybe some basil, but only if it's fresh). Italians are ingredient snobs, and great ingredients are the essence of Italian cooking. Italians may have nothing but olive oil and garlic on hand, but they'll manage to make a great bowl of al dente spaghetti aglio e olio (garlic and olive oil). Italy produces outstanding olive oil, and anything anointed with it just seems to taste better. In fact most people consider it the finest in the world. Especially if it's extra virgin olive oil, which contains less than one percent acidity. Extra virgin olive oil is so aromatic, fresh, and full-bodied that all you really need is some bread to sop it up with. Italian food isn't complicated or fussy, which is part of the reason why it's so satisfying. Scarpetta is still one of the hottest reservations in New York, even though it's been open for well over a year. What did I eat at Scarpetta? Spaghetti with fresh tomato, basil, Parmesan, and olive oil. It was a spectacular bowl of spaghetti. Chef Scott Conant says, "These aren't opulent ingredients, they're simple, humble. You want the diner to say, 'This is the best fuckin' pasta I've ever had.'" It ranks high on my list.

One of the most exquisite and straightforward pleasures in Italian cuisine is mozzarella. The first snowy white, wondrously soft ball of mozzarella originated in Naples in the early 1800s. (I'm not referring to the rubbery, moistureless kind you can buy preshredded in the grocery store. That's low-moisture mozzarella made with skim milk.) I'm referring to the water-packed, tender, and creamy variety. Mozzarella is a general term for any fresh curd cheese in which the curds have been stretched and kneaded in hot water, then molded into a ball. The archetypal Italian mozzarella is made with buffalo's milk, resulting in a glossy, milky lump. Mozzarella di buffalo is much more delicate and expensive than fior de latte, cow's milk mozzarella. (The Italians often use fior de latte for Neapolitan pizzas.) Unfortunately we don't have water buffaloes stateside, so we import it (for a price) or settle for fior de latte, which can be great, too. Italians add mozzarella to everything from salads to pizza, or serve it on its own with a little fresh basil or olive oil. If it's burrata, that's even better. Burrata is a hybrid cheese: a shell of mozzarella containing a cream center and shreds of mozzarella. In Italian, *burrata* means "buttery," which refers to its silky mouthfeel and richness. I'm mad for burrata, and I think Pizzeria Mozza in Los Angeles serves the best in the country. Chef Nancy Silverton drizzles lush burrata, oozing with cream, with a zesty pesto and garnishes it with cherry tomatoes ripened on the vine and a few leaves of basil. It's downright dreamy.

Because purity is so important to Italian cuisine, it's often the simple dishes that best showcase the quality of a restaurant's ingredients. Start with a caprese salad—a classic combination of mozzarella, tomato, and basil. Do the tomatoes look ripe? Are they too firm or not firm enough? Are they tangy and sweet? Nudge the mozzarella with the edge of your fork. If it's stubborn or rubbery or still dethawing, get the check and run for the hills. Mozzarella should be served room temperature. Some restaurants add a little olive oil or sea salt to the plate, which is totally acceptable and brings out the flavor of the cheese. But you don't want a chef who tampers too much with the classics. If a chef respects his ingredients, he won't cover them up with too many seasonings. Lots of condiments usually indicate that the ingredients are inferior or that the chef has something to prove. Unfortunately neither works out in the diner's favor. I once had a caprese salad doused in pomegranate-infused vinegar. Not a good scene. (That poor mozzarella didn't stand a chance.)

Caprese salad is just one useful litmus test of a good restaurant. I usually look for a dish that's populist and relatively straightforward but shows a chef's true colors. A great test of a restaurant's pasta prowess is spaghetti alla vongole. If you see it on the menu, ask if it's cooked to order—it should be. Ask if the clams are fresh or canned. (They should be fresh.) I also judge a restaurant's merits by its fritto misto—a battered dish of deep fried seafood or meat and sliced vegetables, akin to Japanese tempura. Can I still identify all of the ingredients? If you can't tell if you're eating a ring of calamari or a piece of broccoli, it's sorely overbattered. Is the fritto misto—which literally means "fried mixture"—just calamari or mostly vegetables with a token ring of calamari or two thrown into the mix? The best fritto misto should feature a golden, crispy heap of different fish, vegetables, and fresh herbs.

Caprese salad and fritto misto are just two of the Italian specialties everyone should taste at least once in his or her life. Bollito misto is another. La Masseria in New York's Theater District serves an excellent version. Bollito misto literally means "boiled mixture." Doesn't sound too appetizing, right? (Agreed.) But when properly prepared, this Northern Italian dish of meats and vegetables simmered together is anything but boring. La Masseria's broth is insanely rich—a savory backdrop for the tender, juicy slices of chicken, veal, beef, cotechino (a fresh pork sausage), and tongue, all competing for room in the crowded bowl with potatoes, carrots, and chicken agnolotti (stuffed pasta). If that's not enough to digest, it's served with a side of mostarda (mustard-spiced fruit preserves) and salsa verde (an uncooked sauce made of parsley, vinegar, capers, onions, garlic, and anchovies). What I love about bollito misto is the juxtaposition of juicy meats, delicate agnolotti, sweet and sour mostarda, and vibrant salsa verde.

Brodetto di pesce, a traditional fish chowder with as many versions as there are Italian grandmothers, is another do-not-miss. (In Italian, *brodetto* means "broth" and can refer to both meat and fish broth but typically indicates the latter.) Brodetto almost always implies not just one, but several types of seafood. A good brodetto should transport you to the salty ocean waters. I wanted to stick my head into the brodetto at Marea. It was a $45.00 bowl of soup, one of those outlandish purchases you're certain you'll regret. But it was the best soup I've had in years. I'm not sure which was more intense, the briny fragrance or the flavor, but heads turned as the dish made its way to our table. The broth alone is worth the hefty price tag, an intriguingly zesty brew of tomatoes, onions, garlic, olive oil, and fish stock. Marea's brodetto is Chef Michael White's love song to the briny fruits of the sea. His version is filled with a bounty of sweet langoustines, fat scallops, spot prawns, clams, and chunks of striped bass.

Almost everyone has sampled bruschetta—grilled bread rubbed with garlic and olive oil—or some type of crostini (toasted bread), topped with everything from pureed eggplant to pesto. Why not try something new, like crispy-skinned porchetta—roasted suckling pig flavored with herbs, garlic, and pepper—or a classic game dish of capretto, roasted baby goat seasoned with olive oil, garlic, and herbs? (Sounds like heaven to me!) The capretto al forno (oven-roasted baby goat) at Scarpetta was caramelized on the outside, moist and musky within, and scattered with peas, potatoes, and shallots. If you ever crave meat on a sweltering summer day, but you don't want something hot and hearty, vitello tonnato is a great alternative. Vitello tonnato—chilled, thinly sliced veal slathered in a creamy tuna sauce, laced with anchovies, capers, egg yolks, olive oil, and pepper—is entirely original and well worth a departure from "the usual" or the familiar.

In the United States, Italian restaurants tend to fall into two camps: authentic Italian and Italian-American. Italian-American restaurants tend to play it safe and cover their bases—spaghetti and softball-size meatballs, chicken parmigiana smothered in cheese, and gooey baked ziti with plenty of red sauce. A lot of these old-school spots are heavy-handed with their sauces and sizes. They care more about portion than quality. New York City's Little Italy is a hub of Italian-American cooking. If you live in New York and you've never been, or you're coming for a visit, go. It's a New York City rite of passage. Little Italy (*really* little, just a couple of streets now) looks like the Epcot Center's version of Italy: red, green, and white bunting festoons the street lamps, salamis and wine casks hang in storefront windows, tourists clog the streets, and every restaurant has a virtually identical menu. I eat there about once a year, at Angelo's, my favorite. The waiters all have Italian accents (who knows if they're real), and the heaping platters of baked clams, lobster ravioli in vodka sauce, vitello piccata (veal sauced with artichokes, capers, and lemon sauce) and sautéed escarole in garlic sauce are perfect for family-style feasts. For dessert, I head down the street to Ferrara's, famous for biscotti, homemade gelati, Italian sodas, and chewy torrone—the Italian version of nougat, studded with nuts—imported from Italy. But though Little Italy is a sweet piece of New York history, the truth is that with a few exceptions most of the restaurants there are pretty mediocre.

For an authentic Italian meal, visit Sapori D'Ischia, an old-school destination restaurant in Woodside, Queens. The rules are scribbled on a chalkboard at the entrance. "No butter with bread. No cheese with seafood dishes. No lemon peel in your espresso." Those are just three of Sapori D'Ischia's "Ten Commandments." And they're dead serious. New-school spots are more diplomatic about it. Ask for Parmesan on your spaghetti frutti di mare at an authentic Italian restaurant and they'll probably tell you as gently as possible that the chef suggests you skip the cheese. If push comes to shove, they might swallow their pride and spoon a bit over your pasta, but the really old-school joints will flat out refuse. Their attitude is more along the lines of "shut up and like it." And you really can't help but like Sapori D'Ischia's housemade fettuccine swirled inside a hollowed-out wheel of Parmigiano-Reggiano, and tossed with prosciutto and white truffle essence.

How to tell if you're in an Italian-American restaurant or an authentic Italian restaurant, an old-school or a nouvelle joint? Here's a little trick I've learned—ask your server for a list of wines by the glass. If they don't have a list, ask the server to tell you what wines they have by the glass. If he says something like, "Whites, we got a Chardonnay and a Pinot Grigio. Reds, we got a Merlot and a Chianti," you're probably in an old-school joint. But don't immediately run for the hills. Some of the greatest restaurants are old school. They probably make a terrific veal saltimbocca—veal wrapped in prosciutto and sautéed with butter, olive oil, and sage. The servers have probably worked there forever, and the customers are probably regulars who order the same thing every time. I have a restaurant like this in my life, Pietro's in Midtown Manhattan. When my family eats there, we order veal parmigiana and their famous "Shells alla Nat." Ask my sister what's in "Shells alla Nat" and she'll probably respond with something like "cream, butter, oil. I don't know. What?" Between us, it's a bone marrow sauce. (Sometimes ignorance is bliss.) And we always drink the house red with dinner.

But say you ask your server for the list of wines by the glass and he actually brings one to the table. You're in a new-school Italian spot. New-school types have more than three whites and reds by the glass, and they're probably different grapes from different territories—a Brunello, Sangiovese, a Pinot Noir from California, maybe a Cabernet Sauvignon from South Africa. They probably update their wine list all the time and have a sommelier or a beverage director. Locanda Verde in Tribeca has a talented beverage director, Josh Nadel, who's always got something new and interesting to pair with your fish or pasta dish.

Old school or new school, there are many types of Italian restaurants, one for every occasion. There are pasticcerias that specialize in Italian cakes, chocolates, tortas, and cookies; gelaterias devoted to frozen pleasures of the sorbetto and gelato sorts; paninerias that specialize in sandwiches stuffed with Italian meats and cheeses; and espresso shops devoted to Italian-style caffè. Sant Ambroeus, located on Manhattan's Upper East Side, is a pasticceria, panineria, gelateria, and espresso shop rolled up into one. Enotecas focus on wine, not food. They serve snacks, charcuterie, and small plates that require little preparation. Ino-

> • TASTY MORSEL •
>
> *Ever wonder where bologna—commonly known as "baloney"—gets its name? Baloney's Italian cousin, mortadella, a pork sausage larded with cubes of fat, originated in Bologna, Italy. Unlike mortadella, which contains thick chunks of fat, U.S. regulations require American bologna to be finely ground without any visible fat. Instead baloney is typically made of fully cooked and chopped chicken, beef, pork, or veal. Mortadella is cured, not cooked, and made from just pork.*

tecas are even smaller, more casual versions of enotecas. They offer a few items to nibble on, but wines take center stage. At a ristorante you can expect to find multicourse meals, with formal menus and the table service to match. A trattoria is a café where the informal menu may be written or scribbled on a chalkboard—even recited to you by the server. At some salumerias, you can not only buy cheese and salumi, but also sit and eat your purchases as well. Don't confuse salumi with salami, the ground, seasoned pork log that you often find sliced into rounds. Salami is just one kind of Italian cured meat.

Salumi refers to all Italian charcuterie, and as with the French, there's an impressive array of succulent cured meats (traditionally pork) to sink your teeth into. Good prosciutto practically melts on your tongue. Prosciutto is salt-cured, air-dried ham, and sliced impossibly thin. These rosy ribbons, trimmed in fat, are salty-sweet and delicate. Some restaurants serve prosciutto on its own, others serve it wrapped around ripe melon. If there's Prosciutto di

Parma on the menu, I highly recommend an order. Because it's an air-dried meat, climate matters, and Parma's humid climate works magic on ham, producing soft, tender ribbons. If you want something a tad more robust and sturdy, there's sopressata, dry-cured pork salami, which is coarsely pressed—not ground, like traditional salami—and chewier than typical Italian salami. While we're on the subject, there are two types of salami: salami and salame. Salami with an *i* is dry, well-seasoned pork, while salame with an *e* is tangibly moister and less seasoned. And bresaola is salami made from air-dried, salted beef instead of pork—leaner, sweeter, and more tender than standard salami.

You could easily make a meal from all the sensational charcuterie Italy has to offer. There's pancetta, or unsmoked, dry-cured bacon, which is often diced and added to sauce. What would carbonara or amatriciana be without guanciale (unsmoked bacon), for that matter? Speck is essentially smoked prosciutto, made from dry-cured ham that's smoky and sweet (not salty). At Salumeria Rosi on the Upper West Side, there's an entire menu devoted to the fine art of Italian charcuterie, with eighteen meaty options. Servers tote large wood boards, heaped with rounds of salami, fragrant ribbons of prosciutto, pancetta, speck, and mortadella, which is the fattier and tastier Italian version of American bologna. Like most salumerias, they also feature some terrific Italian cheeses to eat with charcuterie.

At most formal ristorantes, cheese not only makes an appearance in many dishes but also gets its very own course—the formaggi (the plural form of formaggio)—eaten just before dessert. Italy makes soft and hard cheeses, fresh and aged, molded blues, some made with cow's milk or goat, others with buffalo or sheep's milk. Each one is distinct and distinguished and can be eaten on their own, with nothing more than a little dried fruit, preserves, and some crusty bread. When you make cheeses as well as the

Italians do, you want to protect their reputation. There are organizations, even laws, to protect Italy's twenty-six most prized cheeses. Some get awarded DOC status, short for *Denominazione di Origine Controllata*, which translates to "Denomination of Controlled Origin." In plain English, in order to be labeled pecorino, provolone, and the like, the cheese has to be made according to strict standards set forth by the Italian government. Those standards are typically established by the region where the cheese was originally produced. There's a world of wonderful cheeses beyond mozzarella, ricotta, and Parmesan. One of my favorites is pecorino, a hard sheep's milk cheese with a terrifically tangy flavor. Pecorino refers to all Italian cheeses, fresh or aged, made with sheep's milk, but some are undeniably better than others. The best is pecorino romano (made in the Rome area), an

---

• TASTY MORSEL •

*DOP is short for* Denominazione di Origine Protetta, *which translates to "Protected Designation of Origin." In plain English, anything labeled DOP guarantees the origin and quality of a product by the Italian government, be it a type of meat, cheese, or pasta. In order to meet DOP standards, a product must not only be made with ingredients from that particular region but also be produced in that same region. For example, prosciutto di Parma DOP guarantees the prosciutto was made with ham from Parma and dried on Parma's soil, according to the high standards designated by the government.*

aged pecorino with a hard, yellow rind and a sharp, salty, and nutty flavor. (It goes great with a bold red wine from Italy, of course.) When I'm in the mood for something soft and creamy, I scan the menu for robiola, a soft, milky white cheese from northern Italy. Like pecorino, robiola refers to a wide range of small, milky white cheeses, made with "mixed milk"—often a blend of sheep's, cow's, or goat's milk cheese—with an earthy aroma and rich, refined flavor. (A bold red wine will clobber robiola. Try a white wine instead.) I'm pretty keen on the bold, nutty flavor of fontina, too. Fontina—a straw-colored cow's milk cheese with an orangish brown rind—is one of Italy's most famous cheeses, imitated around the world (France, Sweden, and Denmark). Fontina ranges from soft to semihard, depending on how long it's been aged. The best fontina comes from Valle d'Aosta, its birthplace, where it's made with raw, unpasteurized milk, resulting in a piquant, full-flavored cheese with notes of honey. I think Gorgonzola is misunderstood, but I may have a stilted perspective. My sister and brother despise the smell of Gorgonzola, a blue cheese made from cow's milk. They won't even sit at the same table with anyone who orders it. So I get my Gorgonzola fix when they're not around. Let me tell you, those two are missing out on not just one, but two very interesting moldy, blue-veined cheeses. There's Gorgonzola piccante, which is hard, sharp, and smelly, and Gorgonzola dolce, which is soft, sweet, and smelly as well. My brother and sister have tasted only Gorgonzola piccante, which I'll admit is an acquired taste, but Gorgonzola dolce is an entirely different breed of blue cheese, one that might make a convert out of them.

Okay, so you've made it through dinner. But wait! There's still dessert. And no one, and I mean no one, should slack off when it comes to dolce, dessert Italian-style. Tartufo! Tiramisu! Panna cotta! Gelato! Semifreddo! And yet, until the eleventh century, prior to the Arab invasion of Sicily, the Italians had never laid eyes on sugar. The most they could hope for at the end of a meal was cheese or fruit drizzled with honey. And even for centuries after the Arab invasion, sugar was an imported extravagance a mere few could afford. Up until the fifteenth century, Italy relied primarily on honey as a sweetener. Their desserts were made mostly from eggs, cheese, and flour. With those ingredients, they created their trademark dense breads, like pannetone, a sweet brioche studded with dried fruit and nuts, or panforte, a dense spice cake chockablock full of nuts and fruits. When Venetian traders started bringing sugarcane from the East, sugar became the new honey. And even though sugar is no longer worth its weight in gold, don't expect to find a peanut butter parfait or chocolate soufflé on an Italian menu. Italian sweets are typically less sugary, less decadent than American confections, though there are some wonderful exceptions. Peek into an Italian pantry and you'll find nuts, cinnamon, honey, dried fruits, cocoa powder, and liqueurs. You'll find cheese, cream, milk, and eggs in the fridge—double-duty ingredients that work for both savory and sweet dishes.

All Italian desserts revolve around bread, cream, or fruit—either singly or in some felicitous combination. One of my favorites is panna cotta—simmered cream set with gelatin, like an ethereal milky Jell-O—with its light, silky-smooth texture and creamy flavor. Panna cotta is a classic and a great litmus test of a restaurant's dessert chops. "It can't be too sweet or gummy. There is a knack to making it light even though it's essentially a jiggle of cream," Gina DePalma says. She should know. Not only is she the pastry chef at Joe Bastianich and Mario Batali's wildly popular Babbo, but in 2009, she also won the James Beard award for outstanding pastry chef. "Our signature dessert [at Babbo] is a saffron panna cotta, so I definitely pay attention when I am eating it elsewhere. It's about caring. If your panna cotta sucks—and it's a dessert of less than five ingredients—then you obviously don't care about details. The glory is always in the details, right?"

Heavenly tiramisu, that rich, fluffy cake made of liqueur and espresso-soaked lady fingers, cocoa, egg, and mascarpone (a soft, triple-cream cheese), is not only the sine qua non of Italian dessert, but it was also invented as a midday pick-me-up for weary prostitutes. In Italian *tiramisu* literally translates to "carry me up" or "lift me up"—an "energy dessert" of sorts. A little protein (eggs), a hit of caffeine (espresso), a jolt of sugar (chocolate), and a little bit of alcohol to smooth out life's rough edges . . . works like a charm. Creamy, fluffy desserts spiked with alcohol are Italy's forte. There's a luscious egg custard known as zabaglione—made with egg yolks, sugar, and a generous splash of Marsala wine—and zuppa inglese, which is the Italian take on the English trifle. While the English soak the cake (or ladyfingers) in sherry, the Italians use rum or other liqueurs, then layer it with cream. One of my favorite ways to end a meal is with a budino, which in Italian means "pudding," but that doesn't really do it justice. A budino is a lot more thrilling than your boilerplate pudding. Most Italian chefs take liberties, thickening their budini (plural form of *budino*) with cornstarch or cookies, and the result is a glorious cross between a ganache and a soufflé. I've had the pleasure of a molten chocolate budino, an earthy, velvety chestnut budino, a dewy apple budino, a criminally rich butterscotch budino, and counting.

Though they're not particularly fluffy or creamy, I also adore Italy's tri-colore cookies, better known in America as rainbow cookies. Rainbow cookies are cakey, almond-flavored cookies, made with marzipan (almond-sugar paste), which taste wonderfully moist and sweet. They're my sister's favorites, so much so that I got her a cake-size rainbow cookie for her birthday one year. Personally I'm not a fan of fried pastry shells stuffed with sweet cream, but if you are, you'll want to make your way to the local pasticceria (pastry shop) for a cannoli.

But if you've gorged yourself on too much pasta, fresh fruit is also a popular end to an Italian feast. Macedonia, a minted fresh fruit salad, or a big bowl of strawberries with freshly whipped cream or aged balsamic vinegar are common meal closers. Fruit also plays into tarts, crostatas (an open-faced tart), chocolates, sorbets, gelati, and other frozen or even half-frozen confections. Spoon your way to the center of tartufo—a chocolate-covered, multilayered ball of ice cream—and you'll discover a maraschino cherry and nut reward. There's spumone, an elegant layered ice cream cake, and a half-frozen dolce known as a semifreddo. Take custard, combine it with whipped cream, and freeze. Voilà, a classic Italian semifreddo.

I haven't forgotten about gelato! You can't possibly write about Italian desserts without mentioning staggeringly creamy gelato. In Italy, gelato is an essential food group. I ate gelato at least once a day when I traveled "the boot," sometimes twice a day. Italians find it insulting when Americans compare gelato to ice cream— don't say I didn't warn you. It's an honest mistake. They're both made with milk, cream, and sugar, but that's where the similarities end. Gelato is denser, creamier, and more intensely flavored than ice cream because it has less butterfat and less air, and is typically served less cold than ice cream. Those three factors make a huge difference. I mean, I thought it was hard to stop eating ice cream, but I'm powerless in the face of gelato. And there are nearly as many flavors of gelato as there are shapes of pasta, so the perils are many. You never know what flavors you'll encounter inside a gelateria, and luckily we've got several gelaterias of our own in the States. (If we didn't, I'd wager quite a few people would made the trek to Italy every summer.) I've had sharp bergamot (the oil of which lends Earl Grey tea its distinctive taste) gelato in Rome and delicate olive oil gelato at Otto Pizzeria in New York City, and I still can't get out of my head the mouthwatering peach gelato pie I ate at Pizzeria Mozza in L.A. Some traditional flavors include fior di latte (sweet cream), cioccolato (chocolate), nocciola (hazelnut), caffè (coffee), stracciatella (chocolate chip), amarena (sour cherry), and fragola (strawberry). I like zabaglione gelato, the frozen form of this wine-laced egg custard, and zingy, bright green pistachio gelato, dotted with real pistachio nuts. Oh, and I'm just as crazy about milk-less sorbetto, made with just fresh fruit, water, and sugar. Sorbetti (the plural form of *sorbetto*) are tremendously refreshing. My go-to gelateria is Sant Ambroeus on New York's Upper East Side. (The first outpost opened in Milan in 1936.) I never thought a fruit sorbetto could make me swoon, but their banana and pear sorbetto taste more intense and sharper than the actual fruit itself. On a summer day when it's too hot to drink coffee, I snack on an espresso granita, a coarser version of sorbetto—an elegant, caffeinated Italian ice.

Pasta. Brodetto. Osso buco. Salumi. Cheese. Tiramisu. All that delicious food definitely takes time to eat—and enjoy. To anyone accustomed to a twenty-minute chow-down (maybe an hour and a half at a nice restaurant), an Italian meal can seem to stretch on for ages. A multicourse meal starts the moment you arrive at a ristorante. Waiting for your table? You'll likely be prompted to enjoy an aperitif—a drink before dinner—at the bar. Once seated, it's time for some antipasti—the appetizers before the meal. The primo—the first course—follows. Italians eat pasta as a primo— not as a main course, secondo, or as a side dish, a contorno. If you want to impress your server or your date, order a primo of pasta to share. And if you really want to mangia the Italian way, fol- low your secondo with a cheese course—formaggio—before dolce (dessert). Oh, and don't order coffee, or as the Italians call it, caffè, before dessert.

Coffee is another important ritual the Italians don't take lightly. A lot of restaurants, Italian and American alike, offer the classic cappuccino—one part espresso, one part milk, one part foam. In fact plenty of servers come to the table and ask: "Does anyone want a cappuccino or an espresso?" But if you're dining by the Italian playbook, then you shouldn't order cappuccino at lunch or dinner. The Italians don't drink cappuccinos after 11:00 A.M. They consider cappuccino food; some consider it breakfast, because it's made with milk. It's a "liquid food" they partake in only in the morning hours because they believe it hinders the body's ability to digest food. So, if after reading this chapter, you remember only one thing, remember this—never order a cappuccino after dark.

Every culture takes caffeine seriously. (I don't dare leave the house until I've had two cups of coffee.) We all have our favorite fix—be it Coke, caramel-whatever-skinny-lattes, or straight-up black coffee. Italians take their coffee so seriously that espresso is the official national beverage. But it's just a dainty cup filled with really strong coffee, right? Actually, no. If you want to get technical, espresso is made by forcing one to one and a half ounces of hot water through seven grams of finely ground coffee at a pressure of nine bars. Because of the pressurization, the flavor of an espresso shot is highly concentrated, and the resulting brew is almost syrupy, with a beautiful golden crema (foam). It should never be bitter. The key to perfect espresso is the skill of the barista pulling the shot—someone who is trained in correctly grinding the beans, tamping the grounds, and operating the espresso machine.

Unlike Americans, who often add lots of milk and syrups to our espresso drinks, most Italians drink straight shots of espresso, the better to taste the coffee itself. And because lattes are so milky, they're not nearly as popular in Italy as they are here. But the Italians are quite fond of the macchiato, a shot of espresso marked with foam. If you'd like a double shot of espresso, ask for a doppio. At an Italian restaurant, but in the mood for a good old-school cup of Joe? Try an Americano, which is a shot or two of espresso with water added to it. Supposedly, in postwar Italy, American GIs used to add water to their espressos to approximate American-style coffee—thus the Americano was born. (But I think it's the Italians' underhanded way of letting us know we can't handle straight espresso!)

I admire the way Italians make the most of every eating opportunity, be it breakfast or a caffè break. There are even cookies specifically created to complement coffee. You can't fit a round cookie into a small cup of espresso, so they made a long, hard biscotti for all coffee-dipping endeavors. Biscotti are indelibly crunchy, twice-baked cookies that soak up a bit of coffee but don't crumble into the cup. There are several flavors of biscotti, including chocolate, hazelnut, vanilla, and anise. The only problem is that once you've had biscotti with your coffee, it's hard to go back to coffee sans the cookies. Italians sometimes serve amaretti, bitter almond macarons, alongside caffè, too. Though they're round and soft on the inside, they're crunchy on the outside and just as good for sponging up hot coffee. Amaretti are versatile; they can be eaten on their own, crumbled over gelato or custard, or served with caffè or even wine.

If espresso weren't the national beverage of Italy, it would probably be wine. Some of the world's oldest and finest wines come from Italy. Big, bold Barbarescos from Piedmont, spicy Chiantis from Tuscany, sparkling Proseccos from Veneto. But even experts have a hard time mastering the more than one thousand varieties of grapes, so don't be embarrassed about asking lots of questions or relying on the sommelier for guidance. That is, unless he steers you to the priciest wines on the list. Give him your price range, tell him what you typically like, and let him direct you to more reasonable bottles (or glasses). Here are a few helpful tips to keep in mind: if you're eating regional Italian, look for a wine made in that region. For instance, if you're dining in a Northern Italian restaurant, drink northern Italian wines. If you happen to be in a Roman-style joint, scan the wine list for Roman wines. Another great way to choose an Italian wine is to consider the character of the region: wines from the north tend to be lean and more acidic with cherry flavors; wines from the south tend to be bold, fruit-forward wines.

In general, red meats and heavy, cream-based sauces pair best with bold, acidic wines that will cut the richness of the dish. Delicate fish or light salads work best with lighter, less acidic wines that won't overpower the flavors of the food. Of course, you don't have to drink red wine just because you're having meat. And you don't have to order white just because you're eating fish. Ask your server what white he would drink with the meat dish you ordered, or what red he would opt for with your fish entrée. Salute!

## Table Setting and Modern Manners

There aren't many rules to eat by at the Italian table. Enjoyment is more important than anything else. Just think about the common Italian phrase: "Mangia, mangia," which translates as "eat, eat." Italians love to share food and feed people. How fantastic is that? If you don't look like you're having any fun or enjoying your food, you'll make everyone else uncomfortable. The dinner table is the center of Italian social life. It's where everyone comes together to bond over food, wine, and exchange stories. If you watch an Italian family sit down to dinner, you'll notice that plates are constantly passed around as everyone takes a little of everything. That's why Italian food is so friendly to a family-style meal.

Really, the only thing you have to show up with is an appetite and a few basic manners. Elbows and hands should remain above the table and plates are passed to the left. They eat Continental-style, meaning the fork is to the left of your plate and the knife is to the right. You pick up cheese with a knife, not your fingers, and cut fruit with a fork and knife. It also helps to know how to twirl your spaghetti, which is not as hard as you might think. Pick up just a few strands with your fork, press it on the side of the bowl and twirl. If you really want to twirl like the Italians, pick up a few strands with your fork, then pick up your spoon in the other hand, and press the fork into the spoon while you twirl, all the better for catching the sauce. As the Italians say, "Buon appetito!"

# · 8 ·
# Japanese Cuisine

*Teach a man to fish, and you feed him for
a lifetime. Give him ramen noodles, and you
don't have to teach him anything.*

LAWRENCE DOWNES

I have no problem committing to one man, but I can't possibly be loyal to just one cuisine. Playing the field is what makes meals so interesting. If I absolutely had to pick a culinary mate, it would be Japanese. For starters, it's a very attractive cuisine—radishes sculpted into flowers, cucumber curls transformed into leaves, and coral fans of salmon sashimi.And there's so much variety in Japanese cooking I could never get bored. Just the other evening, when I suggested Japanese, my friend responded, "I had sushi last night." "No problem," I said. "We could go for soba or udon, tempura, yakitori, kaiseki, or hibachi instead. Or we could go to a robata grill or an inakaya." (I think she learned her lesson.)

Japanese cuisine puts ingredients on a pedestal. Visit any robata grill (robatayaki)—a restaurant specializing in open fire grilling—and you can order garlic. Just garlic. Japanese menus often look more like laundry lists of ingredients than dishes. One of my favorite robata grills in Japan recently opened up a fourth outpost in Times Square. There are sixteen kinds of vegetables on the menu, fifteen types of seafood, three kinds of dried fish, six meats, and seven kinds of seafood. You pick one of two seasonings—lemon and salt, or tare (a sweet soy sauce). That's it. Sounds ho-hum, right? Don't think I didn't roll my eyes the first time I saw a three-dollar order of scallions or ginkgo nuts on a menu. "I could eat in the grocery store if I wanted that for dinner," I thought to myself. But order skewered ginkgo nuts brightened by a squirt of lemon and salt and you'll discover their rich nuttiness and soft flesh. I'd never thought twice about all the ginkgo nuts that fall from the trees in Central Park until I tasted them skewered on a stick. I had no idea how satisfying the subtleties of ingredients could be until I started eating Japanese food. I wasn't a fan of salmon until I tried sake (raw salmon). Sure, it's the same fish, but the nuances of uncooked salmon, plucked from the ocean and served in its original state, strike the palate entirely differently than the flavors of cooked salmon do.

Japanese food engages all five senses—it's incredibly sensual (not to mention great for dates). In fact the Japanese are just as serious about the presentation and texture of an ingredient as they are about its flavor. Some dishes even put texture above flavor. Have you ever tried grated tororo (mountain yam)? It doesn't taste like much and yet it's a staple on most Japanese menus. Why? Because it's worth eating for its slippery, sticky texture alone. Natto, fermented soybean, has almost no flavor at all, but it does have a distinct, some say foul, smell. Though the scent of natto is potent, the gooey texture grows on you almost immediately. And undressed uni is one of my greatest loves. Luscious, custardlike uni is commonly described as sea urchin roe, but if you really want to get specific about it, it's sea urchin ovary. Personally, I prefer to eat it (as often as possible) and not think about its origin. If you want the ultimate carnal experience, try an uni shooter. This divine creation arouses all the senses. Imagine a shot glass filled with bright orange uni tucked beneath a raw quail egg, sprinkled with scallions, and splashed with sake. It's sweet yet salty, delicate yet rich, musty, velvety, and outright extraordinary. I like to close my eyes when I eat sushi because it's as much about mouth-feel as it is about flavor. Shiroebi will do a number on your tongue, too. They're soft, silky baby shrimp that release a sweet, precious flavor as you chew.

But don't close your eyes for *too* long. Next time you go for Japanese, take a minute to admire your plate. You can tell what season it is by looking at the garnish as well as at the ingredients. The collective Japanese kitchen's muse is nature. Chefs often adorn a dish with autumn leaves or spring pansies, and some garnishes are even edible. I'd seen the cherry blossoms in D.C., but I'd never eaten one until I went to Kajitsu, a vegetarian kaiseki restaurant in the East Village, and tried cherry blossom sponge cake. Every dish in our six-course dinner was beautifully ornamented and presented with pride. They seemed as delighted to feed us as we were to be fed. (I almost forgot I was eating in New York City.)

Eating out can sometimes feel like a hit-and-run. Your server whizzes by, tosses a plate on the table, and disappears before you can ask for salt and pepper. That would never happen in a Japanese restaurant. The Japanese embrace the ceremony of eating, yet another desirable attribute in a culinary partner. The ceremony begins the moment you walk through the door. The entire staff stops what they're doing and simultaneously greets you with a warm "Irrashaimase." Servers are attentive but not intrusive; they don't hover annoyingly, and are happy to guide you through the intricacies of a dish. Don't get me wrong; they know how to enjoy their food. They eat sushi with their hands and pour sake until it overflows from the glass. Overflowing sake is a sign of generosity and yet another attractive trait in a culinary partner.

Going for Japanese is a little like going to a culinary spa for dinner. How many cultures greet diners with a hot towel, a glass of water, and a cup of green tea? Usually you begin by ordering

some sake, a bowl of soothing miso soup, and then the rest of the
meal depends on the menu. What you can expect to find in common at all Japanese restaurants is that every dish arrives on its
own plate. Instead of appetizers and entrées, every meal, including breakfast, is a succession of dishes, some bigger than others.
No meal is complete without a small bowl of rice. (Unless you go
for noodles.)

Some Japanese classics recur across menus, no matter the style
of the restaurant. For years I'd spot universal offerings, like oshitashi, hijiki, or oshinko listed on all kinds of Japanese menus, and
yet I was clueless as to what they were. Their names were familiar,
but I never bothered to ask what was in them or try even one. But
I'm the kind of girl who gets jealous of what other people are eating. Food envy and curiosity always get the better of me. Several
times I'd witnessed diners at neighboring tables receive a lidded
porcelain bowl that unleashed a pouf of steam when its top was
removed. One night I couldn't take it anymore, so I leaned over and
asked what it was—and ordered one for myself. Turns out it was
chawan mushi, a steamed egg custard, which feels like cashmere
against your tongue and tastes like an opulent omelet. You never
know what you'll find in your chawan mushi. Some are laced with
sweet nibbles of shrimp, scallion, chicken, or corn; others with
scallops, clams, or mushrooms. My insatiable curiosity also led me
to my love for oshinko, delicate Japanese pickled vegetables that
range from radishes to turnips to mushrooms and vary according to
the seasons. And I'm just flat out obsessed with hijiki, which may
sound strange, considering hijiki is a black, slightly bitter salad of
seaweed that tastes like briny al dente noodles. While I still don't
get the allure of bland oshitashi (boiled cold spinach), I can check
it off my to-try list. You'll find many of these menu fixtures listed
as starters or appetizers, since Japanese meals traditionally begin
with small, palate-cleansing bites like these.

No matter what kind of Japanese restaurant you're eating at, it's not uncommon to find hibachi, teriyaki, and donburi (rice bowls) on the menu, too. Familiarizing yourself with these popular cooking preparations will help you get your footing anywhere. Hibachi beef, chicken, and shrimp are cooked on a hibachi grill; teriyaki beef, chicken, and shrimp are marinated in sweet soy sauce; and the "don" in *donburi* means that the dish is served over rice—the word that prefaces "don" indicates the protein placed on top of the rice. At a mediocre sushi spot, I'll opt for a "buri"—which means bowl—of una-don (broiled eel over rice) or scan the menu for breaded, deep-fried katsu (a meat cutlet), because a crispy-edged cutlet is a lot more satisfying than so-so sushi. Some restaurants offer various types of katsu, while others specialize in one particular style of katsu. Katsuhama in Midtown Manhattan prepares ton-katsu (pork cutlets) ten ways, and they're all excellent. I grew up on ho-hum chicken cutlets, so I know how rare a quality cutlet made with Berkshire pork loin is.

But like I mentioned earlier, one of the primary thrills of Japanese cuisine is its variety. Whether you're a serial monogamist, a heartbreaker, or a casual dater, the only way to find your type is by playing the field. Ready?

## Sushi

Sushi might just be my favorite kind of Japanese food. Scratch that. Sushi might just be my favorite food. Next time you pop a piece in your mouth, pay close attention to its nuances— the warm, slightly sweet rice with a tart whisper of vinegar, the cold, satiny fish and the clean kick of wasabi. Eating good sushi is one of the most thrilling experiences in the world—and it's an experience readily available in almost every American city these days. How lucky are we! But before I start waxing even more rhapsodic, I should admit that I didn't dive into sushi headfirst. I baby-stepped my way in with Americanized sushi, and eventually made a pilgrimage to the Tsikiji fish market—the holy land of raw delicacies—outside of Tokyo.

The first time I tried sushi was in college. Just like the first time I had sex, I had no idea what I was doing, and I was really nervous. I fumbled around, did the best I could, and kept trying until I felt more confident. My college boyfriend had grown up in Los Angeles—the land of exceptionally fresh sushi—so he was a veteran eater of raw delicacies and the perfect guide to show me the way. He suggested that I order from the posted specials—a blackboard scrawled in Japanese listing all of the freshest catches. "No way. I'm not eating anything that I can't read, never mind pronounce," I thought to myself. I ignored his advice and played it safe by ordering rolls with familiar names, like the dragon roll, spider roll, and California roll. My boyfriend tried to dissuade me. "That's beginner sushi," he explained. "It doesn't even count. It's cooked seafood with gobs of rice." But that was fine with me. Sweet, vinegary sushi rice and pungent wasabi were enough adventure for one evening. I also had the pleasure of tasting crispy nori—sheets of pressed, toasted seaweed used to wrap sushi rolls—for the first time, piquant pickled ginger (gari) and seared eel drizzled with a sweet, thick sauce called kabayaki.

For my first year of sushi, I stuck to two kinds of rolls: oversize and Americanized rolls with "the works"—extra rice and lots of fillings, like cucumber, avocado, or asparagus. How do you spot Americanized sushi? Easy. Any roll with a state in its name is unequivocally American. The Philadelphia roll is a prime example. For starters, it's named after an American city and it's made with smoked salmon, cucumber, and cream cheese. I can't with a clean conscience let you order a Philadelphia roll. Smoked fish is bad enough, but I draw the line at cheese consorting with sushi. Even I have my limits. Cutesy names are red flags, too. Case in point: the rainbow roll. Order this roll, which comes with a "rainbow" of fish—typically yellowtail, salmon, crab, and tuna—and you won't taste any of them. Their delicate flavors are canceled out by being lumped together. Personally, I don't think there's anything wrong with a spider roll. It's a crunchy alternative for raw fish phobes. The only way I could lure my mom to a sushi restaurant was to swear on my life there was a spider roll on the menu. She refused to eat uncooked fish, but she was crazy about soft-shell crab, and tempura-battered soft-shell crab is the key ingredient in a spider roll.

Spicy rolls can go either way. They're a Western creation, but some traditional restaurants do serve a spicy roll, like spicy tuna. What distinguishes "traditional" spicy rolls from saucy, sub par ones is the spicy sauce. "Traditional" spicy sauce is made with sriracha, sesame oil, and soy sauce, while saucy, subpar spicy sauce has lots of chile-infused mayonnaise in it, which can camouflage the fish. Mayonnaise definitely crosses the line into American territory—though it's now wildly popular in Japan. The most popular kind of mayo in Japan is Kewpie brand mayonnaise, made with cider vinegar instead of distilled vinegar, which makes it creamier and richer than Hellmann's. (Many homemade versions are made with egg yolks instead of egg whites.) Chefs use Kewpie mayo to make spicy dipping sauces for everything from sushi to baked mussels, or in creamy salad dressings.

And strangely enough, some of our beloved American-style rolls have crossed the Pacific and are now big hits in Japan. When I was in Tokyo, I spotted spicy tuna rolls on a few menus, and even a California roll. (Though I didn't order them.) Many American-style rolls evolved not just because of our initially timid Western tastes but also out of necessity. As Masaharu Morimoto, the original Iron Chef and one of the most celebrated Japanese chefs in the world, explains, "When Japanese food was introduced in the United States thirty or forty years ago, there were few Japanese ingredients or tools available here. So Japanese chefs had to create

Japanese food with what was available. That's how things like the Alaska roll—raw salmon, avocado, cucumber, and tobiko—and the Philadelphia roll evolved. I don't like to hear some Japanese chefs from Japan say, 'This is not Japanese food,' looking at what we make here. They don't know about the history of Japanese food in America." Suddenly I don't feel so bad about my slow road into serious sushi. Besides, it's hard to deny the simple pleasure of a well-made spicy tuna roll or California roll.

I still throw a spicy roll into the mix once in a while, and I occasionally eat fusion sushi with tasty sauces if there's a creative chef behind the sushi bar. But for the most part, I stick to straight-forward pieces of nigiri sushi—hand-molded rice with fish on top—and sashimi with no rice at all. Typically, the more rice in a roll, the less traditional it is. I try to avoid futomaki—big, blown-up rolls, stuffed with multiple ingredients. My motto: If it doesn't fit in your mouth without opening as wide as you have to when you're at the dentist's office, it's too big. If it has more than five ingredients, it's too big. I like to eat my sushi the way the Japanese intended. Yes, the first time you dig into the culinary unknown, es-pecially if it happens to be raw or slippery, is scary. But every time I try something new, my mouth goes somewhere it's never been. If I hadn't experimented, I would never know the briny intensity of sea urchin (uni), the salty, delicate burst of fish roe, the sweet, supple petals of raw scallops, the sweet pink-and-white flesh of porgy, or the slippery tongue-feel of raw abalone. A California roll is a fine way to ease into the unique textures and flavors sushi has to offer. Just don't stay there too long.

No matter what kind of sushi you're eating, there are fundamental components to the meal you'll always encounter: wasabi and gin-ger, sushi rice, nori, and soy sauce. You'd be surprised how many sushi eaters think wasabi is made from horseradish. Wasabi is related to horseradish, but they're not the same thing. True wasabi is grated from the green wasabi root that grows mostly in Japan. It's much more complex than people give it credit for. It's sweet and fruity, and its spiciness, more akin to hot mustard than to chile peppers, doesn't linger. Use wasabi sparingly: a little dab goes a long way. Sushi's not meant to be a fiery food. You want to taste the fish, not numb your mouth for the evening. Wasabi should sharpen the flavor of the fish and awaken your senses. Low-grade wasabi, common in lower quality sushi joints, is often made from a mix of wasabi powder, horseradish, mustard, and food coloring. That breed of "wasabi" lingers longer than true wasabi does and bleeds into the next bite. And the pink stuff on the table is gari, or pickled ginger, eaten between pieces of sushi as a palate cleanser. Neither wasabi nor pickled ginger should be mixed into your soy sauce. Sushi rice is remarkably different from the white rice we eat at home: it's made from glutinous, short-grain Japanese white rice that's cooked with vinegar and sugar, and sometimes kelp or kombu (seaweed).

Raw fish is served several ways: as sashimi, carpaccio, tataki, nigiri, and rolls. Sashimi is a simple piece of fish served without rice. Carpaccio is essentially the same thing as sashimi, except that the fish will be served as paper-thin slices. Tataki is similar to tartare—diced or minced raw fish, usually mixed with other seasonings. Nigiri is a piece of fish draped over a warm nibble of rice. There are many kinds of sushi rolls, and they're almost always made with nori (seaweed), unless the menu specifies otherwise. The most traditional rolls are called *norimaki,* which means "wrapped in seaweed." There are two kinds of norimaki: temaki is a large hand roll, wrapped in a single sheet of seaweed, while maki, which are smaller rolls, are usually cut into six pieces. If you want it inside out—with rice on the outside and more rice on the inside—order uramaki. Futomaki are oversize (usually over-stuffed) rolls.

All raw fish are not alike. If they were, sushi would get very monotonous very fast. There are all sorts of fish to sample in their naked, pure state, and they're all markedly distinct from one another in flavor. I wouldn't jump right in with uni. Oh no. If I had, it might have been my first and last taste of sushi. I'm smitten with uni, and even I can admit how foreign and unctuous it is at first. Start with something milder, like tuna, or as the Japanese say, tekka, and explore the different varieties, like skipjack, albacore, bonito, and bluefin (maguro), which is typically fattier and richer than the others. Generally speaking, the more fat, the more flavor. That applies to cuts, not just species, of tuna. For instance, regular deep-red bluefin (maguro) is leaner, firmer, and milder than pinkish, fatty bluefin tuna (toro). Otoro is even fattier and creamier than toro, and chutoro is the fattiest, creamiest, and most expensive (and most pink) of all bluefin cuts. Now that doesn't mean chutoro is empirically the best. It's really a matter of personal taste. I'd rather eat salmon (sake), or better yet, yellowtail (hamachi) over tuna (tekka), and I like grown-up hamachi better than baby yellowtail (kanpachi). Hamachi is sweet, soft, and buttery, while kanpachi is firm and less sweet. I love both botanebi, small, sweet shrimp, and shiroebi, tiny, sweet shrimp, but I'd choose precious shiroebi first. If you're not fluent in raw fish (most people aren't), the best way to "learn the language" is by trying them for yourself.

Sushi making is serious business. Sushi chefs train for five years before they earn the title of chef, and it takes ten years to train to be a sushi master (shokunin). Have you ever heard of a burger, tamale, or pad thai master? Some sushi chefs remind me of monks whose religion is the sea. (Some masters are so meticulous that they handle the sushi rice so that all of the grains face the same direction.) Next time you go for sushi, sit at the counter so you can watch the chef at work. When Naomichi Yasuda was at Sushi Yasuda in Midtown New York, counter seats were hard to come by. Yasuda is a sushi god who creates transcendently fresh sushi. He wears an almost solemn expression, entirely preoccupied as he molds a small rectangle of warm rice, dabs it with wasabi, and places a glistening sliver of fish on top.

Every sushi chef has his own particular sushi-making style. Yasuda is not only a perfectionist but also a true traditionalist, whereas other chefs might specialize in seasonal sushi, fusion sushi, or even fast-food sushi. While some serve only fresh fish, others will use flash-frozen fish. On Union Square, 15 East specializes in fish flown in from Japan. They have four different kinds of tuna, three yellowtail, seven silverfish, three types of salmon, three eel, and a bunch of live fish, depending on what made it to the fish market that morning.

Some restaurants serve omakase, which translates as "it's up to you" but actually means just the opposite. There's only one menu at a pure omakase sushi restaurant, and it's written in the chef's head. Omakase may change nightly; the chef's whimsy and the element of surprise add to the excitement. Sushi Yasuda offers both an à la carte or an omakase menu. Some sushi restaurants are pure omakase joints, but that shouldn't scare you away. Consider it a night off from menus and decisions. Besides, this is one industry that likes a show-off. Don't you want the best a chef's got? An omakase menu is often a sign of a great sushi chef with confidence in his talents and the quality of his fish. The best omakase I ever had was in Tokyo at five in the morning, following a 4:00 A.M. viewing of the world's largest fish auction at the Tsikiji fish market. Wow, was it something to see: crates of just-caught fish, some still alive, for as far as the eye could see—octopus, shrimp, uni, mackerel, tuna, crab, eel, squid, shrimp, and plenty I couldn't identify. Afterward, as per tradition for buyers, fishermen, and visitors to the fish market, I ate sushi for breakfast at one of the stalls lining the waterfront. It doesn't get much fresher than that. I sat between two old fishermen who had been out all night on their boats. No one spoke a word of English, which was just fine, because the only word I needed to utter was: "Omakase." It was life altering.

There are omakase restaurants that serve the same dishes in the same order every night, like Sushi Sasabune and Sushi Park in Los Angeles. Sasabune and Sushi Park are hard-core. They serve one thing and one thing only: sushi. There's no miso soup or salad, or even a side of white rice. If I were you, I wouldn't make any special requests. Sushi chefs never forget a face or a request they don't want to accommodate. The chef at Sasabune, Nobi San—*san* means "chef"—is slightly flexible when it comes to dietary restrictions. He'll let you skip the scallop if you're allergic, but don't try to add or substitute something else to the omakase. A meal there always starts with albacore sashimi drizzled with a "secret sauce"—made of a blend of soy sauce, ponzu, sake, wasabi, and who knows what else—and always ends with a spicy blue-crab hand roll. Thankfully Nobi will let you order a second round of blue crab hand rolls. I ate my way through the omakase menu twice in one day.

Omakase places excepted, you can order sushi in any order you like, but there's a reason you don't eat dessert before dinner. It's hard to eat a steak after an ice cream sundae, and it works the same way with sushi. Meals often begin with something light, like miso soup, seaweed salad, or a bowl of edamame. Most menus are structured according to the traditional way the Japanese eat. They begin with sashimi, followed by some simple pieces of sushi. As the dishes progress, the sushi gets more creative and ends on a spicy note. No reason to feel rushed. In fact the best way to order is a piece or two at a time. If a sushi chef or server insists you order all at once or makes you feel rushed, you might want to rush out the door. They're missing the point.

There are a few traditions you should observe when eating sushi, though—especially if you want to get the most out of your meal. Did you know that it's proper to eat nigiri sushi with your hands? Originally, sushi was a quick, easy snack that didn't require any chopsticks at all. That's why most restaurants offer you a hot towel at the beginning of dinner. Sushi's very sensual: the chef wants you to experience the freshness of the fish and the flavor of the rice, which is why you should pick up a piece of nigiri from the bottom, so you don't touch the fish directly with your fingers and taint the flavor. Always dip the fish, not the rice, in the soy sauce. If you dunk the rice end in soy sauce, all you'll end up tasting is soy sauce and nothing else. Almost everyone I know mixes the wasabi with soy sauce, and then dips the sushi in it. (I used to.) That's not how it's supposed to work. Here's how my sushi hero, Katsu Michite, puts it: "It's like buttering bread. Spread a thin layer of wasabi over the top of the fish." I also see people put ginger on top of their sushi or in their soy sauce, another no-no. Remember, ginger's meant to cleanse your palate between different bites of fish.

In Japan, when you order a bottle of sake, you offer a glass to the chef. It's a sign of respect and gratitude for his work. Then you offer a glass to your dining companion, and he or she should reciprocate by pouring you a glass. (It's considered bad luck to pour your own.) Sake, shochu (a clear, distilled spirit made from barley, sweet potatoes, or rice, which tastes similar to whisky), or green tea all make great partners for sushi. White wine works, too, but I'd strongly recommend against red wine and fruity cocktails, which often overwhelm the delicacy of the fish.

Definitely don't try and cut a piece of nigiri sushi in half. Nigiri is a one-nibble deal. It will fall apart. A hand roll is a two- or three-bite affair. And there's no black-and-white rule for sashimi. Most sashimi should be eaten in one bite, but once in a while you'll encounter a big piece, so just cut it with your chopsticks and eat one piece at a time.

If you sit at the sushi bar, order everything directly from the sushi chef, with the exception of hot foods and drinks. The server will take care of those for you. Even if you're not seated at the sushi bar, it's a good idea to stop at the sushi bar and ask one of the chefs what's particularly fresh or what he recommends you order. He may have something that's not even on the menu but looked too good to pass up at the market that day. If you don't ask, you'll never know. And don't double dress fish. If you're not sure if it's already been dressed, it's better to ask. Sometimes the chef wants to tease more sweetness from an ingredient by using something other than soy sauce. If it's not dressed, soy sauce and wasabi are all you'll need. Try to follow the sashimi-to-plain-nigiri-to-spicy sequence as best you can. And when you leave, bow your head and say "arigato gozaimasu"—that means "thank you very much" in Japanese. (A little Japanese goes a long way.) If you're looking for bonus points or to get a little respect, graciously say, "Oishii desu ne," which in Japanese means "delicious." (It works for me.)

How do you tell a good sushi spot from a mediocre one? (Or, shudder, a bad one?) On occasion you'll have to go into a sushi situation blind. You may not know the restaurant or the chef's reputation. Look for clues: if you don't see any raw fish on the sushi counter, run. If there's no sushi counter at all, run faster. That can only mean prerolled maki and substandard fish. (Conveyor belt spots are included.) Preprepared rolls and presliced fish are both bad signs as well. Great sushi chefs serve only the freshest fish and rice. They don't remove the rice from the steamer until they're ready to mold you a piece. The rice plays sideman to the fish, but it's a key player nonetheless. It should be warm, slightly sweet, tart, and sticky, but not too sticky. It should never overwhelm the fish or dominate the flavor. Great sushi chefs don't slice their fish until they've got someone to serve it to. Masaharu Morimoto has spent a considerable amount of time behind the sushi counter, so he knows firsthand when to flee. His advice: "Go to popular restaurants because the turnover rate of fish is very good." Crowds are a sign that the fish hasn't been sitting around waiting for an audience. "And make sure the chef's wearing a clean coat and the counter's sanitary," Morimoto adds. Morimoto also judges a sushi spot by its tamago (egg) and marinated fish dishes. "Be careful, since there are two kinds of recommendations: one is what the chef wants to sell because it will go bad soon; the other is what the chef really thinks is good." How do you tell the difference? Look at the chef's coat, counter, and try their tamago.

There are a few other clues you should look for to assess the merits of a sushi restaurant. Read the menu. If it's generic, the food will taste generic. If it's limited to a few basic fish like tuna and salmon, it's going to be mediocre at best. A good sushi restaurant doesn't rush its guests or insist they order all at once. (And remember—they don't rush you, so don't rush them. There are a lot more people working in a typical kitchen than behind a sushi bar. Sometimes there's only one sushi chef to make everyone's sushi. Have some edamame and a little patience.) If you have to stay for dinner at a mediocre sushi place, don't order dangerously. Skip the raw scallops, shrimp, uni, and spicy rolls. Spicy sauces often disguise spoiled or less-than-fresh fish. Stick to cooked foods and Americanized rolls. And I don't say that often!

## Inakaya and Yakitori

It doesn't matter what country you're from: after a long day at work, sometimes you just need to unwind over a drink and a bite to eat. Nothing too complicated or expensive. Americans have neighborhood bars; the Italians have inotecas; and the Japanese have inakayas and yakitori joints. An inakaya is a pub as seen through Japanese eyes. They serve spirits and small plates, but nothing too involved or time-consuming. Expect to find tra-

ditional offerings like edamame, tempura, grated yam, and look
for hiyayakko—a cold block of fresh tofu crowned with ginger,
soy sauce, and onions—a signature dish on many inakaya menus.

A yakitori restaurant is like a combination pub and barbecue
joint. In Japanese, *yakitori* means "grilled bird." Just like Americans, the Japanese like to snack on chicken wings as they drink
beer. Difference is, "grilled bird" ain't just wings—it's the whole,
and I mean whole, chicken. Some people think of Japanese culture as slightly timid. The fearlessness of Japanese foodways highlights perfectly how wrong this stereotype is. Chicken livers, tail,
gizzards, skin, knee bones, and necks are yakitori delicacies, listed
under categories like "Chicken Limited," which usually sell out
before the evening rush. I'm blessed with the good fortune of living near Yakitori Totto, a second-floor yakitori bar in Midtown
Manhattan frequented by Japanese expats, foodies, and lots of big
name chefs like Anthony Bourdain and Eric Ripert. Even I have a
hard time swallowing the idea of knee bones, but hearts aren't bad
at all. They're actually pretty tasty, a little like liver, only smoother
and richer.

But you don't have to be a daredevil to go for yakitori. Actually, most of the menu's quite tame, composed of familiar dishes
with a twist—chicken thigh with scallions, chicken-wrapped asparagus, or chicken coated in miso paste. Everyone should try
yakitori-style chicken meatballs (tsukune) once in their lifetime.
Personally, I try to have some at least once a month. Well-made
tsukune will erase the memory of any bad day. At Aburiya Kin-
nosuke, a sibling of Yakitori Totto, they make magnificently
moist, baseball-size tsukune accompanied by a raw egg dipping
sauce. You can get them plain or shellacked in a sweet soy sauce;
either style is divine. Tsukune are a great litmus test of any yakitori restaurant. Like any meatballs, they should be moist, juicy,
and flavorful. If they're dry, overcooked, or bland, you're in a
subpar yakitori joint.

Yakitori spots don't serve exclusively chicken. The kitchen will likely grill and skewer everything from skirt steak (harami) to Berkshire pork (kura buta) to seafood and vegetables. Unless the menu says otherwise, you'll have your choice of two seasonings: salt and lemon, or tare (a sweet mirin-soy sauce). There's no small print on a yakitori menu. If it says chicken heart (hatsu), it's a chicken heart. If it says pork with mustard and lemon, that's what you're getting. It's amazing how a little lemon can perk up pork. When I now get stuck with a bland piece of pork, I ask for a wedge of lemon for my water, wait until no one's looking, and squeeze.

Going for yakitori is like going to a bar with good food. Most yakitori restaurants are on the smaller side, with wood accents, dim lighting, and lots of smoky haze from the charcoal grill. The menu's traditionally organized according to meat, seafood, poultry, and vegetables. I recommend you try things you can't get at other restaurants, like okra or shisito peppers—blistery green peppers with a mild flavor and delicate skin. (I order shisito every time I go for yakitori.) Like any other bar in the world, yakitori joints aren't big on dessert. They usually offer a few obligatory sweets, like green tea or red bean ice cream, or some sort of jelly or tofu pudding.

## Robatayaki

There's two kinds of Japanese grill cooking: yakitori and robatayaki. Robatayaki are bigger, louder, and generally more entertaining than yakitori joints. If you're ever feeling rejected or neglected, go for dinner at a robata grill (robatayaki). Walk through the door, and you're suddenly the star of the show. The staff simultaneously stops whatever they're doing to bow and greet you with an unusually enthusiastic "Irrashaimase!" You're whisked to a seat at the robata counter, a little like eating dinner around a gigantic campfire. Robata—which translates to "around the fireplace"—is rustic, country-style Japanese cooking. Guests gather around the counter to watch the chefs work the charcoal grill and to ogle the different cuts of meat, glimmering seafood, and elegant and unusual vegetables displayed on ice along the counter.

If you're in the mood for peace and quiet, eat elsewhere. But if you're in the mood for an interactive meal where the food's actually good—no offense to Medieval Times—this is your place. But just because the staff shouts doesn't mean you should shout your order back at them. And don't be a curmudgeon. If everyone's clapping or chanting, join in. The ceremony and celebration is half the fun of robata dining. Order a beer or sake or even a glass of water and the entire staff shouts your order. Order a Sapporo and your kimono-clad chef serves it to you with a long wooden paddle that looks more like a prop than a serving utensil. There's lot of intermissions throughout dinner for birthdays (everyone cheers and snaps photos as if they're tourists, even the Japanese diners), good luck, and sometimes, if you're lucky, a mochi-pounding ceremony. Mochi is a soft, chewy rice flour dough that has a subtly sweet flavor; it's eaten as small cakes, stuffed sweet dumplings, and even wrapped around ice cream. Whatever form you find it in, eat it: just-pounded mochi is heavenly.

Menus at robata grills are often lengthy but super straightforward: everything prepared over the robata grill is broken down into meat, poultry, vegetables, and seafood. Typically, there's a separate section for dried fish, sushi, noodles, and appetizers. Chicken, pork, and beef are sliced, but seafood is cooked and served whole. Some fish is served with sea salt, some with miso paste, so ask your server for specifics. Wagyu, a highly prized beef, is typically served with wasabi and a sweet dipping sauce, and it's an excellent way to experience this tender, marbled meat.

## Hibachi and Teppanyaki

Robata isn't the only kind of Japanese dinner theater. If you've ever been to Benihana, you've experienced hibachi dinner theater. Or a caricature of it anyway. At a hibachi restaurant, the chef cooks your food on a griddle built into your table. Everything's diced, grilled, and sauced right in front of you. The soy-sauce-flipping and knife-juggling are all part of the show. Expect to sit with strangers and leave smelling like whatever you ordered.

Teppanyaki is a branch of hibachi devoted solely to steak, and where steak is concerned, the Japanese mean business. If you've tasted wagyu, you understand. Wagyu beef—often called "the caviar of beef"—comes from black-haired Japanese cattle and is prized for its intensely marbled meat. The result is a spoon-tender texture and buttery, unbeefy flavor. Kobe beef is the king of all Wagyu, raised exclusively in or around Kobe, Japan. If it's not from Kobe, it's not really Kobe. Real deal Kobe cattle receive the royal treatment: massages, sake, and beer feedings. Take a bite and you'll detect sweet and nutty undertones that come from the particular grasses and grains the cattle have been fed. In America we eat mostly American-bred Wagyu and indulge in Kobe if we're splurging.

## Shabu-shabu and Sukiyaki

If you think you can do better than the chef, you can cook your food yourself at your table. There are two types of DIY table cooking: shabu-shabu and sukiyaki. At a shabu-shabu restaurant, you cook raw pieces of sliced beef (and sometimes pork, chicken, or seafood) by dunking them in a pot of simmering dashi broth. We all have hobbies. Some people like to knit, and others, namely me, like to go for shabu-shabu (so named for the sound your food makes as you swish it in the broth). There's something very calming about cooking your own food at the dinner table instead of standing in the kitchen. Meat usually takes a while to cook, but shabu-shabu is crazy quick cooking. I like my beef rare, so I swish it in the bubbling liquid for just a few seconds, but even well-done meat typically takes less than a minute. When it's done cooking, you dip your beef into a sesame sauce or a sweet, citrus-based soy sauce. (I'd go just for the dipping sauces.) All of the shabu-shabu spots I've visited give you an assortment of vegetables and noodles with your meat to cook yourself as well. Instead of swishing your vegetables, you can drop them in the broth for a few minutes, since they take longer to cook. Sukiyaki is less about swishing and more about simmering sliced beef in a salty-sweet sauce made with dashi, mirin, and soy sauce. Beef is the only option, and sukiyaki dipping sauce is raw egg. For me, sukiyaki is about experiencing the sensation of hot beef shavings coated in cool egg.

## Noodle Shops

There I was, lost in a bowl of warm soba noodles at a little place called Soba-ya in the East Village, when I suddenly felt everyone's angry eyes on me—hungry workers on their lunch break waiting for their turn. Oops. Lesson number one: never linger at the noodle counter. See a counter, sit, slurp, and skedaddle. I'm a lingerer. I like long, drawn-out meals. I give food my undivided attention, which is why I had no idea everyone around me had eaten, paid, and left long before me. Noodle counters are the Japanese answer to McDonald's, Subway, or the corner pizza joint.

Japanese noodles come in lots of sizes and styles: smooth, medium, coarse, some hot, some cold, bathing in a dozen different broths, each one a world in itself. Imagine you're peering down at what looks like a glossy spool of yarn unraveling in a bowl. In its midst, an uncooked egg, scallion, sliced cucumber, nori, smoky bonito—an utterly unarchitectural compilation. And when you stir it with your chopsticks—piercing the egg yolk—

suddenly you find yourself staring into a swirling galaxy of soba. It looks like a warm dish, and yet it's surprisingly cold, which is strange, because you knew it was cold when you ordered it. There are so many flavors, and the cold keeps each one distinct. Soba's just one of Japan's glorious noodle dishes. There are four kinds of noodles to know—soba, somen, udon, and ramen—and none of them taste anything like Italian pasta. Especially soba, which is a delicate, earthy noodle made

> • TASTY MORSEL •
>
> *Hot soba noodles call for slurping, because they begin to lose their distinct texture as soon as they make contact with hot liquid. Texture is half the pleasure of soba, so start slurping as soon as the bowl hits the table!*

from buckwheat. There are three types of soba noodles: smooth (seiro), coarse (inaka), and delicate (rino). Somen is a thin, delicate wheat noodle, udon is a thick, white wheat noodle, and ramen are squiggly egg noodles.

The Japanese adapted ramen from the Chinese, but as Masaharu Morimoto points out: "Japanese ramen is totally different than ramen served in China. The Japanese have developed many different types of ramen noodles and soup stocks. The Japanese ramen is still evolving every day, so I like people to try different kinds and discover what they like." There are four different traditional ramen broths: there's a dark, rich soy sauce–based broth known as shoyu ramen; a light, salty shio ramen broth; and a thick, sweet miso broth. Tonkatsu ramen is made with a savory pork broth. There's fast-food ramen and fresh, homemade exceptions like the kind served at Ippudo, a Japanese chain with a New York outpost, where you can watch the noodle maker at work from the storefront window. The best ramen at Ippudo comes with Berkshire pork, scallions, sesame, ginger, and half of a hard-boiled egg. It's so good you'll want to dunk your head in the broth and go fishing for the pork with your tongue.

Asian cultures eat their noodles hot (kake) or cold (zaru), depending on the season and the noodle. In summer the Japanese usually eat cold noodles, in winter warm noodles, but both are tasty year-round. (Ramen is rarely served cold.) The seasonings often come on the side—dipping sauce and simple condiments, like green onions, wasabi, bonito flakes, and sesame seeds. There are noodle salads, too. Instead of a lettuce base, you get cold soba or udon typically topped with shrimp, tempura, tofu, duck, or chicken. On a hot summer day, a cold soba salad topped with shrimp is a refreshing, yet perfectly filling, lunch. Hot noodle dishes are served in big lacquered bowls with soothing, subtle broths—often made from a curry, pork, miso, or salt base—flavored with dashi (a soup stock made from bonito flakes) or mirin (a sweet white vinegar). There's no formula for what you'll find in the bowl. Vegetables depend on the season, and seafood depends on the market. More often than not, you'll find shrimp tempura, tofu, roast pork, or naruto floating in your bowl. Naruto looks like candy but tastes nothing like it. It's a spongy, salty fish cake that brilliantly soaks up whatever broth it's bobbing in.

## Kaiseki

I think it was the words "traditional, multicourse meal" that threw me, but I assumed "kaiseki" was Japanese for an haute tasting menu. Sometimes it is, but more often, it's just the opposite: kaiseki meals are modeled on the way the Japanese eat at home. At a kaiseki meal, diners get something pickled, something raw, something steamed, simmered, grilled, and fried . . . and, of course, a bowl of rice. Kaiseki traditionally ends with a sweet bean cake and green tea. The chef's muse is always the season.

Some chefs keep kaiseki simple, while more ambitious chefs up the ante of the ingredients and the dishes. I dragged a carnivore friend to an ambitious kaiseki restaurant called Kajitsu in the East Village. You should've seen his face when he opened the menu to find: "clear consommé with turnip, bamboo rice, roasted artichoke with diced apple, celery root and soy gelee." I had no idea that vegetarian kaiseki (shojin) even existed. But it has a long history in Japan, beginning with Buddhist monks, who celebrate the end of a fast with a tea ceremony and vegetarian kaiseki. "You're taking me for a burger after this," my friend mumbled under his breath as we surveyed our options. I was nervous: I was sitting across the table from a hungry carnivore with six meat-free courses ahead of him. But he ate his words. Dish after dish was arresting—yam dotted with a cauliflower puree, bamboo-leaf-wrapped sushi, and a phenomenal cherry blossom cake. In keeping with tradition, the chef, Masato Nishihara, prepared something pickled, something simmered . . . and, of course, a bowl of perfectly molded white rice. There were seven seasonal sakes and four kinds of tea on the menu, all served in one-of-a-kind handmade glasses that were over two hundred years old.

The ceremony and experience of kaiseki—the thought that has gone into the design of the meal—is just as important as the food itself. "Don't ask to change the order of courses because it will disrupt the flow, an important element in kaiseki," chef Nishihara says. And don't assume all the ornaments are edible. Some aren't. (Learned that one the hard way.) Nishihara studied kaiseki in Japan for years before opening a vegetarian kaiseki spot in the East Village. He also studied flower arrangement, which is a requirement for kaiseki chefs. Yes, really. If you want to get in good with the chef, admire the flowers and look at the back of your dish after you've cleaned your plate. Kaiseki restaurants pride themselves on the quality and history of the tableware as well.

## Wagashi: Japanese Confections

Unlike the majority of other Asian cultures, the Japanese are quite fond of desserts and confections. They crave many of the same sweets Americans do: cookies, cake, chocolate, pudding, and ice cream. But the ingredients they use are dramatically different and considerably less sweet. For instance, we eat chocolate pudding. They eat black sesame pudding. We like rocky road ice cream. They prefer green tea ice cream. Green tea (matcha) is as prominent in Japanese desserts as chocolate is in American desserts. I've seen green tea mousse, rice cakes, cake, cookies, truffles, and sauce. Yakitori Totto serves a wonderful green tea pudding with adzuki beans.

Buddhist monks first started drinking green tea in religious rituals in the mid-eighth century. Japanese confections (wagashi) were created to complement, not overpower, the character of green tea. That's why wagashi are made with subtle, earthy ingredients, like pumpkin, chestnuts, and cherry blossoms. An overly sweet wagashi that camouflages the tea is a contradiction in terms. It rarely, if ever, happens. The ideal complement for a cup of green tea is green tea wagashi, but adzuki (red bean) confections with sweet and earthy undertones pair well, too. There are red-bean-filled rice cakes, jellies, pancakes, and even red bean soup for dessert.

Wagashi are made with rice flour and sugar, not milk or butter, so they tend to be light. Instead of milk, soy milk and tofu provide the silky texture in parfaits and puddings. It's the confectioner's duty to create a perfect balance between beauty, aroma, texture, and taste. Mousses and puddings are super silky, candy super sticky, and Jell-O jiggly. Chewiness, as in jellies or mochi, is highly prized. The secret to Japanese jellies is agar-agar, red algae that adds gelatinous texture to desserts. Traditional jellies (yokan) are made with bean pastes, but I've sampled a sour plum (ume) jelly with whole sour plums inside and gold leaf sprinkles. Japanese Jell-O is for grown-ups. Instead of strawberry or lemon, there's red bean, green tea, or my pick, plum wine Jell-O.

Hands down, no one makes prettier confections than the Japanese. The first time I passed a wagashi shop in Japan, I did a triple take: for a second I thought I was looking at candy-shaped jewelry in the storefront window, which was lined with hundreds of stunning, edible works of art. I didn't want to leave them behind. I even dumped some clothes out of my suitcase to make room for wagashi. I had no idea there was a wagashi paradise called Minamoto Kitchoan right off of Fifth Avenue. I do drive-bys on a regular basis, so I know that (sakura) cherry blossoms are starting to bloom in Japan when Minamoto begins displaying sakura mochi and sakuranbo jellies. They have a great selection of tsuya—pancake sandwiches with sweet paste fillings, sort of like crepes— and daifuku (bean-paste-filled mochi cakes) made with red beans, chestnuts, and green tea.

## Table Setting and Modern Manners

Did you know the biggest sin you can commit in a Japanese restaurant is leaving your chopsticks upright in a bowl of rice? It sounds harmless, but upright chopsticks resemble the incense sticks lit by the Japanese to commemorate deceased relatives. I've seen three servers simultaneously drop their mouths open and dart across the room to remove the dish from the dining room. They don't teach you that stuff in high school. They should. (I don't know the last time I had to remember that E = MC$^2$, but I dine at Asian restaurants often.) Speaking of which, passing food with your chopsticks is another no-no. Don't suck on your chopsticks or toss them on the table between courses. That's what chopstick holders are for. The pointy end that goes in your mouth rests on the holder. If there's no holder, you can lay them across your plate until the next dish arrives. Do feel free to slurp your noodles and drink your miso soup straight from the bowl! Itadakimasu!

# Reading into Dinner: On Dating and Dining Out

**T**echnically you can live without love, but no one can live without food. Have you ever had mind-blowing uni or a warm chocolate souffle? In my opinion, they both trump love any day. Sharing food with people is just as intimate as, and perhaps even more revealing than, sleeping with them. I never have sex with someone without having had dinner with him first. One, I don't want go to bed hungry. Two, I want to watch him eat.

You can learn a lot about people at the table. Do they share? If they don't, chances are that they hog the covers. Do they order the safest thing on the menu? I bet they also play it safe in bed. Do they wait to hear what you're ordering, then order the exact same thing? No self-confidence. Do they always order the chicken? Close-minded. (It's a fun game to play on a bad date.)

Never mind tea leaves; you can read people by what they order and how they eat it. My sister has portion control down to a science. She's type A. Me, I have no control whatsoever even after I'm full. I'm a glutton and a danger to myself. My brother goes to extremes. He eats very healthfully for the majority of the week, then devours an extra-large tub of popcorn in the movie theater without thinking twice about it. He's the work hard/play hard type. I have a friend who always overorders. She can't make a decision to save her life.

If you're looking for someone who shares, just ask them, "Do you want to share a few dishes?" For me, sharing isn't negotiable. Anyone who says he's going to go off on his own and get the Caesar salad and a steak is a goner. (Oh, and if they don't share soup, they won't share a toothbrush.) You can also tell what people's priorities are by how they order. I love garlic. I'd much rather forgo a kiss good night than just one clove (or an entire head!) of roasted garlic. But I routinely see people choose the possibility of a kiss over the certainty of garlic. I always tell them to get the garlic. It's a sure thing. And if both people eat garlic—even better.

How a person orders his steak is practically a window to his soul. I should know: I stopped eating meat in sixth grade up through the end of high school. I was a nervous child, scared of everything, including sleepovers and field trips. I didn't suck the marrow from life figuratively or literally. Luckily it was just a phase. I'm now a full-fledged carnivore. I'll eat anything. The way you like your steak speaks volumes about your personality. For instance a man or woman who orders a steak black and blue is audacious to a fault. I dated a guy who ordered his steak bloody. He also drove a motorcycle and had a prison record and probably a few illegitimate children. He was a pleasure seeker, first and foremost, and he didn't stick around for long. Then there's the type who likes her steak rare. With a partner like that, you'll have a wonderful, adventurous life filled with discovery. My ideal man likes his steak medium rare. He's fun loving and takes chances, but he's not out of his mind. If your date orders steak medium, you'll have a comfortable, predictable life together. (Not that there's anything wrong with that.) Well done? He might as well order chicken, and you might as well ask for the check, unless you want to sign up for a lifetime of chicken and overcooked steak. That's just my personal preference. You may both like your steak medium. (Not that there's anything wrong with that either.) It doesn't mean you're necessarily soul mates, but you already have something in common. If you both like yours black and blue, not only can you share a steak, but you also might share an adventurous life together. It's not just about what someone orders but about how he interacts with the maître d', the server, or the busboy. Does she answer her cell phone at the table or check her e-mails? Does he snap his fingers to get the server's attention or order before you? Does he wait until you're both served to start eating? Is she more concerned with the decor than with the food? She's partial to atmosphere. If you are, too, you could be a match.

I also apply the same philosophy to friends, coworkers, family members, and strangers. You can tell a lot about people by eating with them or even sitting next to them at a counter. You may end up in bed together, engaged, or negotiating for elbow space. I love my sister, and we spend lots of time together, but we don't play well together at the dinner table. She won't touch pork or consider quail or sweetbreads, and foie gras and rabbit are completely out of the question. It's like eating with some sort of culinary monk. I often wonder whether we're related. She doesn't like to negotiate. She knows what she wants, and she couldn't care less if there are two of the same dish at a table. "What a tragedy," I think to myself. "We could've tasted two different dishes."

When I'm on a review, I have veto power, and I love every minute of it. I can shake my head and put the kibosh on a poor order, but not in a social situation and definitely not with my sister. On a review I can subtly suggest my date order something more creative than a green salad or steamed spinach. I can demand we take risks and order the candy-coated pork chop. Why order it at all? Because it could've been wonderful. Sure, it turned out to be a disaster of a dish, but I still ventured into the unknown, and that's the thrilling part of the experience of dining out.

I'm not proposing you order my way or try things that terrify you. I'm suggesting you observe how and what others eat. You know those couples who eat in total silence, barely acknowledging each other's presence even though they're sitting at the same table? It's depressing. You can't control what you'll have to talk about in fifty years, but you can control what you have in common at the table. When all else fails, we can share the pleasure of food. We can share the sheer satisfaction of perfect pad thai, crispy French-style French fries dipped in aioli, or sublimely fresh sushi.

We all go our separate ways during the day. Some of us head off to work, others to school, but we all reunite at the dinner table at the end of the day. It's where we relax and spend time with people we actually like. Eating together is an intimate ritual that's universal across cultures. Almost every culture has dishes that are meant for sharing. That's what I love so much about Korean food: very few dishes are designed for individual consumption. Hog a dish and you'll get dirty looks or be poked with an angry chopstick. Go for Korean barbecue and you'll eat off a communal grill built right into the center of your table.

When you eat with other people, you don't just learn to share. You also learn how to behave generously, and how other people and other cultures move through the world. The first time I went for Korean food I thought half the guests had the flu. Turns out they were being respectful of their elders. When in their presence, they cover their mouths when they drink soju or beer (traditional Korean spirits). In Italy, children drink with adults long before the legal drinking age. In America you'll see underaged children beg their parents for a glass of wine or a sip of a cocktail, then get denied.

We may speak in different tongues, but we all use our tongues to eat. You don't have to speak Vietnamese to try pho for the first time. All you need is an open mind and an empty stomach. It's the same with love. You can't really fall in love unless you take risks and explore the unknown. So put yourself in the hands of the chef. If you see or smell something you like, order it. Or just close your eyes and point at something and see what arrives. It's like falling in love, except you don't have to give your heart away.

# · 9 ·
# Korean Cuisine

*Eating is heaven.*

KOREAN PROVERB

I t was a hundred degrees outside and I had the flu. I was living alone in Los Angeles, and all I wanted was to be back in my own bed in New York. I was miserable. I'd been holed up in my sublet, subsisting on a diet of chicken soup, pickles, and ginger ale, when a friend stopped by to convince me that all I needed to get better was some samgyetang, Korean-style chicken soup. I'm all about trying new things, but not when I'm running a fever. But my friend insisted, and I didn't have the strength to fight him. Or to change out of my pajamas, for that matter. So I went with him to Keungama, a restaurant in L.A.'s Koreatown. We might as well as have hopped a plane to Seoul. The only Koreatown I was familiar with, in New York, is just a block or so long—Thirty-second Street between Fifth and Sixth avenues in Midtown. But Los Angeles's K-Town (as the Angelenos call it) occupies a substantial part of the city, about three square miles of it, in fact. All the street signs there are written in Korean as well as English, and Korean barbecue joints, supermarkets, saunas, and karaoke halls line the streets.

"There's Keungama," he said as he pointed to the entrance, then pulled around back into a parking lot. Instead of heading to the front of the building, he started walking toward what seemed to be the service entrance. Keep in mind I was running a fever, so I wasn't really up for adventure. Unfortunately I had no choice but to follow him as he disappeared inside, so I trailed in after him, pajamas and all. "Why are we going in this way?" I whispered. "Everyone uses the back door. It's the scenic route," he responded. "And I want you to see their soups," he said, pointing to a series of huge black iron kettles that reminded me of witches' cauldrons in fairy tales, bubbling with mysterious liquids. The aromas emanating from the kettles were incredibly rich, spicy, and meaty.

We made our way to the front of the sparsely decorated dining room and were seated at the last available table. It was only six-thirty in the evening and the place was already packed, mostly with people speaking Korean. My friend ordered me the samgyetang. "I'm not in the mood to experiment," I moaned. "It's just chicken soup, only better for you," he assured me. He ordered himself gorigam tang, oxtail soup, and yakbap ("medicinal rice"), a sweet, glutinous rice dish studded with dates, chestnuts, and beans. The samgyetang looked and smelled like no chicken soup I'd ever seen. The milky, foamy broth was seasoned with generous doses of garlic, ginger, and ginseng. I don't know if you've ever smelled ginseng, but it's not the slightest bit subtle— simultaneously zesty, sweet, and funky. When I dipped below the surface with my spoon, I discovered a small, boiled chicken—the whole damn bird—stuffed with rice, dried jujubes, and fresh slivers of ginseng. In Korea, they say: "Food is medicine." Samgyetang, dosed as it is with all that ginger, garlic, and ginseng, is supposed to have tremendous healing properties. I felt like I was having dinner at an herbalist's. Now, I can't be certain whether it was the change in scenery or the soup, but I felt better the next day, so I'm a believer.

But before the samgyetang arrived, and seemingly only seconds after we placed our order, our server reappeared with a plate piled with cabbage leaves in a powerful-smelling red sauce, and a pair of scissors. "I think I'm hallucinating," I uttered nervously. "It's a fermented cabbage dish called kimchi," my friend said as I stared down at the plate. "It's a Korean staple that's served at every meal." "Uh-huh. Why are there scissors on the table?" I asked nervously. "Most restaurants cut it up for you in the kitchen, but they let you cut it up yourself here. It's more fun," he said excitedly as he picked up the scissors and cut up our cabbage. I rolled my eyes; then I took a bite of the crisp leaves, slathered in an aggressive blend of garlic, ginger, red chile peppers, and fish sauce. Suddenly, I could smell again. The aroma was pungent enough to clear my stuffed-up sinuses, and the taste was salty, spicy, bitter, and oddly pleasing.

Kimchi is probably the single most common kind of banchan (pronounced panchan), the side dishes that accompany all Korean meals. Kimchi is a variant on pickled vegetables, minus the vinegar or brine. Instead the vegetables in kimchi have been fermented and mixed with ginger, garlic, chiles or chile paste, and scallions. There are many different versions of kimchi, some made with cucumbers, some with radishes or eggplant, and depending on the region, a host of other vegetables. But the most common kind of kimchi is made with Napa cabbage. Our meal came with two kinds—one cabbage and one radish kimchi. Both were spicy, crunchy, and cool complements to the hot soups. Korean cuisine adheres to the precepts of the yin-yang philosophy, balancing hot dishes with cold ones, spicy with sour or sweet. If you want to dine by the Korean philosophy of balance, you might follow a savory spoonful of oxtail soup with a light, crunchy banchan, like seasoned sprouts (kong-namul).

Banchan are essential for achieving that culinary balance. That means lots of little bowls packed with big flavors, compliments of the house. Meals typically come with anywhere from two to twelve banchan; the more banchan, the more formal the meal. (In my opinion, the more banchan, the better.) There are over 150 kinds of banchan—hot and cold, spicy and sour, creamy and acidic—all meant to be shared. Besides kimchi, you might find namul—steamed, marinated, or stir-fried vegetables—like bean sprouts (kongnamul); sesame-seed-spackled spinach in soy sauce (sigeumchi namul); and seaweed (miyeok muchim) seasoned with a feisty blend of sesame oil, soy sauce, vinegar, garlic, and hot, dried chile peppers.

There's a whole category of banchan, called boekkum, devoted to chile-pepper-spiced, stir-fried affairs, and another, jjim, devoted to steamed or boiled foods, such as steamed tofu (dubujjim). One of my favorite kinds of banchan is jeon, lacy, panfried pancakes, flavored with everything from kimchi to ground

• TASTY MORSEL •

*The Korean government named kimchi a national treasure. It's rich in vitamins A, B, C, calcium, and iron. There's even a Kimchi Field Museum in Seoul, where visitors can try two different types of kimchi every month in a special tasting room, or observe under microscopes the lactobacillus bacteria that is crucial to the fermentation process.*

meat. I'm just as crazy about the tangy dipping sauce that accompanies them—a blend of vinegar and soy sauce—as I am about the crispy-edged pancakes themselves. Pajeon are scallion pancakes, ·and haemul pajeon are seafood scallion pancakes, typically laced with baby shrimp, oysters, and octopus. Some jeon are made with egg batter, which imbues them with a sweet, soft omeletlike quality. There's even a banchan of fluffy, American-style potato salad with mayonnaise (really!), except the Korean version often includes chopped vegetables, fruit, or ham. Let me tell you, diced apples, cucumber, or ham does wonders for ordinary potato salad.

Walk into any Korean restaurant and you'll look out onto a sea of bowls scattered over the tabletops, not just banchan, but also steaming hot stews, casseroles, noodles, rice dishes, and porridges. I always thought of porridge as bland boiled oats (this was before I had tasted Chinese congee) until I tried the Korean version (juk), studded with pine nuts, sticky rice dumplings, and chunks of seafood, like tuna, shrimp, or abalone. Juk (also spelled jook) is made with boiled rice; it's just as comforting as porridge but much more interesting. There are several variations of juk, including octopus and kimchi juk, mung bean juk, or chicken juk. The most popular is jeonbokjuk, abalone porridge, laced with briny bits of abalone, dried seaweed, and sesame oil, and often served with a raw egg that you mix into the warm, soothing porridge yourself. There are sweet juks, too, like black sesame and red bean, but none of them hold a candle to pumpkin juk. If you like pumpkin, you will likely lose yourself in a big bowl of exceptionally soft porridge, sweetened with pumpkin and riddled with chewy nibbles of sticky rice. (I do.) You can eat porridge for dinner and stew for breakfast at a Korean restaurant.

Most Korean food is intensely comforting. Soups and stews are an integral part of every meal, including breakfast. Open a menu and you'll encounter a rich, spicy bounty of soups (gook, also spelled guk, and tang) and stews (jigae), scattered with kimchi, clams, beef short ribs, and lots more. Koreans have a very different concept of soups and stews than many cultures. For instance, I ordered a soup and it arrived with the entrées, not before it. Soup is served not as an appetizer but as part of the main meal accompanied by an array of banchan. I ordered a stew (jigae), and it came in a large (and very heavy) black stone pot (dolsot), which keeps it hot at the table. (The stone pot is just as hot as the stew inside it, so I wouldn't recommend touching it with your fingers.) Unlike traditional stews that simmer for long hours on end, Korean stews cook for short periods of time, and often finish cooking at your table. Korean stews and soups share many of the same broths and ingredients. For instance, I've eaten spicy kimchi soup (guk) and spicy kimchi stew (jigae), and as far as I can tell, the biggest difference was the amount of ingredients and liquid in the bowl. Soups have fewer ingredients and more liquid than stews. If you want more to chew on, you're better off with a hearty jigae. There are two types of soups: gook and tang. Tang is less watery and more stewlike than gook. While soups are served in individual soup bowls (not for sharing), stews are communal property. It's a double-edged sword: you have to share *your* stew, but you also get to sample everyone else's stew, too. Both soups and stews traditionally come with a bowl of white rice, though the rice doesn't stay on the side for very long. You add the rice to the soup, or mix a few spoonfuls of stew with a few spoonfuls of rice. Restaurants often serve a raw egg on the side, too. Your job is to crack it open into the pot and mix it into the broth. It's a foolproof way to make any soup or stew thicker and creamier. Or, if you prefer, you can add the raw egg to the rice instead. The combination of cold, raw egg and warm, glutinous rice is incredibly comforting. (I highly recommend it.)

One of my favorite "egg-dropped" stews is dubu jigae, firm tofu stew, or even better, soondubu jigae, silken tofu stew. Homemade silken tofu (soondubu) is as silky and creamy as custard; it's the kind of food that makes your heart skip a beat as it touches your tongue. If you think tofu's boring, you'll likely change your mind after eating delicate soondubu in a plenty spicy and sour broth, made with anchovies, sesame oil, garlic, and hot red pepper (gochujang). What I love about Korean heat is the way it ignites all the other flavors in a dish. In this case, the hot pepper awakens the sweet, sour, bitter, and briny undertones of everything around it. If you happen to get a craving for soondubu jigae at four in the morning, head to the nearest BCD Tofu House. They make their organic tofu in-house, and they're open twenty-four hours a day. BCD Tofu House is a popular L.A.-based Korean chain with outposts all over the world, including Japan, Seattle, and New York. The menu features traditional dishes, like bibimbap, galbi, and barbecue ribs, but the best thing on the menu is definitely the soondubu jigae, with your choice of "not spicy," "spicy," or "very spicy" broth. Though its name means "tofu stew," it doesn't mean there's no meat or fish in the mix. (If you're a vegetarian, you might want to ask your server what's meat-free.) Like most Korean restaurants, BCD offers a choice of beef, pork, or seafood.

Just beneath the surface of Korean soups and stews are oodles of hidden pleasures to pluck out with your chopsticks. Besides meat and fish, I've discovered rice cakes, noodles, mushrooms, green onion, and other vegetables. I found oysters and bean curd in my kimchi jigae one evening, and pork, cabbage, and rice cakes another night. Kimchi jigae gets its name from the fermented cabbage and its vibrant, red broth from a spicy-sweet, deep red pepper paste (gochujang). Gochujang (also spelled kochujang) is one-third of the holy trinity of Korean seasonings. The other two are soy sauce (ganjang), made from fermented soybeans, and thick, fermented soybean paste (doenjang). This trinity of seasonings is the backbone of the Korean kitchen, including its stews. There are clear, rich broths flavored with soy sauce; spicy brick-colored broths flavored with red pepper paste; and tangy, sour broths flavored with fermented soybean paste. Just like kimchi, the soybeans are fermented in gobs of garlic, ginger, and red chile peppers. Doenjang jigae, soybean paste stew, tastes distinctly and deliciously sour, bitter, and tangy. And ssamjang is a popular condiment made of a blend of doenjang and kochujang, served with grilled or stir-fried meats.

If you want more to chew on, you might prefer to order a jeongol, or casserole. Jeongol are typically less brothy than stews. While the focus of a soybean paste stew (doenjang jigae) is the soybean paste, the focus of a soybean paste casserole (doenjang jeongol) is everything else in it. Jeongol (also spelled jungol) highlight several main ingredients in one dish, like noodles, mushrooms, sliced beef, and seafood. Casseroles are served in flat-bottomed pans over a hot flame right at the table. Order a jeongol, or any other hot pot, and they bring the kitchen to you. A hot pot—anything boiled or simmered over a flame at the table—is one of the hallmarks of Korean cooking. (I always want to curl up with a hearty hot pot in winter and hibernate until spring arrives.) Jeongol were originally eaten by royalty, so you can expect to find a feast in the pan. There's a place called Kum Gang San in New York's Koreatown (with a second outpost in Queens) that serves a killer seafood jeongol, flush with lobster, clams, shrimp, and octopus in a bubbling, spicy beef broth. There's even dumpling casseroles (mandu jeongol) with mandu stuffed with ground meat and vegetables. Instead of boiling the mandu in water, they're boiled in a rich beef broth, so the savory liquid infiltrates the dumplings, further intensifying the flavor. You can also order these delicate dumplings minus the casserole, boiled (mulmandu), steamed (jjinmandu), or grilled or fried (gunmandu).

Like most Asian cultures, Koreans also embrace a legion of noodles. There are thin and thick noodles, buckwheat noodles, wheat and white flour noodles, stir-fried and boiled noodles, warm and cold noodles. The most common are clear cellophane noodles (jap-chae), made from sweet potato starch, seasoned and served cold as a banchan. I'm always surprised how much flavor you can cram into a little bowl of cold jap-chae noodles. There's regular wheat noodles (guksu) and extra-special galkusu, knife-cut noodle soup in which the noodles are cut by hand into fettuci-nelike ribbons. I love Japan's cold, buckwheat noodles (soba), so I was excited to try the Korean version called naeng-myun, tra-ditionally eaten in summer. Perhaps I was too excited. I acciden-tally ordered a cold buckwheat noodle soup instead of a plate of chilled noodles at Kum Gang San one night. How was I to know Korea's cold noodle soup (naeng-myun) goes by the same name as the buckwheat vermicelli noodles themselves? What a happy ac-cident! What appeared at our table was a nest of wonderfully cold, chewy noodles in an ice-cold, tangy broth, crowned with pickled radish, cucumber, and half of a boiled egg. The buckwheat vermi-celli noodles at Kum Gang San are chewy, slightly resistant, and homemade daily. That's how they should be. Packaged noodles or noodles that sit around too long taste gummy and lifeless. If you want your buckwheat noodles without the soup and a hell of a lot spicier, try bibim naeng-myun, which comes in a sweet-spicy, red pepper (gochujang) sauce. In Korean, bibim means "mixed," and in this case, buckwheat noodles are mixed up with sliced meat, vegetables, and gochujang.

The mother of all bibim dishes is bibimbap, easily one of the greatest single-bowl pleasures known to man. Bibimbap translates to "mixed rice," but the name doesn't do it justice. Order bibim-bap, also known as bibimpap—just saying either is fun—and out from the kitchen comes an enormous bowl of rice topped with (de-pending on what you choose) anything from bulgogi—thin slices of marinated beef, traditionally grilled but sometimes panfried—

seafood, chicken, pork, or even grilled eel, a raw egg, an array of seasoned vegetables, and gochujang. You know those people who can't stand it when their food touches, the ones that hate when the mashed potatoes nudge the chicken or the spinach grazes the salmon? They would recoil from this dish at first sight because bibimbop is all about the interaction of the ingredients and the delicious throng of flavors and textures Korean food has to offer— the crunch of bamboo shoots, the tartness of pickled vegetables, the saltiness of dried anchovies, the crisp coolness of sprouts, the way a runny egg yolk binds it all together. If you've never tried Korean food, it's the perfect starter dish because it embodies the entire flavor palette of Korean cooking. The only thing better is dolsot bibimbap, which is bibimbap served in a hot stone bowl. With dolsot-style bibimbap, you don't want to mix everything together right away. The heat of the bowl crisps the rice, forming an addictively crunchy rice crust at the bottom—sort of like the socarrat in paella.

You know what's even more fun to say than bibimbap? Gogi gui. Just hearing the words *gogi gui*, Korean barbecue, makes me salivate and swoon. There are Korean restaurants—houses of worship, really—that specialize in barbecued meats. (I'm a loyal member.) At these houses of gogi gui worship, the customer gets to play the part of cook. There's a gas or charcoal grill built right into every table, so everyone can cook their own food. It's not the kitchen's fault if your steak's not medium rare, it's yours! You have to keep a close eye on the grill, especially on the fantastically thin slices of sirloin, known as bulgogi. (Bulgogi can also be made with other choice cuts of beef or chicken.) Bulgogi is a first-class and often delicate cut of beef that's been marinated in an addictive blend of sugar, garlic, sesame, and soy sauce. Galbi, beef or pork short ribs, get the same marinade treatment. When either hit the hot grill, the sugar in the marinade instantly caramelizes, sealing in the marinade. The result is meat so insanely tender, chewy, and sweet you'll never see barbecue the same way again. Now, I'm not debating the merits of southern barbecue, but Korean barbecue is extraordinarily sensual—simultaneously succulent, delicate, and aromatic. (Gogi gui is one of the few times I don't mind smelling like my dinner.)

Mention you're going for Korean barbecue, and everyone will want in. On a recent trip to L.A., I suggested such an excursion to a friend, and suddenly we were a table of sixteen with one thing on our minds: gogi gui and lots of it. The group voted on Park's BBQ, located in a strip mall in the heart of K-Town. Park's BBQ is a carnivore's paradise that wheels and deals in deliciously marbled meats on two floors. Smoke wafts up from the grills at every table, disappearing into stainless steel hoods as servers hustle through the dining room, toting large platters of raw meaty delights. Little bowls of banchan pepper the sleek black tabletops, and the charcoal-paved grills sizzle with meat and garlic. As soon as we were seated, we got right down to business, ordering a juicy mountain of galbi and bulgogi. At Park's BBQ, and every Korean barbecue joint worth its salt, both come with ssamjang, a spicy dipping sauce, and lettuce for making your own lettuce wraps. You take a leaf of lettuce, add a dab of ssamjang and some shredded scallions, and a bit of grilled or raw garlic, and revel in the moment.

We also threw in an order of thick-cut bacon (samgyeopsol) and a pajeon, a plate-size scallion pancake laced with shrimp, scallions, and nibbles of corn. Accompanying the food we actually ordered was, of course, a flurry of banchanlike crab legs doused in chile sauce, jiggly squares of acorn jelly, and raw, tender octopus. Not to mention copious amounts of soju, a clear Korean rice liquor similar to vodka in taste, and hof—that's beer to a non-Korean speaker—to wash it all down.

If you get a galbi (short ribs) craving in L.A., but you're not up for cooking it yourself, you can always track down a Kogi truck and order a galbi taco. That's right, Korean barbecue in a Mexican tortilla. I never would've made the connection between the two cuisines, but 54 percent of Koreatown's residents are Latino. Could there be anything more quintessentially L.A.? Back in November 2008, after a long night of drinking and the hunger that follows, Mark Manguera, the owner of Kogi taco trucks (there are currently four of them) came up with the ingenious idea of stuffing galbi in a tortilla, and a whole new taco truck was born. Kogi's chef, Roy Choi, piles soft corn tortillas with barbecued short ribs, spicy pork, chicken, or tofu and an army of toppings like cilantro, cabbage, onions, scallions, and a sesame-chile salsa roja. They also dish out galbi burritos, kimchi quesadillas, and kogi dogs. Frankly I'm glad I don't live in L.A. any longer. Because if I did, I'd spend my days chasing the Kogi trucks around like some crazy person. Word of a Kogi truck spotting draws large, hungry crowds. Wherever a truck stops, a street party ensues—strangers bonding over this brilliant union.

And what could be a better celebration of Korean food? After all, community is the essence of Korean dining. It's a cuisine meant for sharing, for big groups of people eating a myriad of dishes together. The only time you'll see someone eat an entire dish on his own is when he's eating alone, but tables for one are rare. If you're not Korean or Korean-American, and you're eating with friends who are, try not to hog anything (no matter how divine) or eat too fast; otherwise they might think you're going to scarf down your portion and devour theirs next. In Korea, eating is a social experience.

That might be why New York's Koreatown always seems the most alive late at night. Stop by Forte Baden Baden on Thirty-second Street—yes, it's really Korean—at one in the morning on any weekend and you'll find a dining room packed with all kinds of people, gorging on deep-fried chicken and pitchers of beer. Forte Baden Baden is a Korean beer hall that specializes in rotisserie-fried chicken. Unlike American fried chicken, which is battered (often heavily) first and then fried once, Korean fried chicken is barely battered, twice fried, and sauced only after it has been removed from the deep fryer. The chicken gets thoroughly cooked in stage one—moist and juicy—and perfectly crisped in stage two. Baden Baden does it a little differently. They roast their chicken on a rotisserie first, then deep-fry it whole to achieve a crackly-skinned bird with a moist interior. If you like it spicy, there's hot sauce on the table. Korean chickens tend to be much smaller than the American version, and many Korean restaurants dunk the whole bird in the deep fryer—just as they would in Korea—then cut it into lots of little pieces, lacquered with sauce.

After all those banchan, all that bibimbap, fried chicken, and galbi, you'd be forgiven for skipping dessert. But I wouldn't advise it, especially in the summertime when you're craving something cold and sweet. Frozen desserts are Korea's forte and one of my weaknesses. I have no willpower in the face of soft-serve ice cream or frozen yogurt, even in the dead of winter. Did you know that famously habit-forming Pinkberry is modeled on Korean-style yogurt, like that of the Korean chain Red Mango? (In fact, the first Pinkberry in Manhattan opened in Koreatown, and I was there to sample for myself the day they opened.) Korea's tangy, creamy frozen yogurt is a nationwide phenomenon, and so are their toppings. I suspect they have a topping fetish. They also eat shaved ices (patbingsu), blanketed in sweet red beans, canned or fresh fruit, and fruit syrups. Ooh, and sometimes they add condensed milk to give it a creamy dimension, or tteok (rice cake similar to Japanese mochi), candy, or even ice cream or frozen yogurt. I like the two-in-one type of patbingsu with shaved ice, adzuki beans, and green tea frozen yogurt—earthy, creamy, icy, and sweet. Beans and rice often play a role in Korean desserts. They eat sticky-sweet rice balls, rice cakes, or half moons of rice stuffed with dried dates, sesame, chestnuts, or even chrysanthemum flowers. You *could* skip dessert, but why *would* you?

## Table Settings and Modern Manners

In a Korean restaurant you probably won't see knives on the table—that's because they're almost never necessary. The sharpest thing you'll see is a pair of scissors in your server's hand. Meats are usually cut into bite sizes in the kitchen, so most dishes require nothing more than a stainless steel spoon and a pair of metal chopsticks; together, called sujeo, they are the equivalent of our fork and knife. Korean chopsticks have blunted ends, all the better for shoveling rice from the bowl into your mouth! Cold dishes are always placed to the right, hot dishes to the left, kimchi in the back.

Remember, when in doubt, share. Dinner isn't just sustenance in Korea; it's a means of bonding. You won't make any friends if you don't share. (Soup is the only dish that isn't necessarily fair game for the table at large.) And always make sure that your chopsticks or serving spoon is clean before dipping into the communal dishes.

Don't forget, it's bad luck to pour your own alcohol. So offer to pour someone else's, and they should reciprocate. And it may sound strange, but it's proper etiquette to cover your mouth or turn away when you drink in the presence of elders. Gun bae!

# · 10 ·

# Mexican Cuisine

*The chile, it seems to me, is one of the few
foods that has its own goddess.*

DIANA KENNEDY

I'm an East Coast girl, but I have no trouble admitting
that California has the best Mexican food in the country, if just for the sheer number and diversity of options.
Drive up the coast from Los Angeles to Santa Barbara
and you'll discover La Super-Rica Taqueria, the holy
grail of taco shops. (But just remember, they're closed
on Wednesdays. I'd hate to see you drive all that way
for nothing.) A few years ago, I flew into LAX and drove straight
from there to La Super-Rica, even though Santa Barbara is ninety
miles from L.A. That's how much I love La Super-Rica Taqueria. Their tortillas are terrifically fresh and headily aromatic, and
their tamales are to die for. Like most great taco shops, it's not
much to look at. At this worn shack with a tin roof and a covered
patio, you eat off of paper plates and bus your own table. But that
didn't stop Julia Child from swearing by it, and it shouldn't stop
you from visiting, either. This is a real deal Mexican joint, the
kind of spot that isn't dependent on gobs of cheese, spice, and

sour cream. All that creamy stuff we have such a weakness for in the United States? Well, we have Tex-Mex to thank for that.

Have you ever had an order of nachos topped with the works? That's true Tex-Mex innovation at work—Mexican dishes made with American ingredients and a dash of Spanish influence. Translation: cheddar or jack cheese instead of cotija or Oaxaca cheese, sour cream in place of fresh Mexican crema, shredded iceberg lettuce in place of cilantro. Americans have big eyes, and that leads to overstuffed burritos, Frisbee-size flour (not corn) tortillas, and unrestrained doses of cheese. Steak fajitas, chimichangas, and chili con queso (cheese dip) made with Velveeta? All Tex-Mex inventions. (Let's not even get into the complications of distinguishing Tex-Mex-style cooking from New Mexican–style cooking—whew!)

Don't get me wrong; I like Tex-Mex. I have fajitas on occasion, and I even eat chili con carne (a spicy tomato beef stew) during football season, but it's a wholly Texan invention—in fact, it's the official state dish. I like nachos, but I'm not fond of the kind that require you to play "find the chips" beneath an avalanche of cheese, sour cream, and guacamole. I prefer Mexican-style nachos, scattered with cheese and a few slices of fresh jalapeño. Nachos are a good litmus test for determining whether you're in a Mexican restaurant or a Tex-Mex joint. If your nachos are piled with a hefty combination of ingredients, like beans, meat, salsa, guacamole, sour cream, and cheese, you're eating Tex-Mex. Real deal Mexican is much simpler: toppings and fillings are used sparingly, and dishes tend to feature fewer ingredients. Heavy sour cream is a dead giveaway for a Tex-Mex joint. Crema, true Mexican sour cream, is much lighter and thinner than our American version. Tex-Mex is a cuisine unto itself with its own set of rules. If there are beans in your chili con carne or no Velveeta in your chili con queso, it's not true Tex-Mex. Sometimes I think Tex-Mex goes too far. Chili con carne spaghetti is insulting to Mexicans and Italians alike and so are chili cheese fries. (No wonder the French don't like us.)

Thankfully, you don't have to go to Mexico to eat authentic Mexican food. While California may hold the title for the best Mexican food in America, you can find great Mexican all over the country. It's one of those cuisines that seems to be loved universally, from one corner of the country to the other. Faces light up when someone suggests going for Mexican food. Try it—the response is almost Pavlovian. Just the thought of salt-rimmed margaritas, chunky guacamole scooped up with salty chips, and soft, warm tortillas filled with seasoned meats seem to make people giddy with excitement.

So Mexico doesn't need me to campaign on behalf of its cuisine. I'd say almost everyone is convinced of its virtues. And most people have their go-to order, be it chicken enchiladas, steak fajitas, shrimp tacos, or beans and rice. They fall in love with one dish and stick with it. I don't think my brother has ever strayed from his usual nachos and chicken burrito with a side of pinto beans. And that breaks my heart. It's as if the rest of the menu is invisible to him. What about chiles rellenos, chilaquiles, cochinita pibil, or tacos al pastor? There's more to Mexican on American soil than burritos or chips and salsa.

I'd never considered eating cactus until I tried the nopalito (prickly pear cactus) salad at Loteria Grill at the Farmers Market in West Hollywood. Discovering Loteria Grill was pure luck. I had stopped by the Farmers Market to pick up fresh bread and some freshly ground peanut butter for my daily fix, but I was already hungry—on the verge of hanger—and it was unbearably hot out. I saw a free seat at Loteria's counter and grabbed it. The nopalito salad sounded, well, cool—bits of cold cactus consorting with serrano chiles, tomato, onion, and shredded Oaxaca cheese in a lime vinaigrette. I followed it with chicken slathered in a spicy pipián sauce made of pumpkin seeds and peanuts. (I still had peanut butter on the brain.) The pipián was smoky and nutty with a subtle undercurrent of chile heat—just enough to make it interesting without starting a fire in my mouth. On a return visit to Loteria Grill, I discovered their outstanding chilaquiles verdes—tortilla strips sautéed with salsa and often sprinkled with fresh cheese—a traditional Mexican breakfast dish. The sautéed tortilla strips should be tender, but not soggy, a tad crunchy, but not crispy. At Loteria, the tortilla strips are just right. They're sautéed in a mixture of beaten eggs and salsa verde—tangy with tomatillos and spiked with serrano chiles—then sprinkled with cotija cheese. The combination makes a compelling case for changing my breakfast routine and also works wonders on a hangover. (Thank God.)

The dishes we overlook are often more complex and more exciting than our go-to orders—and they don't require a huge leap of faith, trust me: they're made with ingredients we're already familiar with. Corn, chiles, cilantro, cheese, squash, beans, avocados, nuts, tomatoes, tomatillos, onions, and pumpkin seeds—these ingredients are at the heart of the Mexican kitchen. It's the combination of the ingredients, the character of the heat, and the different preparations that distinguish one dish from another.

Corn is a perfect example of the mutability of Mexican ingredients. A soft corn tortilla might sound like nothing special, but have you ever had one made by hand, fresh from the griddle? It's a simple, unadulterated pleasure—a soft, chewy round tortilla with a comforting corn aroma. Fry a corn tortilla and voilà, you have the makings of a crunchy taco shell, a crispy, flaky tostada, or tortilla chips. Tortillas start life as simple masa, which means "dough" in Spanish. But masa refers to a very specific type of dough, one made from dried, pounded corn soaked in lime and ground into a paste. Masa is the starting point for a seemingly infinite array of possibilities: flautas, enchiladas, empanadas, and gorditas all begin with masa. And then there's my favorite, the humble tamale. A tamale looks like an edible present, gift-wrapped in a corn husk. The corn husk functions as a sort of biodegradable double-duty pot and bowl in one—the gift is what's inside it: a velvety pocket of masa, stuffed with anything from shredded meat, cheese, or vegetables to some combination of the three, all of which have been steam-cooked in the husk. It's no wonder every state in Mexico has its own regional version of a tamale—there are close to a thousand varieties of tamales in the country. (Someday I hope to retire to Mexico and try every single one.)

And there are nearly as many varieties of sopes. A sope is a grilled or fried cake of masa that resembles a small, extra-thick tortilla, traditionally topped with crumbled cheese, meat, beans, and red or green salsa. Sopes are shaped by hand and pinched at the edges, so all the goodies on top don't fall off the savory cornmeal cake. (If you look carefully at a sope, you can usually see the finger indentations ringing its edges.) Tehuitzingo Mexican Deli, a teeny bodega near my apartment, serves sopes topped with everything from spiced pork to chorizo (Mexican spiced sausage). The front of Tehuitzingo deli looks like a bare-bones corner grocery store stocked with Mexican sauces, tomatillos, and other imported staples, but head to the back and you'll discover a small counter where you can order tortas, tacos, and sopes. Their sopes are phenomenally

> **• TASTY MORSEL •**
>
> *You can often judge a Mexican restaurant by its tortillas. Authentic Mexican joints use only corn tortillas, and the best ones make them in-house. If the corn tortillas are thin and chewy, and fresh from the griddle, you're in good hands. A tortilla should be pliant, not rubbery or thick. While they do eat flour tortillas in Mexico, they're considered inferior to corn.*

> ### • TASTY MORSEL •
>
> *Baja California, Mexico's northern and westernmost state,
> is an eight-hundred-mile-long peninsula jutting into the
> Pacific Ocean. Because almost no point in the state is more
> than fifty miles from water, the regional cuisine has a
> decided emphasis on seafood. Baja-style fish tacos—light,
> flaky, battered fish on corn tortillas topped with cooling
> shredded cabbage, creamy white sauce, a sprinkle of salsa
> fresca, and a hit of lime juice—are enormously popular in,
> you guessed it, California, Baja's northern neighbor.*

fresh—supple cakes piled with savory meats like braised pork or beef tongue.

It's pretty amazing what you can do with a simple ear of corn, husk and all. Even the fungus that grows on the cob is a delicacy. Called huitlacoche (pronounced weet-la-coh-chay), this inky brown truffle is surprisingly complex—moist, musty, sweet, and smoky. Huitlacoche is the most affordable truffle available and the only canned truffle around. It's great in soups or as a filling for tacos, tamales, and quesadillas. Tehuitzingo makes a huitlacoche quesadilla that is sensational, which goes to show that you can't judge an eatery based on its looks.

When it comes to all things corn, there's also hominy (dried corn with the germ removed). For some reason, when you soak corn in water and lime to remove the germ, it swells up and takes on an entirely new mouthfeel that I'm just crazy for. It's firm yet chewy, excellent in a traditional stew called posole. Posole is one of those comforting foods that words can't do justice to—a

soul-soothing stew thick with hominy and shreds of pork or sometimes chicken, dosed with chile peppers and garlic. Most restaurants serve posole with a side of raw onions, avocado, radish, and
fresh cilantro to add texture and brightness to the broth. Elotes
give buttered corn on the cob a run for its money. Just picture a
roasted or boiled cob, slicked with mayonnaise, and dusted with
chile powder and crumbled cotija cheese. The crowning touch is a
zesty squeeze of lime. If you don't feel like gnawing on a cob, you
should try esquites, a lush, savory parfait of layered sautéed corn
kernels, cheese, lime, and mayonnaise. My favorite rendition of
this creamy, corny goodness is served in a flimsy plastic cup at La
Superior in Williamsburg, Brooklyn. To say the dining room at this
taquería is understated is an understatement. The table settings
are disposable—red and blue plastic plates, flimsy supermarket
napkins in battered napkin holders, and salsa-stained menus.

This is Mexican street food with the luxury of a roof and a
scattering of tables. And the epitome of Mexican street food is the
taco. A true Mexican-style taco should be simple: a fresh, soft, and
small corn tortilla topped with a measured amount of meat or veg-
gies, and a sprinkling of onions and cilantro, served with a wedge
of lime. Those extra-large soft tortillas and U-shaped hard shells
you often see are an American invention. Technically, so are flour
tortillas. They do eat flour tortillas in Mexico, but mostly in the
northern border regions, where cheap white flour is imported from
the United States. La Superior's tacos are uniformly excellent, like
fiery chipotle-sauced shrimp strewn with a few shreds of cooling
cabbage and cilantro, and a dollop of guacamole. Even more thrilling are the tacos piled with Mexico's signature seasoned meats,
including perfectly charred carne asada (tasty bits of grilled skirt
steak) and heavenly carnitas, braised, pulled pork melting in its
own delicious fat. Tragically, al pastor is a no-show on La Superior's
menu. Al pastor, like carnitas, is a preparation of pork, but unlike
slow-braised carnitas, al pastor pork is marinated for days in an

achingly flavorful blend of achiote, chiles, and citrus, then spit-roasted and shaved. (Think souvlaki in a Mexican marinade and served in a soft taco.)

La Superior's menu features many traditional dishes, including tinga de pollo. Tinga de pollo—shredded, stewed chicken in a tomato and chipotle pepper sauce—is a wonderfully versatile dish that can be served as a stew or as a topping for tostadas, tacos, or tortas. At La Superior they serve tinga de pollo as a taco filling—a moist tangle of chicken sparked by chile peppers, which practically melts into the tortilla beneath it. (Yum!) Birria—goat stew—is another classic dish you might see on a menu, and if you do, I highly recommend you sample it for yourself. I've had my share of goat, but nothing as intense as birria. This is a smoky stew with gamey shreds of goat, loads of chile peppers, and hints of cloves and cumin. It usually comes with a side of fresh cilantro and onions, which you scatter over it. Interestingly enough, this brooding stew is traditionally served on special occasions, like weddings and funerals. (Personally, I think this intense dish is better suited to funerals.)

But if you try just one new dish, let it be mole. I discovered it by following my nose—really. I was at Alegria on Sunset, a Mexican restaurant in Los Feliz, California, when I smelled something irresistibly smoky and sweet coming from the table next to mine. Without an ounce of shame (or manners, admittedly), I followed the fragrance to a plate of a mysterious substance bathed in a tar black sauce spackled with sesame seeds. "What is that?" I leaned over and asked my neighbor eagerly. "Chicken enchiladas," he answered. It didn't look like any form of chicken enchiladas I had ever seen. "What's on it?" I persisted. "Oh," he responded, leaning back in his chair and nodding knowingly. (He really did.) "It's mole." So that's exactly what I ordered. The chicken enchiladas were a bonus, but the real find was the devastatingly thick, spicy-sweet sauce, flavored with dozens of spices, chiles, and plenty of other seasonings.

I've eaten mole hundreds of times now, but I'm still captivated by its complexity and wealth of ingredients—chiles, chocolate, nuts, seeds, cinnamon, garlic, coriander, onion, and tomato. Eating mole engages the senses in a push-pull seduction—hints of earth and heat, undercurrents of cocoa and coriander.

There are many kinds of mole: some are red, green, or yellow; some are made with chocolate; some with pumpkin seeds, others with almonds or peanuts; some with tomatillos; some with poblano chiles, still others with ancho chiles (which are the dried form of poblanos). Mesa Coyoacán in Brooklyn has a thirty-seven-ingredient mole poblano that requires its own chef and features six types of chiles. Mole isn't something you whip up at the last minute. In Mexico, mole is a celebratory food, savored for special occasions like weddings and holidays because of its extensive list of ingredients and preparation time. It's a labor of love that requires hours, patience, skill, and an army of ingredients cooked separately from one another. No two moles taste exactly alike.

Mole wouldn't be possible without chiles. Ancho, guajillo, and pasilla chiles are like the holy trinity of mole. And chiles, like corn, are one of the fundamental foods of Mexican cuisine. There are over one hundred types of chiles used in Mexican cooking, employed fresh, dried, whole, powdered, roasted, and smoked. When you think of chiles, you might think of the kind of spice that makes your eyes water. That's like saying all red wines taste exactly the same. Chiles are misunderstood. And this is coming from someone who's not a fan of turning purple at the table. Sure, the heat of some chiles hits you instantly, but they're not all spicy. Yes, some are ferocious, especially the fresh little ones. (I stay away from those.) A good rule of thumb I dine by: fresh chiles are generally hotter than dried chiles, and the smaller the chile, the hotter it is. Dried chiles are earthy and fruity. Some taste mild and sweet, others smoky with just a whisper of heat.

I navigated the landscape of chiles by eating my way through all of the different chile-spiced moles, salsas, and sauces. For years I neglected chiles rellenos because I assumed a stuffed chile pepper was out of my league. But chiles rellenos is surprisingly mild. When it comes to heat, poblano chiles, the core of the dish, are more akin to bell peppers than they are to jalapeño peppers. The classic preparation of chiles rellenos is a battered, pan-fried poblano filled with a mixture of seasoned ground meat (picadillo), dried fruit, nuts, and cheese. (There are vegetarian versions, too, filled with cheese, nuts, or vegetables, so be sure to ask, if the menu isn't clear.) Chile en nogado is another great—and mild—introduction to chiles. This dish also features a poblano pepper stuffed with picadillo, but the pepper is left unbattered. Instead this beautiful dish, which reflects the colors of the Mexican flag (and is a traditional Independence Day treat), is doused in an ivory walnut sauce and sprinkled with ruby pomegranate seeds, which pop against the glossy green flesh of the poblano.

My next conquest was the ancho chile. Anchos are dried, purplish poblano chiles that range from mild to tepestuous, and are sweeter and fruitier than fresh green poblanos. Ancho chiles are one of the most commonly used chiles in Mexican cooking and are often ground into a powder and added to everything from mole to tamales. After cleaning a plate of ancho-crusted shrimp, I felt brave enough to take on chile colorado, a brick-red chile sauce made with garlic, onions, cumin, and a mixture of red chiles (every cook has his or her own preferred blend of chiles). Chile colorado is traditionally served with pork, as a filling for tacos or enchiladas, or as a stew. I could eat bowfuls of chile colorado, but I'm not foolhardy (or courageous) enough to eat more than one bowl of chile verde, a pork stew made from crushed green chiles and tomatillos. Rule of thumb: aside from poblanos, fresh green chiles—jalapeños, serranos, and habaneros—tend to be spicy. Habaneros are some of the hottest of all chiles, and sometimes ripe habaneros turn red, so watch out for those, too. (When in doubt,

ask your server.) The chile verde I ordered was spiked with serrano chiles—slender green fireballs—and tomatillos, which are
not chiles at all. Tomatillos are a tart green fruit that resembles
tomatoes—they temper the
heat of the chiles.

Chiles are also central to salsa.
What most people think of as
capital *S* salsa—pico de gallo, a
combination of diced tomatoes,
onion, cilantro, jalapeños, and
lime juice—is just one variety of
salsa. Mexico has a huge arsenal
of salsas at its fingertips. Salsa—
which simply means "sauce" in

> **• TASTY MORSEL •**
>
> *Pico de gallo is also known as
> salsa Mexicana, because it's the
> colors of the Mexican flag (red,
> white, and green).*

Spanish—really refers to *any* sauce at all. But restaurants stateside
rarely refer to a cooked sauce as a salsa. For the most part, salsa refers to an *uncooked* condiment made with chopped or whole fruit or
vegetables. Some are smooth, others chunky, and not all salsas are
tomato based. Don't limit your tongue to just pico de gallo when
there are fruit salsas, tomatillo salsa, and salsa borracha (salsa that's
made with alcohol—*borracha* means "drunk"). I've had pork with
mango salsa and tilapia with tequila-spiked salsa.

One of my favorite "uncooked" dishes of all time is ceviche.
I think of it as a refreshing "seafood salsa." In ceviche, fresh raw
fish is mixed with lime juice and other ingredients such as onions,
cilantro, tomatoes, or vegetables. The acid of the lime juice essentially "cooks" the raw fish without tampering with its freshness
and character. The point of ceviche isn't to show off what you can
do with it, but rather how little you have to do. As for the fish, anything just hooked goes—shrimp, squid, scallops, octopus, tuna, and
sea bass are traditional players. Whenever I'm in Mexico, I devote
much of my mealtime to soft, sweet parrot fish ceviche. While the
West Village may look nothing like Mexico, Yerba Buena Perry's

ceviches go a long way to make up for it. The chef, Julian Medina, makes a fantastic flounder ceviche with lime, Amarillo chiles, onions, cubed sweet potato, and bits of grilled corn. You'd think the flounder would be overwhelmed, but somehow all the ingredients just intensify its delicacy and flavor. (It takes just as much talent to "uncook," too.)

From delicate ceviches and bright salsas to complex moles and beautifully braised meats, there's so much more to Mexican food than chicken burritos. These aren't unusual dishes that require a Google search. Just read the menu a little more closely next time you go to dinner. You could order fajitas. Or you could wander off the beaten path and try cochinita pibil. Get cochinita pibil. (Trust me.) This isn't just slow-roasted suckling pig. It's achingly tender and savory-sweet—marinated in sour oranges and achiote chiles. You could order the nachos. Or you could order queso fundido, cheese fondue made with tangy Mexican cheeses. It's served with spicy homemade chorizo for dipping. Doesn't that sound so much more interesting? The chef, Zarela Martinez, is a missionary of sorts, determined to protect her culinary tradition. She's written four books on the subject. Her cuisine features rustic home cooking: flaky, fresh snapper hash, barbecued lamb, and pan-seared trout in a puree of hoja santa, garlic, and jalapeños. Hoja santa means "sacred leaf"—a heart-shaped herb with hints of pepper, licorice, anise, and tarragon—used as a wrapper for fish and meats, or blended into sauces.

Even at Mama Mexico, a New York minichain, where it's Cinco de Mayo year-round and they embrace Tex-Mex—there's chili con carne, deep-fried chimichangas, and combo platters—they still serve regional family-style dishes like enchiladas suizas, chicken in mole poblano, and tamales. Or grab a torta for lunch instead of your usual turkey sandwich or cheeseburger. A torta is the equivalent of a Mexican hoagie, served on a crusty white roll (bolillo), and stuffed with traditional meats like chorizo or tinga de pollo, and sometimes cheese, onions, peppers, or even a dab of guacamole. In the end, it's not about eating at the "right" restaurant or the most authentic one. Really, it's about exploring the other half of the menu.

Same goes for desserts. Until just a few years ago, dessert menus at most American Mexican restaurants were limited to fried ice cream, flan, and churros. That was pretty much the extent of it. Nowadays the dessert menu has become much more exciting. Have you ever had buñuelos? I highly recommend you put these warm doughnut fritters on your to-do list. They're doughy and pliant on the inside, crusty on the outside, and often dusted in cinnamon or sugar or drizzled with honey. Most restaurants serve buñuelos with chocolate or dulce de leche dipping sauce. Dulce de leche—a thick caramel sauce made from sugar and condensed milk—is like liquid crack. It's used as an ingredient in ice cream, flan, and cake. While pastel tres leches isn't made with dulce de leche, it is made with three kinds of milk. Just imagine a sponge cake soaked in heavy cream, evaporated milk, and condensed milk and you've got the moist, milky idea. One of the most traditional Mexican desserts is arroz con leche, creamy rice pudding sprinkled with cinnamon. Are you noticing a pattern? Mexican desserts are very sweet and very rich. After all that chile-spiced food, something sweet balances out the meal perfectly.

Horchata is essentially the liquid form of arroz con leche. It's made with rice milk, sugar, almonds, cinnamon, and lime zest. Like dessert, Mexican drinks work wonders to balance out a spicy meal. Mexico also has its own sodas (sweeter than traditional sodas), flavored with lime, tamarind, lemon, and plenty of other tropical flavors. Most are made by Jarritos, which is like the Coca-Cola of Mexico. If you want something really thick and chocolatey, there's Mexican hot chocolate. This is no ordinary cup of hot chocolate. Mexican hot chocolate is vibrantly spiced with cinnamon, anise, vanilla, and often chiles.

You *could* eat Mexican food without drinking tequila, but it wouldn't be nearly as much fun. What would chips and guacamole be like without margaritas? (I don't even want to imagine.) Tequila is a distilled spirit made from a blue agave plant called *Agave tequilana*. Forget the worm in the bottle. That's a myth. No Mexican-made tequila has a worm in the bottle. (Apparently it's illegal to put insects in tequila in Mexico. Thank God.) Tequila is a type of mescal, but not all mescals are tequila. Mescal refers to all distilled spirits made from agave, and that includes tequila. If it says *mescal* on the bottle, that means the alcohol inside has been distilled from blue agave—or ten other varieties of agave plant. Tequila is 100 percent blue agave, and I happen to like it much better than mescal. Then again, I'm a serious fan of tequila, so I might be biased.

There are three classes of tequila—anejo, reposado, and blanco—that correspond to the length the tequila has been aged. Tequila blanco doesn't usually age at all, and if it does, it's for no more than two months, resulting in a clear tequila with a strong flavor. Reposados, on the other hand, have been aged in oak barrels for anywhere from a few months to just under a year. Reposados are also clear but much more smooth and complex than blancos. And any tequila aged over a year, but less than three years, qualifies as anejo. Anejos are darker and more complex than both reposados and blancos. (If it's been aged in oak for over three years, it's extra anejo.) Generally speaking, the longer a tequila has aged, the better it is. The best tequila—usually reposados or anejos—is meant to be sipped on its own, not used as a mixer in a cocktail. Some restaurants serve sipping tequilas with sangrita—a tequila chaser made from orange juice, pomegranate juice, grenadine, and chiles. If you're offered the option of a "sangrita back," take it. Blancos are mixing tequilas, meaning you mix them into a cocktail, namely a margarita. In Mexico, tequilas are traditionally drunk before the meal to stimulate one's appetite or after the meal to stimulate digestion. In America, we drink them throughout the meal, which works for me!

## Table Setting and Modern Manners

Did you know that it's inappropriate to be on time for a meal in Mexico? Arriving thirty minutes late is actually the norm. In the States that policy doesn't really apply, though I have noticed Mexican restaurants are rather relaxed about tardy guests. Many Mexican dishes are meant to be eaten with your hands—tacos, tortas, and sopes are a perfect example. But your hands should remain above the table at all times. (This implied dining rule dates back centuries, when people used to hide weapons beneath the table.) For dishes that do require utensils, lay them across your plate with the fork prongs facing down and the handles to the right when you're through with a dish. Before beginning a meal, the customary cheer—akin to "Bon appétit!"—is "Buen provecho!" which literally translates as "good privilege" (perhaps because enjoying the meal—and the company—is a privilege), and the traditional toast is "Salud"—to health!

# Diners' Rights

If I wanted to be mistreated, I'd go to one of my relative's houses for dinner. If I wanted a hassle, I'd cook. Dining out is a pleasure, a minivacation where someone else takes care of dinner and the guests are there to enjoy the show. Hospitality comes first, and so should the customer.

I like my steak medium rare. If it's cooked any more than that, then I might as well be eating dirt. If I order it medium rare, I have the right to send it back if it comes out well done. A good restaurant will offer to remake it. Register your complaint right away, however. Don't wait until the check comes to say something. Don't clean your plate, then complain. You ate it, after all!

Do you know what the word *tip* stands for? It comes from the acronym T.I.P., which stands for "To Insure Promptness." It seems to have lost a bit of its meaning. I'm not suggesting you should stiff your server. That's mean-spirited, but I do think restaurants and servers should make more of an effort "To Insure Promptness." If your server is missing in action, you have a right to ask the manager for a new one. The state of the stock market and your personal financial situation shouldn't affect how much you tip, however. If you're usually a big tipper but financially strapped, you might want to tip a little less, but don't take your personal situation out on a server. Everyone's just trying to make a living, and servers make the bulk of their income from tips, not from their hourly minimum wage (in fact, many states have an even lower minimum wage for servers).

Unless you had wretched service, you ought to tip at least 15 percent of the check. (No, you don't have to tip on tax.) I usually tip 18 percent. If you have truly wonderful service, I believe in a 20 percent tip. If the service is just fine, go the 15 percent route, but anything less is unacceptable. I usually like to give 18 percent anyway, just to be a better person. Kill them with kindness.

The real aim should be to head off potentially disastrous meals before you have to deal with poor service or inferior food. If a restaurant looks dicey, perhaps you should order a glass of wine and then study the menu. If your gut says no, call it a day. Pay for your drinks and leave. Ask questions and protect yourself from a bad situation and a bad meal as well! (And should you be having that glass of wine or cocktail at the bar, transferring the tab to your table is a diner's right. Why should you have to pull your credit card out twice in the same restaurant? Just leave a cash tip at the bar, so the bartender doesn't get stiffed by the house.)

Finally, if you haven't eaten all of your food, don't be embarrassed to ask to have it wrapped up. Why waste good food? I've taken home doggie bags from Le Cirque, Monkey Bar, and Minetta Tavern, and no one flinched when I asked for one. It's not tacky. It's a compliment to the chef that you liked it enough to take it home with you. Restaurateur Keith McNally, of Balthazar and Minetta Tavern fame, thinks leftovers are underrated, too. "So many things taste better the next day," he insists. It's like eating something good twice.

· 11 ·

# Middle Eastern
## Cuisine

*He who has no bread has no authority.*

TURKISH PROVERB

The only thing they can agree on in the Middle East is food. I think everyone should sit down and settle their disputes over a little baba ghanoush and baklava. And falafel. Falafel's practically the universal language of the Middle East. Hell, they can swap recipes for firearms. Make mezze, not war. (While the Greeks spell *meze* with one *z*, most Middle Eastern countries spell it *mezze*.)

They'll realize how much they have in common. Like tabouli, tahini, and shawarma for starters. Israelis eat *felafel* and the Arabs eat *falafal*, but there's no reason to quibble over spelling or pronunciation. Dining and religious habits vary from country to country, but they vary within each country, too. Some Israelis eat pork and some don't. Neither do most Muslims, which is why kosher Jews and Muslims often dine in the same restaurants. They're bonded, for better or worse, by land, and this is a land of figs, dates, pistachios, pomegranates, pine nuts, parsley, chickpeas, sesame seeds, mint, and wheat. The entire Middle East shares a biblical menu that originated in ancient Egypt.

And many of the countries in the Middle East border the Mediterranean—Lebanon, Syria, Israel, and Turkey—so it's no surprise that Greek and Middle Eastern food share a lot of similarities as well. Greek food is like the offspring of Middle Eastern and Mediterranean parents. Nothing happens in either culture's kitchen without chickpeas or tahini (sesame paste). They share dips, salads, and other signature dishes, like stuffed grape leaves, baba ghanoush, egg-lemon soup, yogurt sauce, and moussaka. But in the Middle East, there's less phyllo dough and more pita and flatbread, and lots of vegetarian options for kosher and Muslim diners. Really, the biggest distinction between Greek and Middle Eastern cooking is the volume and intensity of spices used in seasoning. The Greeks don't make a habit of spicy food, and they don't like to mix too many different spices together in one dish.

It doesn't matter whether you're dining in a Turkish, Israeli, or Lebanese restaurant, all Middle Easterners eat by the "a little of this, a little of that" dining philosophy. I have a tough time choosing between all the thick, tangy dips and fragrant, fresh salads, so I don't. Instead I'll drag a warm triangle of pita through hummus and then another through yogurt, and so on. If you're in a hurry, stuff a little of everything into a pita and eat it on the run. It's sensational grab 'n' go grub, a lot more interesting than a street cart hot dog or a ham and cheese sandwich, not to mention fresher, healthier, and vegetarian friendly. Not only is falafel the most common manifestation of "fast food" in the Middle East, but it's also probably its most famous food export, too.

These tremendously crispy fritters are made from spiced ground chickpeas or ground fava beans, or a blend of the two. Falafel are usually seasoned with some combination of onions, garlic, parsley, cumin, and coriander. Every chef has his or her own recipe; some chefs swap mint for parsley or leave out coriander and add

more cumin. If all goes well in the kitchen, falafel should be perfectly crispy on the outside, moist and flavorful on the inside. Some
falafel emerges from the fryer too wet and without a crunchy exterior, others as heavy as paperweights. (Boo!) There's nothing worse
than overfried, dry, or leaden falafel so dense it tears through a pita.
Falafel isn't boilerplate food. I wouldn't go so far as to say falafel
is an art, but I'd wager the chefs making them would. There are
thousands of spiced chickpea balls being dropped into deep fryers
and stuffed into sandwiches all
over America every day, which
means you can eat around and
find your favorites. One of my
favorites is the irresistibly fragrant falafel at Rainbow Falafel
& Shawarma in Manhattan, just
off Union Square. (Locals simply
call it "Rainbow.") The aroma of
garlic, parsley, onion, cumin, or
coriander is released with every
perfectly crunchy-tender bite.

> • TASTY MORSEL •
>
> *In Egypt, McDonald's features
> the "McFalafel," a falafel patty
> topped with lettuce, tomato,
> and "secret sauce" on a ham-
> burger bun. The secret sauce is
> actually just tahini.*

Unfortunately Rainbow is not
a well-kept secret, thus the line trailing down Seventeenth Street
at lunchtime. I suspect the real holdup happens at the window.
I've witnessed it plenty of times. A guy catches a glimpse of a
passing chicken shawarma (sliced, spit-roasted meat) and freezes
up. He had his mind set on falafel until this unforeseen distraction
came along. "Get both," I murmur to myself. "Eat half and half.
The falafel's only $3.50. A Frappuccino at the Starbucks next door
costs more than that." When *I* can't make a decision, I get both.
I'm a both kinda girl. You can't go wrong with both. Just broke.
Although at $3.50, how much damage can you do? And this is the
best $3.50 you're likely to spend on a meal. Just make sure to grab
a bunch of napkins: between the tahini sauce (ground sesame paste

often thinned with lemon juice, olive oil, or water), hot sauce, and shredded lettuce, tomato, and onions, it can get very messy. Those are just the basics. For an extra dollar, you can get hummus or fried cauliflower in your falafel sandwich. (In Israel, it's not uncommon to get French fries and pickles in your pita.)

Part of Rainbow's magic is how utterly unassuming it appears—if it weren't for the line, you could walk right by it and not even notice. It's basically a three-by-six hole-in-the-wall with a counter. There are no seats, not even sidewalk seats, just the counter, a vertical roaster stacked with lamb twirling in the back, and a refrigerator case full of Snapple next to the cashier. But all you need is a falafel sandwich, and that's what most people are there for. In fact Rainbow's customers are so falafel-fixated that most of them don't even know what *kind* of food they're waiting for. I took an informal poll once while waiting in line, so I know this for a fact. One girl said, "Falafel." Her friend responded, "It's Middle Eastern, silly." That's true, but what kind? Technically, Rainbow is Syrian. The only reason I know that little tidbit is because there are Syrian-style soups on the takeout menu, and I read menus on the subway. But that's my point. Syria, Israel, and Iraq are like relatives who bicker all the time. They should all wave flags with a falafel emblem, or better yet, chickpeas. They're essential to falafel and hummus, a thick, tangy blend of chickpeas, tahini, lemon, and olive oil. The entire cast of mezze makes a compelling case for becoming a vegetarian. You don't even miss the meat.

Many Middle Eastern restaurants offer mezze platters, where you can choose from a variety of mezze, the better to share and to try lots of different dishes. Hummus is so commonplace in America now that you can buy a premade tub of it in any old supermarket. And while freshly made hummus is still hard to beat, it's worth venturing further afield, just for muhamarra alone. This jewel-toned dip of roasted red peppers, ground walnuts, and pomegranate molasses is such an interesting combination of flavors and textures; it's velvety, yet grainy, smoky and sweet and often spicy, with an undercurrent of lemon juice that balances the flavors. One of my favorites is thick, creamy labneh, a homemade strained yogurt cheese—almost like sour cream—often blended with olive oil and fresh mint. I'm perfectly content with tangy labneh all by itself, but most people smear it on just-baked pita. I also love a lemony baba ghanoush—roasted eggplant blended with olive oil, tahini, and garlic. And if you're not crazy about beans, you might change your mind after an order of ful mudammas, a dry fava bean stew, with buttery, slightly bitter fava beans, onions, and often tomatoes and garlic. Ful mudammas is a nice change of pace from the same old chickpeas, and so are spiced cauliflower florets or simply grilled eggplant rounds. Moujadara might sound ho-hum—after all, what could be so exciting about lentils mixed with rice or bulgur (cracked wheat)?—except it's also loaded with crispy caramelized onions, lending this Lebanese dish an earthy, nutty sweetness that makes it pretty tasty.

Grains like bulgur are a staple ingredient of Middle Eastern cuisine and a common feature of mezze platters, including salads. Tabouli is the Middle Eastern "Greek salad." You'll find tabouli in every Middle Eastern joint, not always prepared exactly the same way or with the same ingredients, but still the same basic, vibrant salad of fresh herbs, bulgur, and lots of lemon. (You can also add tabouli to your falafel sandwich at Rainbow.) There are restaurants in New York and Washington, D.C., named after this lemony, hand-chopped mix of parsley, mint, tomato, onion, and bulgur with a touch of black pepper and cinnamon. Fattoush is like the Middle Eastern version of Tuscany's bread salad, panzanella, only made with toasted pita, of course. The vegetables in fattoush depend on what's in the market (though you're likely to encounter cucumber and tomato), but you can count on lots of garlic and lemon.

Perhaps because Middle Eastern food is so similar across many

countries, restaurant owners don't feel compelled to identify themselves. The sign outside Alfanoose in Manhattan's Financial District reads MIDDLE EASTERN CUISINE, leaving curious diners like me
to wonder exactly which Middle Eastern cuisine they serve. Is it
Lebanese, Turkish, or Egyptian? Maybe Syrian or Iraqi? The most
common kinds of Middle Eastern restaurants in the States are
Turkish, Israeli, and Lebanese, or a sort of mash-up of all three.
I think the ambiguity of Alfanoose's sign is a strategic move by
its Lebanese owner, Mohammed Shami. The more territory you
cover, the bigger your audience. Pita sandwiches have a huge audience. If your notion of pita is lifeless rounds stacked in plastic
bags, you're in for a fantastic awakening. Alfanoose bakes their
pitas in-house and serves them fresh from the oven. Nothing's hap-
hazardly stuffed in—which can happen at a busy falafel shop with
a long line—and though the pitas are amazingly thin, I've never
had my freshly baked pita tear once. Their vegetarian sandwiches
are thoughtfully assembled flavor bombs. You could order a different mezze sandwich every day of the week.

But Alfanoose makes an even more compelling case for carnivo-
rous endeavors of the shawarma sorts. I feel like one of Pavlov's
dogs just thinking about their succulent, vertically roasted meats.
All of the meats—chicken, beef, or lamb—marinate for what
tastes like a delicious eternity in coriander, cumin, and vinegar before they're roasted on a spit and sliced to order. (I'm not a fan of
presliced shawarma in my pita pocket.) There's not a bad one in
the bunch, but I most adore the lamb shawarma. Slivers of spice-
crusted lamb are tucked into a pita along with lettuce, tomato,
pickles, and an arresting garlic sauce. Like so many other Middle
Eastern dishes, the secret to the garlic sauce is tahini. Shawarma
without garlic sauce is like a Caesar salad without Caesar dressing. Alfanoose also serves a great lamb kibbe, which happens to be
Lebanon's national dish. (Mr. Shami does his native country proud.)
Fried or grilled kibbe looks like a Middle Eastern meatball, made

with not just ground meat and spices, but also with bulgur and a spice mix called baharat—an enchanting blend of cinnamon, clove, cardamom, nutmeg, and coriander—that brings out the sweet side of meat. Kibbe aren't like other meatballs. For starters, they really look more like minifootballs than meatballs. There are two parts to kibbe: the shell and the filling. First, the shell (made with meat and bulgur) is molded into a small torpedo and then filled with the stuffing of minced, seasoned lamb. And then they're fried until they're a deep tawny brown. Raw kibbe—where the raw meat and bulgur are mixed together—is a traditional Lebanese dish (and one of my favorites), sort of like a cross between steak tartare and pâté, traditionally served with a side of chopped onions and fresh mint.

People often confuse kibbe and kafta, another traditional ground meat dish. Kibbe is not kafta, but they are close relatives. I liken them to fraternal twins. They have a lot in common: they're both made of spices and finely ground meat—usually lamb—and both are baked, grilled, or fried. Kafta is essentially kibbe minus the bulgur and the baharat. (And kafta look more like traditional meatballs.) If you're ever uncertain which is which, look for the meat and bulgur shell or sniff for sweet baharat. Kafta is 100 percent succulence, ground meat flavored with parsley, onion, and other spices.

If you've got a lamb fetish, you'll want to familiarize yourself with your local Middle Eastern restaurants, especially the Turkish ones. The Turkish kitchen practically revolves around lamb. Whenever I crave it, I go to Ali Baba in Murray Hill. There are nineteen lamb options, including eggplant-wrapped lamb shank, lamb chops, baby lamb chops, sautéed lamb with peppers, and lamb-stuffed cabbage. Lamb comes kafta-ed, kibbeh-ed, and kebab-ed every which way, every one juicy and tender. (I could've used a kebab manual the first time I ate there.) I had no idea what a narrow understanding of kebabs (also spelled kababs) I had. I was raised to believe that all kebabs were skewers of meat and charred vegetables. Au contraire. Meat combined with vegetables is *shish* kebab, and it's only one kind of kebab. The key to knowing your kebabs is learning how to decode the word *before* kebab.

You're already familiar with kafta and kibbe—Adana kebabs are like their long, spicy cousin. Instead of ground meat molded into balls or patties, Adana kebabs are made of minced meat (usually lamb) laced with hot red peppers that is molded into long brochettes and grilled on skewers. My favorite incarnation of Adana can be found under "Yogurtlu Kebabs," which must be Turkish for "splashed in cool yogurt and tomato sauce." That's how I learn about food. I eat something I don't like. I cross it off my list. I find something I do, and I learn what it's called. Maybe I should get a "yogurtlu kebab" tattoo in case I lose my memory in my old age. (You never know.) That's how sad I'd be to go without them. Adana yogurtlu does a number on your tongue—the heat of hot-pepper-laced adana, the cool, creamy yogurt, the fruity tang of tomato sauce, and the crisp flatbreads that accompany everything out of the kitchen. Like ketchup and French fries, yogurt and lamb are practically inseparable in Turkish cooking. Some menus—both in Turkey and in America—specify the kind of kebab but not the meat. It's safe to assume they're using lamb unless it says otherwise. If you're dead set against lamb, try yogurtlu tavuk or yogurtlu tavuk Adana. (*Tavuk* is chicken.)

Some people travel to Paris to see the Eiffel Tower; I traveled to Turkey to eat herds of lamb and yogurtlu kebabs. While I was there, I realized kebabs aren't just fast food or something you order at a takeout counter. In Turkey white-tablecloth-and-wine institutions serve kebabs. There are even kebab houses that focus solely on grilled, skewered meats. But you don't have to travel to Turkey for Middle Eastern kebabs. When I returned home, I went into serious lamb withdrawal, so I went to Ali Baba for lamb doner. Doner kebab is like the granddaddy of shawarma, Greek gyros, and Mexican al pastor shaved pork. Ground, pressed lamb is roasted on a vertical spit and shaved off to order in juicy, crispy

sheets of meat. The doner of all doners is iskendar kebab: a grati-
fying mess of diced pita topped with doner meat, and smothered
with tomato sauce and browned butter—outstanding, disastrously
sloppy Turkish comfort food.

Doner kebab is extremely popular throughout Europe—it's the
de facto late-night snack of practically all EU night-clubbers—
but it's just one sliver of Turkish cuisine. There were probably
more cooks in the imperial kitchen than officials in government,
and they all specialized in different dishes. Stuffed grape leaves
are just one of many dolma (stuffed vegetables) possibilities; there
are cabbage, pepper, and eggplant dolma, filled with a mélange
of rice, nuts, dried fruit, and spices. If you don't like any of those
vegetables (or vegetables at
all), you can try mussels stuffed
with the same ingredients. (I'm
a big fan of those.) There's cold
marinated octopus or warm,
grilled octopus, eggplant salad
or fried eggplant. Jump in with
an assortment of mezze. At Ali
Baba I graze on fried zucchini
pancakes (mucver), grilled
calamari spackled with parsley, and lebni—a fresh cheese
made from strained yogurt,
just like labneh—flavored with
walnuts, dill, and mint. Like
all Turkish mezze, Ali Baba's
collection is best eaten with an

> **• TASTY MORSEL •**
>
> *Turkish immigrants first
> brought doner to Berlin in the
> 1970s, and there are now over
> 15,000 doner kebab shops in
> Germany. They collectively
> sell four hundred tons of doner
> meat every single day—making
> it the single most popular fast
> food in the country.*

anise-flavored spirit called raki. As ouzo is to Greece, raki is to
Turkey. It's Turkey's national drink, and it's much easier going
down than ouzo and stronger.

Ali Baba serves pizza, but it's not what you're thinking. It's not the bleak cardboard you'd associate with a shoddy pizza joint, nor does it bear any relation to Italy at all. It's called pide—the Turkish word for long, thin flatbread shaped like a banana—and it comes topped or stuffed with everything from ground meat to pomegranate seeds or mashed potatoes. Turkish pide is something delicate. The crust is a chewy, gently crispy flatbread made from the same dough as pita. The most classic pide is lahmacun, paved with moist minced lamb, herbs, and chopped vegetables. Ali Baba's pides are easily the best thing on the menu—even better than their doner, and that's saying something. Their tour de force is the "special" pide, and by special they mean the works. I highly recommend you sample this puffy creation filled with spiced sausage, chopped hard-boiled egg, ground meat, and mozzarella-like kashar cheese.

Not everyone bakes Turkish pide, so seize the occasion when it presents itself and don't despair if it doesn't. Add a few mezze to any flatbread and you've got yourself an ad hoc pide pie. For me the beauty of Middle Eastern food is its wealth of flatbread pleasures. There's aromatic zaatar pita, dusted with thyme, sesame seeds, salt, and red sumac berries—which is sufficiently seductive on its own but also pairs well with labneh. Ezekiel bread—not the packaged kind you find in the supermarket—is what some refer to as "Bible bread," made of wheat, barley, beans, lentils, millet, and spelt. And if you want something super crispy, there's lavash (also spelled lavosh), a cross between a cracker and flatbread, dusted in sesame or poppy seeds. Turkish cuisine has other crispy wonders. Borekas are flaky, triangular-shaped pastries with a savory filling, such as spinach, cheese, or ground meat. They are made from borek, or phyllo dough, which is cut into triangles and layered for borekas, or rolled into a cigarette-shaped pastry, called sigara (cigarette) boreka, which remind me of the grown-up (and savory) version of candy cigarettes.

Ali Baba has sticky sweet baklava, but it doesn't compare to Güllüoğlu's, in Brooklyn. It's tough to compete with a Turkish chain that's been in business since 1871 and boasts twelve types of baklava. I didn't even know there *was* more than one kind of baklava before I visited Güllüoğlu's American outpost in Brooklyn's Flatbush neighborhood. If it weren't a safe distance outside Manhattan, I'd have a bad baklava habit. Güllüoğlu's baklava is just as good as any I ate in Turkey. Maybe that's because their pistachios, butter, and wheat flour are all shipped directly from Turkey. They bake the archetypal baklava with vibrant green pistachios, but they also make baklava that's rare in the States, like a hazelnut and milk version. Güllüoğlu manages just the right ratio of phyllo to pistachio to sugary give. I'm most charmed—code for infatuated—by their milky pistachio baklava, which tastes like a phyllo-endowed pistachio custard. Milk is much more popular in Turkish food than any other Middle Eastern cuisine. You'll also come across rice puddings, milk puddings, and thick yogurt topped with fresh fruit.

The most famous Turkish dessert is called Turkish delight—a chewy combination of sugar and cornstarch—scented with rosewater, dusted in powdered sugar, and often studded with pistachios. I didn't like Turkish delight until I ate it in Turkey. I didn't really have a choice. They offer you Turkish delight everywhere you go. But I came home a convert, toting a very large suitcase—the kind you have to check—packed with all kinds of Turkish delight, including rosewater, pistachio, and chocolate-covered jellies.

All of these sticky sweet treats were made to be eaten with a tiny demitasse cup of strong Turkish coffee. Turkey is known for its muddy unfiltered coffee made from finely ground beans boiled in a beautiful copper pot. The best part is the coffee froth—not milk froth—that forms on the top as the coffee boils. And you might want to check your teeth when you've finished a cup. (The grounds that settle at the bottom of the cup often end up in your mouth.) At the end of the meal, they also serve a sweet, soothing apple tea—made from black tea, apple flavoring, and spices—that reminds me of pleasantly watered-down hot apple cider, and fragrant unsweetened Turkish black tea. Both are served in small, dainty glasses, so you can admire the color of the tea.

There's a lot less mingling of dairy and meat in Israeli cooking, and a hell of a lot less pork. Kosher Jews can't even think about lamb doused in yogurt sauce or milk pudding at the end of a meaty dinner. While I can't imagine a yogurtlu-less life, Israelis carve other ambrosial paths to contentment, such as lamb chops in pomegranate sauce or honey-glazed chicken with almonds. It's a seesaw effect of savory meat in delightful negotiation with vibrantly sweet sauce. Of course not all Israelis are observant Jews who keep kosher or strict Muslims who eat only halal food, but most Israeli eateries hedge their bets and serve milk-less baklava, just in case, or go the vegetarian route with the entire menu. In lieu of kebabs, you'll find an assortment of dips, hummus, couscous, cheese-filled borekas, and stuffed pita sandwiches. Taim—an Israeli vegetarian joint in the West Village—specializes in three flavors of falafel: one made with harissa; one made with sweet, roasted red pepper; and another version made with parsley, cilantro, and mint. You could visit three times to find a favorite falafel, or you could just order the sampler platter, which includes all three. Most of the time, I order the sabich, a classic Israeli sandwich stuffed with fried eggplant, a hard-boiled egg, and tahini sauce, and an Israeli salad made with finely chopped vegetables dressed in lemon and olive oil.

At Miriam, a quaint neighborhood spot in Brooklyn, a regular crowd drinks Israeli wines and nibbles on inspired Israeli creations until late in the evening. Out from the kitchen come meatballs in pomegranate sauce, roasted beets in a tangy green tahini sauce, and Jerusalem bread filled with jalapeños, scallions, and feta. But honestly all I could think about during dinner was dessert. I say *could* because, tragically, Miriam no longer serves halva mousse. (I'm thinking of organizing a rally to have it put back on the menu.) Halva (also spelled halwa or halvah) is a popular Middle Eastern confection, made with ground seeds, nuts, or grains and honey or sugar (and sometimes dried fruits). It's a many-splendored confection: there's semolina halva, walnut halva, almond halva, and my darling, sesame halva. I love tahini (ground sesame paste), period. I love savory tahini sauce in my pita just as much as I love honey-sweetened tahini, cooled and cut into halva bars or blocks. I buy packaged halva bars (plain or chocolate-covered) at specialty candy stores or homemade blocks of chocolate-covered halva at Jewish delis. Miriam used to whip this sweet sesame paste into a satiny mousse. The only way I can now get my fix there is by having it crumbled over vanilla ice cream. I'm still praying for the return of the mousse, but I'll take my halva any way I can get it.

Even Miriam is a pretty casual affair. "A nice night out" and "Middle Eastern" aren't often mentioned in the same breath, but it does exist. It's just not as common. In my experience, the fanciest Middle Eastern restaurants in America tend to be Lebanese. Lebanese spots, like Ilili and Byblos in Manhattan, have wine lists, candlelight, and atmosphere. Unlike most Middle Eastern restaurants, they feature not just one or two seafood dishes, but several options, or even a separate seafood section. The most classic fish preparation is whole fish coated and cooked in tahini sauce (samak bi tahini). I was skeptical of this combination, but the outcome is blessedly moist meat, imbued with a light, nutty flavor. Whether it's cooked in tahini or drizzled in tahini after it's cooked, the pairing of tahini and seafood is divine.

Lebanese is a lot more fish friendly than most Middle Eastern cuisines. Ilili's menu features marinated sardines draped over tabouli and an unusually supple black cod cooked in a tagine over tahini sauce and rice. They serve traditional kebabs of beef and lamb, and less conventional variations with duck or spiced cubes of tuna. Like most Lebanese restaurants, Ilili deploys hot spices and sauces more than other Middle Eastern countries. You can order your lamb kebab or whole fish slathered in the archetypal yogurt sauce or hot yogurt sauce.

You'll probably walk into Ilili, take one look at the swanky setting and well-clad crowd, and dismiss it as fashionably ethnic. (I did.) Stay for dinner anyway. I could do without the clubby scene, but the food's excellent. Ilili is an extreme case of Middle Eastern chic, furnished with dark wood walls, red velvet banquettes, and high ceilings. There's pop music in the background and vibrantly colored cocktails with Lebanese twists, like the Sumac Margarita. (Skip those.) As for the food, it's Lebanese enough for most ethnic eaters and sexy enough to entice beginners. The dips are exotically perfumed with thyme, sumac, cumin, and pepper, and the salads are herbaceous and crisp. While it probably sounds unoriginal to get falafel, you should get around to trying Lebanese falafel with not just chickpeas, but fava beans as well. Ilili modernizes a dish or two, but for the most part, the kitchen stays true to Lebanese tradition. A humble side of spiced potatoes may not fit with the setting, but batata harra—fried, cubed potatoes slathered in red pepper, chile, garlic, and coriander—goes well with any of the grilled meats on the menu.

Places like Al Bustan in Midtown Manhattan dig a little deeper into Lebanese food, and I'd take advantage of it if I were you. If you really want to sink your teeth into Lebanese cooking, sample their version of beef pastrami called basturma, a feisty, chewy sun-dried meat, spiced with fenugreek, cumin, and hot pepper. Taste a traditional spicy fish dish called samakeh harra—dosed with cayenne pepper, cumin, and black pepper—and sambousseks, often dubbed Lebanese dumplings or meat pies. To me they look and taste more like empanadas with Middle Eastern fillings, like ground lamb or spinach and feta cheese. You'll find more in the way of vegetables, like okra, squash, and string beans as well as bean soups and salads. And nobody loves bread more than the Lebanese. (Even moldy bread gets a superstitious kiss good-bye, as a sign of respect, before it's thrown away.) They eat spiced lavash crackers with mezze, pita with their shawarma, and sticky cakes for dessert. My favorite Lebanese sweet is fried doughnuts alongside an orange blossom dipping sauce, rice pudding, or a very traditional cheesecake (knefe) crusted in what else but phyllo. (Pita would've been a good guess too, but we're in dessert mode.) Finish the night with a glass of arak, a clear, anise-flavored spirit that packs the same punch as Turkish raki.

## Table Setting and Modern Manners

Dining is a casual, communal affair throughout the Middle East. How formal can it get when everyone is using their pita as silverware and then eating it? It's hands-on dining, so it's a good idea to wash your hands before sitting down to dinner. Dirty hands or nails are frowned upon at the collective Middle Eastern dinner table. (Just a century or so ago, it was customary to set a finger bowl next to every diner's plate.) As is traditional with most grazing cultures, sharing is obligatory. But don't take bread from someone else's plate. And don't reach over people or stand and lean over another guest for a dish. Ask for it to be passed to you, and be an able and willing passer.

Middle Easterners tend to eat with their right hand. Left is for shaking hands. Me, I'm a lefty. As far as I can tell, no one seems to mind, and it's not a rigorously enforced rule. While the complex politics of the Middle East may be famously hostile, the dinner table is a place of hospitality. Even in restaurants, the host offers guests the best table available, unlike some trendy joints that save the best ones for regulars or celebrities. They overfeed rather than underfeed to ensure there's enough to go around. In the domain of a restaurant, that's a very good idea. So, afiyet olsun, b'tayavon, and bil-hanā 'wa ash-shifā'!

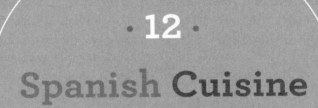

· 12 ·

Spanish Cuisine

*I drink when I have occasion, and*
*sometimes when I have no occasion.*

SANCHO PANZA IN *DON QUIXOTE*

Maybe I should move to Spain. I'm always hungry and always eating, and the Spanish are grazers. Where do you think tapas come from? The Spanish verb *tapar* means "to cover"——one popular explanation has it that at inns in old Spain, drinkers used to cover their glasses of sherry with a slice of bread, to prevent fruit flies from hovering over the sugary alcohol. Innkeepers began adding nibbles of food to the bread "lids" to lure more customers, et voilà, tapas were born. Another theory holds that innkeeps would serve strong cheese with cheap wine to mask or "cover" its subpar quality. And some think it's metaphorical——a "lid" to fend off hunger between lunch and dinner. Whatever the true origin of tapas, they are much more than just snacks. Tapas are a way of eating, a culture unto itself. In fact they're such an integral part of Spanish culture that there's even a specialized verb dedicated to the

· TASTY MORSEL ·

*Since sherry might be the reason tapas were first invented, it's the perfect drink for all tapas endeavors. Sadly, sherry is often overlooked and misunderstood. Many people think of sherry as an outdated spirit, but it's actually an elegant amber wine made from white grapes grown in Jerez and fortified with brandy. There's a wide range, from dry to sweet and light to dark sherries—something for every kind of drinker. So give it a whirl. If you don't like it, you can always go back to whites or reds, preferably from Spain.*

activity of eating tapas: tapear. (Every culture needs one of those verbs.) I "tapeo" all day. I just wish we had a tapas bar on every corner, as they do in Spain.

In the United States, a regimen of three square meals a day is standard: breakfast, lunch, and dinner. That's not Spain's style. They start with a light breakfast—maybe a cup of coffee and a pastry or pan (bread)—then eat a succession of tapas straight through to bedtime, and dinner to boot! Why commit to one large dish when you can sample half a dozen different tapas? No one does bar food better than the Spaniards. They are virtuosos at creating small bites packed with flavor and texture. Take a traditional tapa, like bacon-wrapped dates: a chewy, sweet date, stuffed with a crunchy, smoked almond (and often cheese, too), and wrapped in salty bacon. What more could you want from a bite of food?

Nada. Tapas are strong, spirited snacks, like warm, gooey ham and cheese croquetas, stuffed mussels, or tomato-rubbed toasted bread (pan con tomate). Rub that toast with a little garlic prior to the tomato, and you have the classic Catalan tapa, pa amb tomàquet, a favorite of mine and remarkably simple: just a little olive oil, sea salt, and ripe tomato on warm, crusty bread. A tapa will often showcase just one ingredient: a bowl of grassy green olives, sweet, fire-engine red piquillo peppers, or the rich, unusually creamy Marcona almonds that Spain is so famous for.

At Tia Pol in Manhattan the tapas are so well crafted that if you didn't know better, you might think you were in Spain. It's a teeny spot, but that doesn't seem to stop everyone from cramming in for the most perfect ham croquetas (breaded, fried fritters with a mashed potato and béchamel base—if there are no croquetas on the menu, it's not a real tapas joint), chorizo al jerez (spicy sausage finished with sherry), pinchos morunos (juicy skewers of spiced lamb), and tortilla Española (also called tortilla de Patatas), a cakey potato and egg omelet, served in room-temperature wedges. Before I went to Madrid, I had never considered eating eggs at a bar, no less with a glass of Spanish red wine, but it's a surprisingly smart and satisfying pairing. In a good tortilla Española, the potatoes should be tender and unctuous (in chef speak, that's a good thing—buttery and rich) and the eggs creamy, never rubbery. Tortilla Española is such a staple food in Spain that it's even served as a filling in bocadillos (crusty Spanish sandwiches).

Patatas bravas are another emblematic tapa. Spanish for "fierce" or "brave" potatoes, this famous dish of crispy, olive-oil-fried cubed potatoes is almost always served with a spicy tomato-garlic sauce. (Spaniards don't do ketchup.) These roughly cut potatoes—crispy on the outside, creamy on the inside—are prepared in the most humble tapas bars (tascas) and by the most famous chefs alike. José Andrés, perhaps the most prominent Spanish chef in America (he trained with Spain's legendary Ferran Adrià, molecular gastronomy trailblazer and chef-owner of the world's hardest reservation, elBulli), is still perfecting his version of patatas bravas. (I think they're perfect just the way they are.) Andrés pioneered the tapas trend in America when he opened Jaleo, in Washington, D.C., back in 1993, with a whopping sixty tapas spread over two menus. One features traditional tapas and the other modern tapas that showcase cutting-edge techniques and Andrés's creativity.

Since then, Andrés has opened a Los Angeles outpost called Bazaar that makes the best pa amb tomàquet I've had to date. Bazaar's menu pays homage to classics, like tortilla Española, gazpacho, scallops with salsa verde, and chicken croquetas. None of this is fancy food, even in a renowned chef's hands. It doesn't take an army of chefs to prepare these dishes. Tapas are laid-back, no-reservations food meant to tide you over until dinner, which, in Spain, is typically eaten between nine and eleven at night. That's where I take issue with Spain. I don't want to go for the early bird special, but I do need the ball to be rolling by nine. By that time, I like to be seated with an appetizer in front of me, or at least have placed my order with the kitchen. Otherwise I get hangry, and that's never a pretty sight.

In my experience, an empanada happens to be a wonderful way to ward off hanger. These savory, fried pastry turnovers satisfy even the most severe case of low blood sugar–induced grumpiness. I was smitten with the cinnamon-scented beef empanadas laced with crunchy bits of marcona almonds at La Fonda Del Sol in Midtown. It's almost a good thing they're no longer on the menu, given the limits of my self-control. If you have problems with restraint— you know, if you can't keep your fingers out of that bowl of nuts on the bar?—don't order garbanzos fritos (fried chickpeas) at a tapas joint. They're warm and crunchy, and you'll keep putting them in your mouth no matter how many times you promise yourself you'll stop. Orders of garbanzos fritos line the bar tops at many tascas in Spain, as well as the tables at Tía Pol, where they're gently dusted in sweet paprika.

Though Tía Pol (2004) arrived on the scene two years before Boqueria (2006), Boqueria marked the tipping point for New York City's considerable tapas trend. The opening chef, Seamus Mullen, cooked his way through Spain, and it came through on the menu, which is littered with traditional Spanish snacks— cojonudo (one of my favorites!), quail egg and chorizo on toast (dainty-looking, one-bite wonders); albóndigas, golf-ball-size lamb meatballs; and buñuelos de bacalao, salt cod fritters served with citrus aioli.

Like most tascas, Boqueria devotes a considerable portion of its menu to charcuterie and cheeses. Often I only "window shop" in these departments so I can devote my full appetite and attention to new discoveries and chef-stamped creations. But Spain is not a country where you want to skip this section. Their cured meats are spectacular. People smuggle this stuff back in their suitcases for good reason. Spain is the largest producer of ham in the world, and they take great pride in their hogs, displaying them at the bar or in the window. Boqueria keeps their leg of serrano ham in the storefront window, where the chef sheers off orders of pink, paper-thin ribbons of meat. They peddle plates piled high with spiced chunks of chorizo and morcilla, an unctuous blood sausage, and the sausage of all sausages, salchichón de bellota, made from prized and pricey acorn-fed pigs.

France and Italy used to hog all the attention—no pun intended—for their distinguished charcuterie, but these days Spain deservedly receives just as much love. The turning point was 2008, when importing jamón ibérico from Spain to the States finally became legal. (What a splendid day that was for America.) Also called pata negra (black foot), this cured meat comes from the leg of an Iberian black hog, famous for its delicate nutty flavor and silky texture. It gets even better. Jamón ibérico de bellota is the holiest of all hogs, raised on an all-acorn diet. Apparently pigs love acorns, and nothing tastes better than a happy pig. Bellota is a delicacy, the "Wagyu of Spain." When the opportunity to try jamón ibérico presents itself, seize it. Before it became legal to import, travelers would smuggle bellota into the country in their luggage, and certain Spanish grocers sold it under the counter for a small fortune.

Spain's famous for all of its cured meats (not just the black hog variety), especially jamón serrano made from white pigs. Makes serrano ham so special is that it's air cured at a high elevation (jamón serrano literally means "mountain ham") and then aged anywhere from twelve to eighteen months. It's what I refer to as "au naturel" ham. While white pigs are considered inferior to Iberian black hogs, they taste pretty splendid, too. Hams from other countries tend to be saltier, fattier, and aged for less time. Serrano ham is cured in sea salt and aged like a fine wine, to experience the seasons.

But there's much more to prized pigs than cold charcuterie. Where do I begin? Chorizo with melted bittersweet chocolate or chorizo doused with sherry (both classic combinations) come to mind. If you're a pig lover, it doesn't get better than cochinillo asado. I've eaten hordes of roast suckling pigs, so I feel confident asserting that nobody roasts a better suckling pig than Spain. They have their way with the pig—teasing maximum crispiness from the skin while producing fork-tender meat. La Fonda Del Sol has a dazzling cochinillo asado, paired with figs and an almond puree. (All I need is a spoon and some quality time alone with this crackly-skinned hog.)

What goes well with such robust cured meats? Robust cheeses—and Spain's got quite a few of them. The most well known is La Mancha's nutty Manchego, a semifirm sheep's milk cheese aged a minimum of sixty days. The buttery, piquant flavor of Manchego is beautifully underscored by a swipe of dulce de membrillo—sweet quince pâté. Mahon, a semihard cow's milk cheese, has a flavor that's similar to but slightly saltier than Manchego. Idiazabal is a traditional Basque sheep's milk cheese with an elegant, layered flavor. Basque shepherds kept their flocks high in the Pyrenees throughout the spring and summer. When they descended in autumn, before the first snows, they brought with them this rich, smoky cheese, which they preserved throughout the summer season by storing it in the chimneys of their mountain shelters.

Consider yourself warned: Spain doesn't make beginner blue cheeses. These are strong, smelly cheeses. If you can handle an in-your-face blue, try Cabrales, the most pungent and spicy of them all. (It also pairs well with jamón serrano and a spicy red wine.) If you're up for a blue, but looking for one that's a tad more subdued, there's slightly sweet and complex Valdeón cheese. Wheels of Valdeón always come wrapped in sycamore leaves, which adds to its complex flavor. In Spain, where the best cheeses (including Manchego, Mahon, Idiazabal, and Cabrales) have Denomination of Origin protection, cheese is a dish in its own right. It's not something you add to an omelet or bocadillo.

Technically bocadillos are sandwiches, but you might want to adjust your expectations. Let's start with the bread: all bocadillos (nicknamed bocatas) start with a crusty baguette—no Wonder Bread or sliced rye or multigrain healthy stuff . You're probably familiar with minimalist art. Well, bocadillos are minimalist sandwiches. They're not loaded with fixings: no smear of mayo, mustard, cheese, or lettuce. The baguette is sliced in half, hollowed out, and filled (not stuffed) with anything—from charcuterie, fried calamari, or tuna to tortilla Española—but only one. We have ham

and cheese. They have ham *or* cheese. If you see a chorizo bocadillo on a menu, that's what's in it: chorizo. Bocadillos are often
part of a tapas menu. If you don't see a bocadillo section on the
menu, look for a "Bocata" section. Tapas are typically organized
according to food type or plate size. For instance, you might find
midsize tapas listed in a "Media Ración" section and larger plates
listed under "Raciones." Alternately, dishes might be grouped by
whether they're served hot or cold ("caliente" or "frio"), or by
genre: "queso" for cheese, "embutidos" for charcuterie, "ensala-
das" for salads, and "postres" for desserts.

Of course, there's delicious Spanish food to discover beyond
tapas—though both tapas and larger, family-style dishes share
the same palette of flavors and ingredients. If someone brought
you to a Spanish restaurant blindfolded, you could probably
identify the genre of cooking by the smells wafting through
the dining room: saffron-scented rice, paprika-perfumed paella; fragrant, roasted tomatoes; and briny notes of calamari,
shrimp, and other seafood. Those ingredients aren't particular to
Spain, of course, but they do lie at the heart of Spanish cooking.
Without paprika (smoked pimentón) there would be no chorizo
or patatas bravas. Without garlic, there would be no gambas al
ajillo (garlic shrimp), garlic soup (caldo de ajo), or aioli (garlic sauce). If you don't like garlic, you won't like Spanish food.
There's garlic in almost everything—salsa verde, soups, almond
sauce, patatas bravas, and so on. Spain's pantry isn't stocked with
a blizzard of seasonings, but olive oil, garlic, onions, saffron, almonds, and mild, sweet, and spicy peppers are absolutes. Spanish food is mostly Mediterranean—fish, olive oil, wine, fruits,
vegetables—with a dash of the Romans, Moors, Greece, France,
Africa, England, and even American tomatoes thrown into the

mix. José Andrés likens Spain to a "delta." The Moors introduced nuts and dried fruits, England contributed its sherry, France its madeleines, and Rome its olive trees.

Even within Spain, there are vast regional differences. "Don't think of one Spain. Think of multiple Spains. We are an incredibly diverse country geographically speaking and a country of many cultures, and the cooking reflects this," José Andrés suggests. The Catalonian region of northwest Spain perfectly reflects this diversity; Catalonians speak their own indigenous language: Catalan. And Catalan cuisine reflects the abundance of the region. It's got everything going for it—the mountains, the coast, and the sea. It's a cuisine that pivots around Mediterranean ingredients, like tomatoes, red peppers, artichokes, and chickpeas. Yet it's one of the biggest pork producers in the world, so imagine their massive selection of cured meats. This is a charcuterie lover's paradise. They have lots of cooked duck and rabbit in their repertoire, too. Catalonia is also famous for romesco sauce (a garlicky red pepper and almond puree), gazpacho, bacalao, sweet and sour combinations, and allioli (Catalan for aioli). So it's no surprise that there are restaurants devoted to the region's prodigal cuisine. Mercat, located in the NoHo section of Manhattan,

> **• TASTY MORSEL •**
>
> *Catalan is a Romance language that is similar to but distinct from Spanish, with its own grammar, syntax, vocabulary, and spelling. At a Catalan-style restaurant, for example, embutidos (charcuterie) become embotits. Arroz becomes arros. Patatas bravas become patates braves. Go with your gut—if a dish looks familiar, it is probably just what you think it is.*

specializes in Catalonian classics, like grilled botifarra sausage with butter beans and sautéed spinach (espinacas) with chickpeas, raisins, and pine nuts, as well as seared monkfish with romesco sauce. Mercat's all-Spanish wine list features wines from all over Spain, particularly Catalonia, as well as its cavas, sparkling wine from the Penedes region of Spain.

My family ate a lot of Spanish food growing up. In fact, we went for Spanish food almost as often as we went for Italian or Chinese. Back then there were no tapas restaurants in New Jersey, never mind the country. Every few weeks, we'd pile into the car and drive to the Spanish Tavern in Mountainside, New Jersey. It was twenty-one minutes from our house, twenty-three minutes tops. (When you love a restaurant, you know exactly how long it takes to get there.) My father didn't drink, and he never let us have even a sip of alcohol, but he made an exception for sangria. Sangria is Spain's signature wine punch, composed of wine mixed with brandy, sugar, club soda, and fruit—a fruity, full-bodied concoction. (Red sangria is made with red wine, and white sangria is made with white wine.) He'd order a big pitcher of ruby red sangria and pour each of his three underaged children half a glass, then fish out all the red wine and brandy-soaked chunks of apple and orange with a wooden spoon. My brother, sister, and I rarely fought, unless there was food or sangria involved.

No matter what you ordered for dinner at the Spanish Tavern, the servers brought you a bottomless bowl of garlic soup (caldo de ajo), and my father took full advantage of it. The man could (and often would) down five bowls of this thick, rustic soup made of stale, crusty bread, chicken stock, vegetables, and a mess of garlic. (I'd wager that when the staff spotted our name in the reservation book, they would make an extra pot that morning just to feed him.) We ate what the Spanish eat: plump shrimp slicked in habit-forming garlic and paprika sauce (gambas al ajillo) that we mopped up with bread; crab-stuffed portobello mushroom caps; chicken in a sherry-inflected almond sauce; and a piping hot pan of paella marinera packed with seafood and yellow rice.

For dessert we shared a silky flan sheathed in a translucent layer of caramel and took turns sipping from my mother's Spanish coffee, which was spiked with brandy and set on fire at the table. (You can imagine how disappointed I was to grow up and find out that a regular cup of Spanish coffee doesn't come with fireworks and a nice buzz.) My parents sure knew how to eat. They loved the simple pleasures, which is why they loved Spanish food so much. They loved the bright, defined flavors, the straightforward preparations, and the abundance of seafood.

Spain's surrounded by waters that are flush with sardines, anchovies, octopus, calamari, tuna, and mussels. They're one of the largest seafood consumers in the world, and the country is home to the world's second largest fish market, MercaMadrid. Spaniards eat oceans of seafood. Go out for tapas and you'll find out how commonplace grilled sardines, marinated white anchovies (boquerones), and marinated seafood salad (salpicón) are. They snack on anchovy-stuffed olives and crabmeat-stuffed mushrooms the way Americans eat bar nuts.

Chances are you've tried canned sardines and generic anchovies at some point and called it a day. I don't blame you. I used to cringe when I saw them on a menu until a date brought me to Tía Pol for dinner. It had just opened, so seats in under an hour were still a possibility. "You don't mind if I order for us, do you?" he asked. (Actually, I do.) But I thought it was too early in the relationship to argue, so I bit my tongue. Sure enough, he ordered the boquerones. To top it off, he casually remarked, "I hear you're a big foodie," just as the food arrived. In my book, that's a challenge. Now I had to eat the damn anchovies. So I did. I didn't like my date, but I loved those parsley-flecked and vinegary boquerones.

They were meaty and rich, and nothing like all the salty, fuzzy filets I'd tried in the past. And there's sure to be bacalao (dried, salt-cured cod) in some form on any Spanish menu. A Spanish restaurant with no bacalao is like a Chinese restaurant without pork dumplings. Nothing else keeps cod quite this tender, firm, and flaky as this old-school salt-preservation method, which also makes it easy to shred and mold the fish into popular finger foods like croquetas and buñuelos (imagine croquetas made with bread instead of potatoes). I'm partial to brandada, a gloriously garlicky salt cod mousse, spread on a baguette or eaten straight from a spoon.

Tapas joints like Tía Pol and Boqueria are newbies to New York compared to Sevilla, a landmark Spanish restaurant on a charming corner in the West Village. Since 1941 they've been serving Spanish classics like fried calamari à la Romana (deep-fried battered squid) and pulpo gallego, a Galician dish made with octopus, boiled potatoes, paprika, and salt. Sevilla excels in sangria and mariscada (shellfish stew) every which way. I'm a maximizer, so I like mariscada because you get a little of everything—a generous mix of scallops, lobster, shrimp, clams, calamari, and mussels. (Give or take a shellfish or two.) Sevilla makes five versions of mariscada. There's mariscada al ajillo (garlic), al salsa verde (green sauce made from parsley, garlic, onion, and olive oil), al sevilla (spicy tomato sauce), and al egg sauce. Egg sauce is unique to Sevilla (the restaurant, not the city). But switch it out for marinera (fish-stock-based sauce with white wine, onions, and parsley), and you have Spain's trademark seafood sauces. Not that you won't run into an occasional white wine sauce, or even better, a tangy, thick romesco sauce. Now and then you'll stumble upon salsa al madrileño, which is Madrid getting credit for spicy tomato sauce instead of Sevilla. Once you learn these principal sauces, you'll be able to navigate any seafood section. I'm a big fan of salsa

verde because I love how the clean, fresh flavor of parsley illu-
minates any fish. Sevilla's menu features scallops, shrimp, clams,
crabmeat, mussels, bacalao, and flounder, all in a salsa verde—you
could eat a different one each day of the week.

"A la plancha" is to Spain what smoking is to southern barbecue, so consider it required learning. This is Spain's favorite
cooking preparation, especially when it comes to seafood. The
plancha is a hot metal plate, and what it does to anything grilled
on it is phenomenal. In cooking, you often have to make sacri-
fices. If you want crispy octopus, you also get a dry, rubbery interior. But octopus cooked "a la plancha" is both juicy and crisp.
Thankfully, chefs don't reserve the plancha solely for affairs of
the sea. Steak, carne a la plancha, has the benefit of crusty edges
and a juicy interior. "The sign of a good Spanish chef is whether
he knows how to cook on the plancha," Seamus Mullen asserts.
José Andrés agrees, adding that he should also know his way
around a paella pan.

Not many dishes have a pan devoted entirely to them. *Paella*
actually means "frying pan"—the dish takes its name from the
pan, not vice versa. If paella isn't cooked in a wide, flat-bottomed
pan with two handles, it's not paella. It's just arroz (rice). It's the
magic of the pan and the stove (never an oven) that bequeaths
the socarrat—the nutty crust of rice that forms on the bottom
of the pan. Paella without socarrat is like an apple pie without
the crust. And the more socarrat, the better. My parents never
taught me the word *socarrat*, but they did teach me to dig down
to the bottom and scrape off all the crunchy rice. (I just wish they
hadn't taught my brother and sister, too. Something about loving
all their children the same, blah, blah, blah.) Paellas vary from
region to season, but saffron-stained rice and olive oil are non-
negotiable fixtures. The base is either bomba or Calasparra rice,
both short, absorbent grains, great for soaking up the cooking

liquid. Most feature paprika, saffron, tomatoes, and beans (often lima or green beans), and the protein will vary, depending on the style of paella. Some are seafood-studded paellas, rich with bacalao and fat, sweet scallops; others showcase various meats, like sausage and chicken; and some throw in a little of everything. Paella isn't a casual fling. It requires commitment—rescuing briny, supple clams from their shells, searching for buried chunks of chorizo, and scraping at socarrat. It requires partners in crime as it serves two, and easily feeds three.

I studied Spanish in high school. For our class trip, we went to Don Pepe in Newark, New Jersey, to eat paella, Spain's national dish. But tell that to someone from Spain and they'll protest that tortilla Española and patatas bravas are the country's heart and soul foods. Unless, of course, they're from Valencia, which is where paella originated. It's also where rice is widely grown. Valencians think there is one way and one way only to make paella—the way they do. That's how it works in every culture. A Valencian paella requires chicken, rabbit, white snails, tomato, haricot beans, saffron, paprika, olive oil, and Calasparra rice (rosemary and red and green peppers are optional) all of which happen to be available in fertile, coastal Valencia, but not all over Spain. True Valencian paella should not contain onion, garlic, chorizo, or peas. And most importantly, no seafood! In Valencia, paella was cooked by men only on Sundays, or for special occasions. (Women have paella cooking rights nowadays.)

I'm not going to lie to you: some dishes just taste better in their homeland. For instance you're not going to get better jamón ibérico than in Spain. "Pata negra is the first thing I consume (in great quantities) before I even leave the airport," Seamus Mullen says. But you don't need to be in Spain to find great paella. There are many great variations served across the country, including Washington, D.C., and New Jersey. If you happen to be in New York, Socarrat Paella Bar has a sensational Valencian paella. Get there early or be prepared to wait outside. It's a sliver of a space with two-sided communal tables paved with golden yellow paellas. It's a gold mine for a grazer like me. Nobody's pan is safe. There are no strangers, only plates I haven't tasted yet. Here's what usually happens: I offer the guy next to me a little of my paella, he offers me some of his. It's a chain reaction, and soon everybody's sharing and we've eaten our way through the menu. If the name's any indication, the owner, Jesús Lolo Manso, certainly has his priorities straight. Socarrat's namesake paella has a little of everything, including chunks of beef and chicken, briny, supple mussels, cuttlefish, and an outstanding crust. There are five paellas on the menu, including paella de la Huerta, a vegetarian paella with asparagus, and a paella carne with wheels of chorizo, pork, and chicken. Pasta made in a paella pan, so that the noodles get nice and toasty, is called fideuà. When faced with the dilemma of choosing between two paellas, don't. Instead order one paella and one fideuà, especially if there's squid ink-stained fideuà available—the briny intensity of the ocean painted on noodles.

In Spain cocida madrileno, or simply cocido—a stew of fresh meat, salted meat, sausage, and chickpeas—is as common as paella or tortilla Española, particularly in Madrid, where the dish originated. Abroad, cocido is a rare find, because it's a dish you eat at home. You don't go out for dinner and hope to spot a casserole on the menu. Soups are another story. Sevilla has four soups on its menu: there's hot garlic soup (sopa de ajo) in winter and cold garlic soup (ajo blanco) in summer. Spain has bragging rights to gazpacho, the most famous cold soup in the world. Period. This quintessential summer soup is so widely eaten most don't even know its origin. Often referred to as a liquid salad, gazpacho is a tomato-based, raw vegetable soup made with garlic, onions, cucumber, peppers, vinegar, olive oil, and bread. It's the stale, crusty bread that adds body and thickness to most Spanish soups, including the garlic soup my father used to pound at the Spanish Tavern. Spain has fish soups, shellfish soups, chicken soup, potato soup, and caldo gallego—a Galician soup-cum-stew filled with meats, like pork or chorizo, beans, and potatoes. Hearty soups and thick stews often come with arroz abanda, which means "rice on the side," for mixing into the broth.

## Traditional versus Molecular Gastronomy

Bazaar is an extraordinarily unique restaurant with one foot anchored in tradition and the other in the fantasy of a mad scientist. There are two menus, and they reflect the two schools of cooking: "Blanca" and "Roja." If you want to understand the difference between them, order the olives from both sides of the menu. The traditional, grassy green olives are stuffed with anchovy and wrapped in a shiny red sliver of piquillo pepper. The modern version looks exactly like an actual olive, cautiously spooned out of a glass jar, but is a liquid sphere of olive juice that bursts in your mouth.

Modern Spanish cooking transforms the kitchen into a laboratory and turns conventional technique on its head. José Andrés explains, "I think the avant-garde movement definitely is Spanish in origin and spirit. It is reflective of this creative rebirth, but it is beyond borders in the sense that it looks outward and touches people outside. I think this stuff is bizarre to some now, but in a hundred years it will be classic." The man behind the molecular gastronomy revolution is Ferran Adrià, the legendary Spanish chef. Adrià runs elBulli in Spain, the most famous culinary laboratory in the world, open only six months a year. What does Adrià do the other six months? Tinker with food at the molecular level. He changes liquids into solids and solids into air. Molecular gastronomy is a subject of great debate: Is it cooking or science? Does it threaten traditional Spanish cuisine?

José Andrés doesn't take sides on the subject. Instead, he meditates on both schools of cooking. You can eat like you're in a meson (a traditional inn) at Bazaar, or you can eat like you're at a cutting-edge restaurant that transforms tortilla Española into a liquid served inside a delicate egg shell. "For some reason, people have a hard time understanding that these two styles of cooking can coexist." As my friend Juan Mari Arzak says, 'There is really only one kind of cooking: good cooking.'"

While the technique is sophisticated and scientific, the dishes and the ingredients are essentially the same. The modern approach doesn't forsake the flavors or dishes of Spain. At the end of the day, it's still a tomato, olive, or Valencia orange, albeit a molecularly rearranged version. José Andrés hates the term *molecular gastronomy*. "It means nothing and most of us that cook this style reject the label. I like Spanish avant-garde or techno-emotional cooking. I'm Spanish, and you could say my cooking is Spanish, whether it is modern or traditional, but in the end it is me, a reflection of who I am and the experiences in my life. I cook to please me."

## Desserts

Spain's selection of desserts is short and sweet. (Kindly indulge the pun.) If Spain had a national dessert, it would be flan. The best end to a meal is often this creamy egg custard, traditionally topped with caramel sauce and served cold. The vanilla flan at Bazaar is phenomenally silky and light and as good (if not better) as any I ate in Spain. Tía Pol serves an orange flan, while Sevilla flavors theirs with caramel. Caramel and cream are running themes in Spanish sweets. Cream lays the foundation for a classic caramelized custard called crema catalana with a crunchy, caramelized lid—a lighter version of France's crème brûlée. Spain also makes a milky rice pudding (arroz con leche) and tor- rija—the incredibly crunchy Spanish spin on French toast. They take several sweet cues from France, including sponge cakes, like the buttery, shell-shaped madeleines. You'll often find chocolate or apple tarts, or even better, a torta de Santiago, a moist, rich al- mond tart. And you'll definitely see cinnamon and sugar-coated churros, especially if you go for tapas. One of my favorite end- ings to a meal is a sampling of Spanish cheeses. Or Spanish-style hot chocolate, which is nothing like instant hot chocolate with those miniature dehydrated marshmallows. Their hot chocolate is wickedly concentrated, like a melted chocolate bar served up in a glass.

## Table Setting and Modern Manners

On the whole, Spain is a pretty laid-back country. They're not sticklers for rules. Food isn't a means to an end but rather an opportunity to socialize, snack, and drink. Loud conversation and debate are par for the course in Spain. Drinking between meals is not. But there are a few dos and don'ts you might not expect to find in the rule book.

I had no idea I could be brought up on bread charges. The Spanish way to eat bread is to cut a piece off, not tear it with your hands. I say this from experience. (I've been handed my knife when caught in the act.) They also frown upon dipping your bread in soup, stew, or sauce. (I don't like that rule, especially when there's leftover garlic sauce in sight. I dip when no one's looking.) Put your bread on your plate, not the table. No elbows on the table either, and no hands under the table. It sounds extreme to me, too, but apparently it suggests that you're doing something naughty to yourself or someone else if your hands aren't showing. When in doubt, use your fork and knife. They don't even eat fruit with their hands. Most importantly, enjoy, or as they say in Spain, "Buen provecho!"

# · 13 ·
# Thai Cuisine

*Love is the same as food. It can be sweet,*
*sour, and spicy.*

THAI PROVERB

This is one cuisine where I urge you not to be fearless, at least at first. People who grow up eating Thai food have an incredible threshold for spice, far beyond that of the Thai newbie. It's like some kind of spice superpower. In a good Thai restaurant, mild means spicy, medium means super spicy, and hot means on fire. Unless you are a professional fire-eater or Thai, start with mild. You can always turn up the heat on your next course, but too much heat can take you out of the game for the rest of the meal. (Believe me; you don't want to miss out on Thailand's tempestuous curries, lush coconut soups, and sweet black sticky rice.) I was once bushwhacked by a roast duck salad at SriPraPhai in Woodside, Queens. I'm wild about roast duck, but I didn't see the red chiles coming. For the next twenty-four hours, all I could taste were chiles, and there was no mention of spiciness in the menu's description of the salad. Just imagine how spicy the "spicy beef salad" is!

Before I ate that duck salad, "blazing hot" and "salad" were not words I'd ever used in combination. Thai salads are the sneakiest spice culprits, and they're unusual in other ways, too. In European and American cuisine, "salad" traditionally implies a light, straightforward mix of greens and vegetables tossed in vinegar, oil, or a creamy dressing. But Southeast Asian salads can be complex—and often surprising to the uninitiated. I thought my friend was having dessert before dinner when she ordered som tum—papaya salad—to start. But the papaya in som tum isn't ripe; it's green, crunchy, and slightly sour, almost citrusy. Let me tell you, I could eat green papaya salads every day of summer. The tropical medley of roasted peanuts, dried shrimp, tomatoes, long beans, garlic, and bird's-eye chiles is at once cooling and invigorating.

In Thai cuisine, shredded green mango and green papaya often occupy the spot that lettuce or other greens would in an American or European salad. And instead of oil or a creamy concoction, Thai salads are dressed with fish sauce, lime juice, honey, and chiles. That combination of ingredients and the resulting vibrancy of flavor is what I call the "S Factor" of Thai cuisine. Apart from dessert and rice, everything is salty, sweet, spicy, and sour all at once. It's this bold juxtaposition of flavors that makes Thai food so exciting to eat. Food writers often refer to it as a "balance of flavors," but I think that's misleading. The sweetness of the honey in SriPraPhai's green papaya salad and in the roasted duck salad doesn't neutralize the sear of the chiles. They're still packing heat, so proceed with caution.

There are many paths to achieve the S Factor that embodies Thai cooking. Most Thai food gets its spice from chiles and black pepper; its sweetness from coconut milk, fruits, honey, and palm sugar; its saltiness from fish sauce, shrimp paste, nuts, and dried fish; and its sourness from tamarind, lime, vinegar, and fish sauce. They add coconut milk to curries, and papaya to pork in sweet and sour sauce. They stash crushed peanuts inside vegetable dumplings and shower cashews over wok-fried shrimp in plum sauce. The most traveled route to salty and sour is nam pla, pungent fish sauce—a pale, amber liquid with a potent, briny aroma. The Thai cook with it, dress with it, use it as a table condiment, and add it to another ubiquitous table condiment, prik nam pla. Prik nam pla is what I call Thai hot sauce—a mix of fish sauce, chiles, and lime juice—served in a shallow bowl, the fresh chiles bobbing on the surface. But prik nam pla is not the same "hot sauce" as the thick, ketchup-colored sauce you find in those plastic bottles with a rooster logo and a green squeeze top. That's sriracha—hot chile sauce made from chile peppers, vinegar, garlic, sugar, and salt—which non-Thais add to everything from Malaysian to Chinese food when they crave a little extra heat. I haven't even gotten to the abundance of herbs that lend aromatics, color, and freshness to Thai food, such as lemongrass, cilantro, garlic, ginger, scallions, basil, and mint.

One of my favorite ways to travel to Bangkok, Thailand (without hopping a plane), is by way of tom yum, hot and sour soup teeming with mushrooms, red chiles, chile paste, lemongrass, garlic, cilantro, fish sauce, kaffir lime leaves, and lime juice. But the most pronounced flavor in tom yum is galangal, a gingery root with undertones of pine, which imbues the gutsy broth with a sharp, almost citrus perfume. A Thai restaurant without tom yum on the menu is like an Italian joint with no tomato sauce. And just as with Italian tomato sauce, there are hundreds of takes on this popular soup: the most common are tom yum goong (or kung), made with shrimp, and tom yum gai, made with chicken. Tom kha soup combines tom yum broth and coconut milk into one sumptuous, silky blend. Kaffir lime leaves, fresh lemongrass, chiles, fish sauce, palm sugar, and onions infiltrate every drop of the coconut milk. In my not-so-humble opinion, I think tom yum goes best with shrimp and tom kha goes best with chicken. There are plenty of other sassy soups, including a curative chicken and galangal soup thickened with coconut milk, or a spicy shrimp and seafood soup replete with an embarrassment of shell-on shrimp, cod, crab, fish balls, and other fish riches.

Where Thai is concerned, there's no such thing as too many flavors or textures in a dish, or in a meal. In most cultures you have to make choices: you pick a meat or a fish, a salad or a soup, rice or noodles. A typical Thai dinner includes all of the above, the more variety the better. So eat like a native and order a little of everything. Technically there are no starters, entrées, or sides. In the United States, Thai menus are usually divided into appetizers, entrées, and sides, but take those categories as suggestions, not absolutes. Everything is on equal ground, and everything is shared. The rest is fair game for everyone at the table. Rice is served at every meal, and it's the only thing you can claim as yours.

Thai rice (called khao) is one of life's cheapest and most rewarding pleasures. There's moist sticky rice, coconut rice, white rice, jasmine rice, and black rice. I refuse to choose between them. I never say no to banana-leaf-wrapped bundles of steamy, sticky white rice, or better yet, exotic black rice: just unwrap and nibble the glutinous grains right out of the wrapper. Black rice is also called purple sticky rice because it turns purple when cooked. And there's coconut-milk-bathed white rice, or white rice bathed in a savory chicken stock. One of my favorite Thai desserts is a luscious black rice pudding, steeped in coconut milk. I love jasmine rice (also known as Thai fragrant rice), just not for dessert. Jasmine's much better suited to rich savories and curries because of its potent and nutty aroma.

In Thailand, Thai rice is like edible Play-Doh for grown-ups, which you get to eat with your hands. Scoop out a little with your hand (make sure they're freshly washed), roll it into a ball, and go to town. The rest of the dishes should be eaten with a fork or a spoon. The Thai are the only Southeast Asian culture that doesn't use chopsticks. They use forks in lieu of knives, and spoons

### • TASTY MORSEL •

*There's a good chance pad thai wasn't originally created by the Thai at all. Most believe it was first introduced to Thailand by Vietnamese traders centuries earlier, and the dish didn't become commonplace in Thailand until World War II. During the 1930s and 1940s, Thailand's prime minister, Luang Pibulsonggram, promoted and encouraged the production of rice noodles as a way to stem unemployment and grow the Thai economy. His government even distributed pamphlets detailing how to produce rice noodles and dishes to use them in, including recipes for pad thai. Before long, pad thai carts were popping up on street corners from Bangkok to Chiang Mai.*

for everything else. You wouldn't put a knife in your mouth, so—when eating Thai—don't stick your fork in your mouth, either. A fork is for shoveling rice, noodles, and whatever else you're eating onto your spoon. For some strange reason, Thai restaurants in the United States sometimes place chopsticks on the table. And I've only seen a few people eat rice with their fingers, but hopefully that will catch on soon in the States.

Rice is Thailand's main staple. The sauces and curries are there to complement the rice, not the other way around. Without rice, there would be no dumplings, wrappers, or rice noodles. There would be no pad thai. (That should get people's attention.) Pad thai is a gateway drug to Thai food. People get hooked on the thin rice noodles glossed with fish sauce, lime, tamarind, garlic, and chiles. They crave the feast of flavors and textures—the supple noodles, crunchy bean sprouts and peanuts, the fragrant herbs, egg, and plump shrimp or chicken. It's hard to believe that pad thai is street food. In Thailand, they have hawker carts that peddle spring rolls, pad thai and other noodles, and barbecued satays. Pad thai is a great litmus test of a chef. If I get gloppy, overly sweet pad thai, I grab the check. Pad thai is supposed to be a delicate noodle dish, so look for pad that's dressed, not drenched, in sauce. Life's too short for subpar food, and there are plenty of cheap and tasty Thai restaurants all over the country. In fact, some takeout places make the best pad thai. I don't have to leave my apartment, never mind the island of Manhattan, to get Wondee Siam's sensational shrimp pad thai.

There are four Wondee Siam outposts in Manhattan, but my favorite spot to eat their pad thai is on my couch. I usually start with an order of duck spring rolls filled with crispy bits of duck, bean thread noodles, basil, julienned cabbage, taro, and shiitake with a plum dipping sauce, and the barbecued chicken satay— a snack-sized skewer threaded with chunks of grilled marinated meat, which comes with a toothsome peanut sauce and cucumber sauce. The beef and chicken satays at Wondee Siam are first marinated in a blend of coconut milk and curry powder, then imbued with the grill's smoky char. The Thai people immigrated from south China in the tenth century and brought a few Chinese influences with them, including satays. I've had chicken satays at Chinese restaurants, and Thai satays blow them out of the water. (No offense, China.) Southeast Asian satays win my vote on the basis of the dipping sauces alone. (The Chinese usually serve hoisin sauce with satays.) Fried rice (kaw pad) also made its way from China to Thailand. I often order Thai fried rice studded with pork, pineapple, cashews, and tomato. I'm not going to take sides on this one, though, because they're so different. Instead of white rice, the Thai use jasmine rice, which imparts an elegant aroma and a nutty flavor. And they season with lime juice, fish sauce, chile peppers, and soy sauce.

Just like Chinese food, most Thai food is wok cooked. You could eat wok-fried squid with basil-chile sauce one night and wok-fried duck with ginger-chile sauce the next. No matter which you settle into, you'll notice how much sweeter the dark soy sauce tastes in Thai stir-fries than salty Chinese soy sauce. The wonders of the wok also account for most noodle dishes, including "drunken" noodles (pad kee mao), sautéed with garlic, dark soy, chiles, and basil leaves. Drunken noodles is a hearty, warming dish—the kind you eat after a long night of drinking, thus its name. (The chiles are supposed to wake up drunk, drowsy night owls.) The rice noodles in pad kee mao are much wider than the ones in pad thai, a bigger canvas for the feisty seasoning. For the spice fearing, there's pad see ew, a classic noodle dish made with the same kind of panfried noodles as pad kee mao, except these are sautéed with Chinese broccoli, egg, and a sweet brown sauce. Following the wrath of the roast duck salad my first night at SriPraPhai, our server took pity on me and suggested rad na, a delightfully mild sauté of beef, Chinese broccoli, extra-wide rice noodles, mushrooms, garlic, and a thick, savory gravy. If you want to taste the scope of noodle dishes, SriPraPhai is the place to do it. The menu features over twenty noodle dishes. Some noodles arrive in dark, spicy sauces or colorful curries; others are dropped into rich, fragrant broths. And noodles are just the beginning of it—SriPraPhai's menu is over twenty-five pages long. I could eat here every night of the week for a year and never tire of the phenomenal selection or the food. (Maybe I'll write my next book about that. It sounds much easier than trying to cook Julia Child's recipes for 365 days.)

SriPraPhai is no secret, despite its out-of-the-way location in faraway Woodside, Queens. Word leaked years ago, and this former hole-in-the-wall has since tripled in size, received a fresh coat of paint and some flat-screen televisions. But the food's just as delightful as it ever was, and that's all that really matters. I've never seen a concise Thai menu, so don't get caught up in the vastness or order-by-number system many Thai restaurants use. It's a lot easier to repeat a number than try to correctly pronounce unfamiliar dishes, like pad kra-prao gai (stir-fry chicken with chile-basil sauce) and gaeng khiao wan goong (shrimp green curry) anyway. Instead of skipping a dish because you can't pronounce it, use the number! Most menus are organized into sections that include salads, soups, rice, noodles, curries, seafood, meat, and duck. The majority of people in Thailand are Buddhist, so there's almost always a tofu and vegetable section for vegetarian foodies as well. There's really no wrong way to order, as long as you play the field.

Think of it as a choose-your-own-adventure meal. In most Thai restaurants, you can pick your sauce and your protein. (For instance, I like green curry with shrimp and red curry with chicken.) Start with a salad or two, like gingery squid or crispy-skinned duck in a cool tangle of papaya. At SriPraPhai, I break my cardinal rule and start with the same thing every time. I'm a hypocrite. I can't help it. I have no willpower in the face of larb. Larb is a Thai salad with ground meat. In my case, I always go for moo—pork—but you can switch out the pork for chicken (gai) or beef (nuea) if you like. My eye automatically does a search for moo. It's like a tick I can't control, especially when it comes to larb moo, a toothsome union of tender ground pork punched up with dry chiles, ginger, mint, lime, and toasted rice. SriPraPhai also dishes up homey, savory chicken curry puffs, which aren't so much puffs as fried flour pastries filled with chicken, potatoes, and onions, loaded with curry and black pepper. They serve sweet, pork sausages mingled with cucumber and onions; fried spring rolls stuffed with crabmeat and pork; and build-your-own lettuce wraps with ground gai, nuea, or moo, too. (You just learned three juicy Thai terms.)

Here in the States, an English translation will almost always

appear right below the Thai name on most menus, so you don't
need to learn an entirely new language just to eat new things.
The only place I've ever been without an English menu was in
L.A.'s Thai Town. I used the plates floating around the room as
my visual menu. Really, everything you need to know about Thai
food can be learned sitting in the restaurant. Instead, imagine
what's in the kitchen's pantry. You can't cook Thai food without
coconut milk, bird's-eye chiles, cilantro, fish sauce, dried shrimp,
basil, lime, lemongrass, garlic, and nuts. (If you're allergic to
nuts, this is not your cuisine.) The Thai are ingredient addicts
who can't get enough variety and texture. Thai is crack for flavor
addicts. Crunch is key: nuts, toasted rice, sprouts, and raw vegetables come to mind.

Thailand's surrounded by water, so consider it your duty as
a diner to delve into the seafood selection. And nobody makes
crispier fried fish than the Thai. Terrifically crispy sea bass, trout,
and snapper, served whole, come flavored every which way. Take
your pick of curries, or sweet and sour, tamarind, chile, and garlic
sauces. I often marvel over SriPraPhai's fried snapper anointed
with a lemongrass sauce so herbaceous I wonder if they picked the
herbs just before depositing the sauce on my plate, or the steamed
trout heaped with fresh ginger and scallions. If you have trouble
making decisions, you'll have a hell of a time picking a fish, its
preparation, and flavor. But I surprised even myself when I fell for
a friend's fried snapper in a chile-dosed red curry sauce. I assumed
I'd take a bite and instantaneously combust, and that would be my
first and last taste of Thai curries. Instead, the curry's heat built
slowly and subtly, just enough to ignite my mouth without sear-
ing my taste buds, while the coconut milk in the sauce seemed to
keep the chiles in check. Being the nosy eater that I am, I asked
our server to list the ingredients in the red curry. "A lot," she
snipped, then stormed off. (If you want to piss a busy server off,
that's the way to do it.) I looked up the recipe when I got home

that night, and after reading the laundry list of ingredients, I don't blame her for being annoyed. There are dried red chiles, garlic, galangal, shallots, shrimp paste, lemongrass, coriander, cumin, and whatever else the chef at SriPraPhai felt like tossing into the mix on that particular night.

While Indian curries are traditionally made with dried spices and herbs, most Thai curries are made with fresh herbs, and many look more like soups or stews than sauces. (Thai curries are composed of a chile and herb paste mixed with either water or coconut milk.) The best way to differentiate among curries is by color. Red curry gets its reddish hue from dried red chiles and its briny undertones from shrimp paste. It's a mild, versatile curry, as good with beef and bamboo shoots as it is with shrimp. Green curry is—no surprise—made with green chiles. I am smitten with Thai green curry; its vivid broth is an aromatic result of the fresh coriander, basil, kaffir lime leaves, and green chiles that form its base. (I like green curry with seafood, but I'll happily make an exception for roast duck.) Mild yellow curry, colored with turmeric, tastes great with coconut milk and chicken, or with seafood. But for most affairs of the sea, I like orange curry, sometimes called "Jungle Curry," spiced with dried red chiles and made tangy and sour with tamarind. Panang curry and massaman curry are both great beginner curries—not too spicy and richly flavorful. Panang is a dry curry—that means the curry paste is fried in coconut milk (or coconut cream), not boiled in coconut milk. As a result, the liquid burns off, and it's a thicker, pastier curry than the more soupy red curry, which it resembles in color. Massaman curry is like the love child of Thai and Indian curry, usually made with a spice mixture of cardamom, cumin, cloves, and cinnamon. Most versions of massaman curry that I've seen are made with coconut milk and feature meat, potatoes, and peanuts.

I lost a lot of time with Thai desserts because I assumed that they weren't worth considering. I was devastated to find out how wrong I was. Black rice pudding and coconut custard both rank high on my list of all-time favorites. What makes most Thai desserts so damn irresistible is how sticky, moist, and luscious they are. Instead of butter or dairy, they depend on coconut milk, rice, palm sugar, and exotic fruits. They drizzle fried bananas with honey and crown coconut sticky rice with sliced mango. The owners of Sri-PraPhai must know that diners won't have the discipline required to save room, so they keep a refrigerator case in the dining room stocked for to-go orders of marzipan candies, syrup-poached egg yolks, and sticky rice treats. It's nice to have an emergency backup plan, but you'll miss out on the warm, just-steamed cakes made from chestnut flour and filled with deeply earthy mung beans. The menu features coconut milk studded with tapioca pearls and lycheelike longan fruit, and lots of exotic fruits and flavorings, like jackfruit custards, mango puddings, and pandan-leaf-scented ice creams and cakes. My favorite is the black sticky rice crowned with custard. If you're looking for something to cool down your mouth, you might try a sweet and creamy Thai tea, a floral, spicy black tea sweetened with condensed milk. During dinner, they like to drink a mild Thai whiskey, or any Southeast Asian beer, including Singha.

## Table Setting and Modern Manners

The Thai season liberally, so you never have to worry about insulting the chef by adding more nam pla or any other sauce. Since spoons are the primary utensil, it's important not to dip yours into any communal dishes. There will be serving spoons on the table for that. If necessary, there's a fork on the table to shovel food onto your spoon, but remember not to put the fork to your mouth, or your soup bowl for that matter. The Thai live for eating, but they always leave enough for everyone at the table. They usually take enough for a three- or four-mouthful serving at a time, then pass it on. They also frown upon putting too much in your mouth in any one bite. The most serious offenses are chewing-related ones, so try not to chew loudly or with your mouth open. On a brighter note, they don't mind elbows on the table one bit. Enjoy dinner! Or, as the Thai say, "Kŏr hâi jà-rern aa-hăan!"

# · 14 ·

# Vietnamese
# Cuisine

*Rice and fish are as inseparable as mother and child.*

VIETNAMESE PROVERB

I magine that you sleep in a serene bamboo hut on stilts overlooking acres of rice paddies. Hot, coastal country. Wandering rivers, mountains, and beaches. Your backyard is flush with wild lemongrass, lettuce, basil, cilantro, perilla, pandan leaves, and mint bushes. If you reach up high enough, you can pluck a coconut, a lime, or a banana from a tree limb. You can even fish for your dinner, then wrap your fresh catch in a banana leaf and cook it over an open flame. Break open a coconut and cook a handful of rice in the luscious milk. Voilà, dinner is served.

Vietnamese food is sexy. You may never have been to Vietnam, but you can still taste the land and the sea in its cooking. My first trip there was by way of Nha Trang in downtown Manhattan. Apart from a few plants and pictures of Vietnamese idylls along the walls, it doesn't look remotely like the subtropics. But what comes out of the kitchen tastes romantic and unexpected. There are steamy soups perfumed with herbs, cool salads that pack a seductive heat, slippery noodles, and sultry finger foods, skewered on sugarcane or stalks of lemongrass. Dinner at Nha Trang was like taking an advanced class as a beginner. There are exactly one hundred dishes to choose from, and I didn't know what a single one was. I was in way over my head. There was talk of foreign dishes—frog legs with curry sauce, shrimp with preserved sour vegetables in oyster sauce, and barbecued pork paste. "Exactly how do you make a paste out of pork?" I wondered. "And how do you barbecue a paste?" This was one of the few times I was happy to be at a big group dinner, where someone else was ordering for the table. I figured the more dishes on the table, the more likely it was that I'd find something "safe" to eat. I felt like Alice after she'd fallen down the rabbit hole, desperately in need of my own White Rabbit to guide me through this mysterious culinary adventure.

We began with cooling goi cuon (summer rolls, also called salad rolls)—sheets of translucent rice paper wrapped around shrimp, carrots, onions, cilantro, and cold vermicelli noodles—served with a thick peanut dipping sauce. The rolls were refreshing and re-splendent with texture—the crunch of carrots, the slight resis-tance of shrimp, the slippery vermicelli. We followed the summer rolls with addictively crispy squid in garlic sauce that I could snack on all day. The rest of the evening is a blissful but blurry memory, though I vaguely recollect delicate chunks of lobster skimming the tangy, tart surface of a sweet and sour sauce, lemony canh chua ga (hot and sour chicken soup), and a steamed pork casserole bathed with a mysterious "special Vietnamese sauce" so addictive that the bowl was practically clean by the time I was through with it. On a return trip to Nha Trang (I couldn't get that "special Vietnamese sauce" out of my head, so I went back for more) I ended up fall-ing for the chao tom, an appetizer of moist, ground shrimp paste formed into patties—reminiscent of giant meatballs—and grilled on sugarcane skewers. The banh cuon (Vietnamese ravioli made of silky rice sheets), stuffed with minced chicken and mushrooms and steeped in lemongrass, garlic, and nuoc mam (fish sauce), were yet another revelation.

I had no idea a restaurant like Nha Trang existed in New York, especially on the edge of Chinatown. The only Vietnamese restaurants I'd been to featured Vietnam's "greatest food hits," like sates (the Vietnamese spelling of satays, grilled skewered meats served with peanut sauce), spring rolls, sticky rice, and bowls heaped with bun (rice noodles), but nothing as unfamiliar and exciting as the Nha Trang menu. For most of my life, I had equated Vietnamese cooking with just the "greatest hits" until I stepped foot inside Nha Trang. That was in 1995, and Vietnamese food wasn't as commonplace in New York then as it is now.

These days, there are pho shops all over the city, banh mi trucks roaming the streets of Los Angeles, and even a Vietnamese beer garden in downtown Manhattan. In 2009, Michael Bao Huynh began building an empire of Vietnamese eateries in New York City, including a restaurant called Bia Garden on the Lower East Side. If I weren't the kind of person who hunts down restaurants, I might have missed it, and I would've missed out. There was a dinky grill out front, the kind you'd find in someone's backyard. Stepping down a flight of stairs, I found myself at a grungy takeout counter. When the hostess appeared, she escorted me through a walk-in refrigerator

• TASTY MORSEL •

*Beer Lao is the national beer of Laos, especially popular with backpackers and travelers throughout Southeast Asia. Its limited availability outside of Laos has turned it into something of a cult item—"Beer Lao" T-shirts are prized souvenirs in the United Kingdom.*

door and then down a narrow hall with beer bottles lining one wall and an open kitchen along the other. At the end of the hall, I suddenly found myself in a dimly lit covered garden. I had the sense I was in on a secret: diners sat on long benches at rough wooden tables topped with Café du Monde coffee cans repurposed as chopstick holders, and ice buckets filled with twelve different kinds of Asian beers, like Tiger, Tsingtao, Taj Mahal, and Kingfisher. My favorite was Beer Lao, a refreshing rice-based lager that paired well with all the sumptuous meats and spicy options, like barbecued pork spring rolls and the spicy seafood hot pot.

I nibbled on crispy pork belly drizzled with nuoc mam, and the classic Vietnamese dish bo luc lac or "shaking beef," so called because of the action of "shaking" the beef in a hot wok, which consists of tender cubes of beef sautéed with nuoc mam, garlic, and onions, served over a bed of watercress. Baked whole fish can at times be bland and tedious with all the deboning, but at Bia Garden it was a deliciously vibrant feast that required—and deserved—every inch of table space. A shimmering pink snapper arrived crowned with a fistful of scallions and crushed peanuts, trailed by a basket of fresh herbs, a bowl of pickled onions, another of fish sauce, and two small plates, one of mushrooms and one of rice paper. You dipped the rice paper in warm water and built your own fish wrap with a little of everything in it. If you headed back through the long hallway to the takeout counter, you could've even ordered a banh mi (a Vietnamese sandwich) to go.

A sandwich—the functional lunch box food of children and office workers the world over—may not be the first thing that comes to mind when you think of Vietnamese food. But if you know anything about Vietnamese food, then you've probably heard of banh mi (pronounced "bun me"), a bit of a paradox in terms. A banh mi—a crusty French baguette larded with anything from pâté to grilled meats, fragrant herbs, and pickled vegetables—is much more than just a sandwich. It's the delectable love child of the French colonization of Vietnam, a chic hoagie with everything going for it: spicy, sweet, salty, and crunchy. And the crustier the baguette, the better. Instead of one world of meats to choose from, you have two: you can fill your sandwich with France's rich pâtés, sausages, bologna, and ham, or Vietnam's barbecued beef, pork chops, lemongrass chicken, and crispy catfish (many banh mi shops offer tasty vegetarian options like curried mock duck and grilled tofu). The toppings are all Vietnam's doing: crunchy pickled carrots and daikon, fresh cilantro and cucumbers, jalapeño, spicy chile mayonnaise, and native coriander (rau ram).

My favorite banh mi in New York happens to be made in the back of a jewelry store in Chinatown, at a place called Banh Mi Saigon Bakery, where you can get the world's biggest and best banh mi for $3.75. I'm tempted to tell them they're undercharging, but I don't think their customers would appreciate it very much. My go-to order is the roast pork banh mi and a Vietnamese rainbow ice—a dessert of shaved ice topped with red beans, jellies, and condensed milk. But I always have a hard time choosing: there's a terrifically salty sardine banh mi, and a tropical papaya and shrimp banh mi, which are also great. Really, the only one they're missing is, oddly, the great and classic banh mi dac biet, stuffed with the works—pâté, head cheese, and a variety of thinly sliced cold cuts. And whether they're referred to as "Vietnamese hoagies," "Vietnamese subs," or even "Vietnamese po'boys" (as they are in New Orleans), banh mi are hugely popular across the country, especially in Houston, Dallas, Los Angeles, the Twin Cities, and Northern California, where the first Lee's Sandwiches—which sells Vietnamese and European-style Sandwiches—opened in 2001. There are more than three dozen Lee's outposts in the country, many doling out banh mi's from a drive-thru window.

Before banh mi got big, there was pho and its fanatics. Simply speaking, pho (pronounced "fuh") is simmered beef noodle soup, but it's a deceptive bowl of soup, with a bewitching aroma that smells curiously sweet and redolent of anise, ginger, cinnamon, and cloves. The first thing Michael Bao looks for at a pho shop is a cloudy broth. If it's cloudy, pho-get it. (I couldn't resist.) The clearer the broth, the better the pho. Pho broth's flavor comes from slowly simmered beef bones, and it must be skimmed frequently to remove the liquefied fat. Pho should taste delicate and complex, not heavy. The broth is brightened by lime, basil, bean sprouts, and a hint of cilantro. Some pho parlors serve the garnishes on the side, while others toss them into the broth on their way out the kitchen door. (Garnishes on the side are a good sign of quality pho.) How do you eat pho? Garnish as you go, so you don't get stuck with soggy sprouts or herbs halfway through the bowl. Pho has come a long way from the streets of Vietnam to trendy parlors with cutesy names, like Absolutely Phobulous in L.A., Pho Show, Pho and I, or Phobulous in Edmond, Oklahoma.

You can get the hang of a pho menu fast. Once you understand that pho is beef noodle soup with wide white rice noodles (banh pho) made just for pho, you can pick your protein by looking at the word that follows it. If you want beef in your soup, look for pho bo, or if you prefer chicken, look for the pho ga. Can't make up your mind? Get the pho bac diet, which like the banh mi bac diet, translates to a little of everything. Anything with *bac* in the name, like the pho bac, means it's a traditional dish prepared the way it used to be back in the day. Pho bac is the original, Hanoi-style soup, with notably wide, soft noodles. I like my meat rare (tai), so I scan the pho selection for "tai" and work backward. I'm crazy for pho tai nam gan with meltingly soft, rare beef brisket and saw-tooth herb (not always available)—the edges look like the teeth of a saw—on the side. Some pho fanatics swear this exotic, serrated coriander makes or breaks pho. I'm not sure it's a deal breaker, but I love the fragrance it emits when you tear up the leaves. When the opportunity of the sawtooth herb presents itself, remember to tear and inhale before dropping it in the bowl.

Noodles play a pivotal role in the Vietnamese kitchen. With the exception of pho noodles, they don't play second string to broth. I used to take noodles for granted. In fact it wasn't until I took a liking to Vietnamese cooking that I appreciated the unique texture of different noodles in different cultures. My awakening happened at lunch, over a cold glass noodle salad with crab—and I was never quite the same. When I first saw the plate, I rushed to judgment. "Where's all the crab? And there's barely any vegetables," I said bitterly inside my head. (I have lots of conversations with myself.) I fished out some crab, and then I finally gave in, and scooped up a bunch of glass noodles (aka cellophane noodles). Glass noodles are made from mung bean starch, and as a result, they're pleasantly elastic. The second the translucent strands touched my tongue, the seduction began. They were cool, smooth, and slippery, and my tongue had to chase them around. The balance between the noodles, crab, and vegetables ended up being absolutely perfect. After my lunch of glass noodles, I quickly began experimenting with other Vietnamese noodles: tender egg noodles, delightfully chewy arrowroot noodles, and the quintessential Vietnamese noodle, bun, vermicelli rice noodles that are skinner than pho noodles and less slippery than glass noodles.

I took a crash course in bun at the eponymously named Bun in SoHo. I climbed mountains of soft, springy bun noodles piled with grilled meats such as pork chops, lamb sausages, shrimp, and even slices of crispy, slender spring rolls. The best part of eating a bowl of bun is the delightful layering of all the ingredients. The bottom of the bowl is filled with fresh herbs, cucumber, bean sprouts, lettuce, and fish sauce. Then come the noodles and, finally, the protein, and my crack—crushed peanuts. Give it a good toss with your chopsticks to reap the reward of the raw vegetables and seasonings at the bottom of the bowl and go to town. It's a high-octane symphony of textures and salty, sweet, and sour flavors—a little like Korean bibimbap, though I'm sure the Vietnamese would see it the other way around. I couldn't keep my chopsticks out of a bun at Bun that was topped with searingly spicy chicken. The genius of bun is balance: every time my mouth was set ablaze with red chiles, it was promptly subdued by tart shavings of pickled papaya, minty hints of fresh coriander, crunchy carrots and daikon, and the aggressive pungency of fish sauce. The food at Bun is modern Vietnamese: instead of plain old pork, bun noodles are crowned with Berkshire pork belly and jumbo shrimp. Instead of sirloin, there's bun with hanger steak, chopped apples, and mint. Bun—the noodles, not the restaurant—also make an appearance in soups, stocked with seafood or chunks of pork. Bun also serves a marvelous dish called Mekong bun soup, filled with crab, shrimp, and basa, a flaky white fish that soaks up the full-flavored seafood broth.

The Vietnamese make very good use of all those rice paddies. Bun and pho noodles wouldn't exist without rice flour. Neither would rice paper, and you can't make summer rolls or spring rolls without it. Rice is also served in its original state with almost every meal. There's warm sticky rice, or jazzed-up bamboo-studded rice, coconut-bathed rice, fried rice, fragrant jasmine rice, and broken rice, made from fractured rice grains. If you're looking for rice-based dishes on a Vietnamese menu, look for the com dia (rice dish) section of the menu. Just like bun, com dia plates come topped with anything and everything—grilled pork chops, lemongrass chicken, caramelized tofu, or vegetables. Nha Trang has twenty different com dia dishes, which makes choosing just one extremely difficult. My top com dia is crowned with squid, lemongrass, and chile.

The Vietnamese seem to bring out the best in squid. I'm not sure what goes on behind kitchen doors, but what comes to the table is crispy at the edges, chewy within (but not at all rubbery), and tremendously sweet. They take full advantage of the waters that surround and run through the land, which may account for the frequent squid sightings on Vietnamese menus. They eat small fish in stews, in dumplings, and in stir-fries. Canh chua is a radiant seafood soup made with tomatoes, okra, pineapple, sprouts, and spices. Canh chua tom is a wonderfully acidic, hot and sour shrimp soup similar to Thai tom yum. Bigger fish are typically steamed in banana leaves or cooked in clay pots, and often served whole. One of my favorites is their whole fish glazed in Vietnamese-style sweet and sour sauce. Like so many cultures, the Vietnamese make their fair share of stews, casseroles, and curries. Vietnamese curries are soupier and milder than Thai curries. I love chicken curry creamy with coconut milk and laced with fish sauce, curry powder, ginger, and lemongrass.

Vietnamese seasonings fall into four categories: sweet, sour, spicy, or all of the above. Think of fish sauce (nuoc cham) and chile sauce (sriracha) as the Vietnamese salt and pepper. Almost every dish that comes out of the kitchen is seasoned with one or the other, or both. Look around a pho parlor and you'll see patrons igniting their pho with a squirt (or two) of sriracha, which is a blend of garlic, sugar, and chiles. The dipping sauce is made of nuoc mam, chiles, garlic, and sugar. Nuoc mam—umami in a bottle—is a pure fish extract, and it's the main ingredient in nuoc cham. In the early

> **• TASTY MORSEL •**
>
> *Fish sauce, an essential ingredient that imparts umami (the "fifth" taste, savoriness) to Vietnamese and Thai food, may seem like a condiment particular to East and Southeast Asian cuisine. But the classic British condiment Worcestershire sauce is a kissing cousin to fish sauce. Worcestershire sauce's primary ingredient is, yep, fermented anchovies.*

days, it was actually a primary source of protein for those unable to
venture into deep ocean waters for large fish. As with wine, there's
a serious fermenting process that goes into producing nuoc mam,
which involves salting anchovies, then pressing and aging them in
barrels for six months to a year. You don't want to dip your finger
in the fish sauce and eat it on its own. It's too pungent and salty,
but when you mix it into a dish, the pungent aroma mellows out
and adds a lot of flavor.

Despite France's historical colonial influence, dessert isn't a
huge part of Vietnamese cuisine. They do eat sweets in Vietnam,
but usually as a snack between meals, not at the end of the meal.
The Vietnamese mostly drink their desserts. When you have such
unusual fruits like jackfruit and durian at your fingertips, that's a
wonderful thing. Everything from longan to pineapple, and even
avocado, makes its way into delightfully thick fruit smoothies,
sweetened with a small splash of condensed milk. In the same way
that fish sauce is crucial to savory dishes, condensed milk is crucial
to sweets. You'll find condensed milk in custards, yogurts, ices, and
even Jell-O. In fact, instead of adding milk to coffee, in Vietnam
they add coffee to condensed milk. Iced Vietnamese coffee happens
to be one of my favorite desserts. It's super-sweet, super-silky, and
super-strong. Vietnamese tea is also strong but usually unsweetened. The caffeine-sensitive might want to opt for a salty lem-
onade (chanh muoi) instead, made with muddled pickled limes
and a dash of sugar. It's true to its name: salty, sweet, sour, and
refreshing. Of course, if there's che on the menu, all bets are off.
Che refers to any sweet soup or pudding, and for me, it ranks right
up there with Vietnamese iced coffee. There are hundreds of kinds
of che: hot, cold, some made with coconut milk and beans, others
with fruit, seeds, jellies, rice, and tapioca. I've had che served in a
bowl with a spoon and served over ice in a plastic cup, and both are
equally delicious.

## Table Setting and Modern Manners

This is sultry food, the kind you can eat with your hands. (Think rice paper purses and shrimp and short rib lollipops with lusty dipping sauces.) Obviously you don't want to toss your noodles with your hands, but you can hold the bowl as close to your face as you please. (It's not bad manners in Vietnam.) That includes a bowl of rice, too. You can eat your rice straight from your bowl, using chopsticks to maneuver it into your mouth. Since Vietnamese rice tends to be sticky, you can also use your chopsticks to take communal rice, too. They eat with long chopsticks with blunted ends, and they always use both at once. It's tradition to pick up your bowl with your left hand and pass plates with both hands. When you're through with dinner, set your chopsticks across the top of your bowl or plate. Save some bun and com dia for me! Chúc suc khoe!

# Index

# Index